CITY OF CAPITAL AND LABOUR

City of Capital and Labour

The Making and Transformation of Industrial Manchester

Tom Saunders

https://www.openbookpublishers.com

©2025 Tom Saunders

This work is licensed under a Creative Commons Attribution-NonCommercial 4.0 International (CC BY-NC 4.0). This license allows you to share, copy, distribute and transmit the text; to adapt the text for non-commercial purposes of the text providing attribution is made to the authors (but not in any way that suggests that they endorse you or your use of the work). Attribution should include the following information:

Tom Saunders, *City of Capital and Labour: The Making and Transformation of Industrial Manchester*. Cambridge, UK: Open Book Publishers, 2025, https://doi.org/10.11647/OBP.0459

Further details about CC BY-NC licenses are available at https://creativecommons.org/licenses/by-nc/4.0/

Copyright and permissions for the reuse of many of the images included in this publication differ from the above. This information is provided in the captions and in the list of illustrations. Where no licensing information is provided in the caption, the figure is reproduced under the fair dealing principle. Every effort has been made to identify and contact copyright holders and any omission or error will be corrected if notification is made to the publisher

All external links were active at the time of publication unless otherwise stated and have been archived via the Internet Archive Wayback Machine at https://archive.org/web

Digital material and resources associated with this volume are available at https://doi.org/10.11647/OBP.0459#resources

Information about any revised edition of this work will be provided at https://doi.org/10.11647/OBP.0459

ISBN Paperback: 978-1-80511-556-4
ISBN Hardback: 978-1-80511-557-1
ISBN PDF: 978-1-80511-558-8
ISBN HTML: 978-1-80511-560-1
ISBN EPUB: 978-1-80511-559-5
DOI: 10.11647/OBP.0459

Cover image: Rand W. Dean & Co., A Plan of Manchester and Salford (1809), https://commons.wikimedia.org/wiki/File:A_Plan_of_Manchester_and_Salford,_published_by_Rand_W._Dean_1809_-_btv1b8443186z.jpg
Cover design: Jeevanjot Kaur Nagpal

Contents

Acknowledgements	vii
List of Illustrations	ix
Introduction	1
1. The Georgian Boom Town, c.1720–c.1780	15
2. The 'Shock City' of Industrial Capitalism, c.1780–c.1840	35
3. City of Triumphant Liberalism, c.1840–c.1860	97
4. City of Civic Pride and Industrial Paternalism, c.1860–c.1890	149
5. City of Ambition and Popular Culture, c.1890–c.1920	213
Conclusion	285
Bibliography	293
Index	299
About the Team	309

Acknowledgements

Although writing a book can feel a lonely business, it is an inherently social activity involving the contributions and input of numerous people. I would therefore like to thank a range of individuals whose help has been essential for publishing this work, in particular, Dee Hawes and Steve Roskams for their detailed feedback and suggestions on earlier drafts. Thanks are also owed to Michael Reeve, Terry Jackson-Baker and Tony Martin for reading and commenting on the text (as well as to two anonymous referees). But in addition, I am greatly in debt to friends and family who provided encouragement and support throughout, especially the 'chuckle brothers' Chris Rowell and Martin Bennell, and my long-suffering partner Ragnhild Steinshamn, and our daughter Ella Saunders (whose participation in this project, willing or not, is recorded in several photographs in this volume). Finally, I'm grateful to Dr Alessandra Tosi and the team at Open Book Publishers to agreeing to publish this book and seeing the process through to its completion, especially to Adèle Kreager for the copy-editing and help with the illustrations.

Levenshulme, May 2025

List of Illustrations

I.1	Back Pool Fold, off Cross Street (Author, 2021).	p. 4
I.2	G. W. Bacon's Plan of Manchester and Salford, c.1900. Image provided by The John Rylands Research Institute and Library, The University of Manchester.	p. 8
I.3	Manchester and Salford conurbation from the air (looking east with Trafford Park and Salford Quays in the foreground). Photograph by M. J. Richardson (2010). Wikimedia Commons, CC BY 2.0, https://www.geograph.org.uk/photo/2103101	p. 9
I.4	Manchester Royal Infirmary, Piccadilly (just before its demolition in 1910), photographer unknown. Image courtesy of Manchester Libraries.	p. 10
I.5	Piccadilly Gardens today. Photograph by And-Rew (2007), Wikimedia Commons, CC BY-SA 3.0, https://commons.wikimedia.org/wiki/File:Piccadilly_Grdns.jpg#/media/File:Piccadilly_Grdns.jpg	p. 11
1.1	Hough End Hall, Chorlton (Author, 2020).	p. 17
1.2	Platt Hall, Rusholme (Author, 2022).	p. 17
1.3	Heaton Hall, Heaton Hall (Author, 2023).	p. 18
1.4	Casson and Berry's 1746 'A plan of the towns of Manchester and Salford'. Image provided by Manchester Central Library/Bridgeman Images.	p. 20
1.5	Manchester Cathedral (Author, 2023).	p. 21
1.6	St Ann's Church and St Ann's Square (Author, 2023).	p. 22
1.7	Cross Street Chapel, 1900, unknown photographer. Image courtesy of Manchester Libraries.	p. 23
1.8	Moravian Church, Fairfield, Droylsden (Author, 2023).	p. 24
1.9	Sacred Trinity, Chapel Street, Salford (Author, 2020).	p. 25
1.10	35 King Street, Manchester (Author, 2020).	p. 25

1.11	Old Wellington Inn and Sinclair's Oyster Bar, Shambles Square (Author, 2022).	p. 26
1.12	William Green's 1794 'A plan of Manchester and Salford'. Image provided by The John Rylands Research Institute and Library, The University of Manchester.	p. 27
1.13	Cobden House, 10 Quay Street (Author, 2025).	p. 28
1.14	The Infirmary, Dispensary and Lunatic Asylum, Manchester, England. Line engraving by J. Davies after S. Austin (1831). Wellcome Collection, https://wellcomecollection.org/works/trrq4wes/images?id=vd63xnfr, public domain.	p. 29
1.15	New Cross, c.1800 painting. Unknown artist. Image courtesy of Manchester Libraries.	p. 30
1.16	Grocer's Warehouse, Castlefield (Author, 2023).	p. 31
1.17	Reconstruction of Grocer's Warehouse (© Michael Nevell).	p. 31
2.1	James Pigot 'A plan of Manchester and Salford', 1836. Image courtesy of Manchester Libraries.	p. 38
2.2	The distribution of Manchester's textile factories by 1800. The base map is Green's map of Manchester published in 1794. Key: dots = cotton spinning factories; diamonds = finishing works (© Michael Nevell).	p. 39
2.3	Murrays' Mills, Redhill Street, Ancoats (showing the blocked entrance of the arm of the Rochdale which led to a basin within the mill complex), Photograph by Clem Rutter (2010), Wikimedia Commons, CC BY-SA 3.0, https://commons.wikimedia.org/wiki/File:Ancoats_Redhill_Street-_4557.JPG#/media/File:Ancoats_Redhill_Street-_4557.JPG	p. 40
2.4	Plan of Murrays' Mills complex, Redhill Street, Ancoats (© Michael Nevell/Historic England Archive).	p. 40
2.5	Entrance to Beehive Mill, Jersey Street, Ancoats (Author, 2012).	p. 42
2.6	Marsland's Mill, Chester Street, Chorlton-on-Medlock (Author, 2021).	p. 43
2.7	Chorlton Old Mill and Chorlton New Mills (far-left building with chimney), Cambridge Street, Chorlton-on-Medlock (Author, 2021).	p. 44

List of Illustrations xi

2.8	47–53 Tib Street, Northern Quarter (showing workshop attic with windows and 'taking-in' door) (Author, 2022).	p. 45
2.9	Cutaway reconstruction of a weaver's workshop dwelling (based on 1–5 Kelvin Street, Northern Quarter) (Taylor and Holder 2008, 16, all rights reserved).	p. 47
2.10	The canal network in the Manchester and Salford conurbation (© Michael Nevell).	p. 48
2.11	Dale Street Warehouse (Author, 2012).	p. 50
2.12	Merchants' Warehouse (left) and the Middle Warehouse, Castlefield (Author, 2023).	p. 51
2.13	One-up, one-down houses at Bradley Street, Northern Quarter (Author, 2012).	p. 54
2.14	Development of urban housing at Bradley Street (Taylor and Holder 2008, 24, all rights reserved).	p. 54
2.15	Distribution of Manchester's religious buildings by 1838, shown on James Pigot's 1838 'A plan of Manchester and Salford', annotated by the author (blue dots = Anglican churches; yellow dots = Commissioners' churches; green dotes = Catholic churches; red dots = Nonconformist chapels; pink dot = synagogue).	p. 55
2.16	Independent Chapel, Chapel Street, Salford (Author, 2023).	p. 55
2.17	St Philip, Salford (Author, 2023).	p. 57
2.18	St Thomas, Pendleton, Salford (Author, 2021).	p. 58
2.19	Distribution of institutions of coercion and institutions of culture, shown on James Pigot's 1838 'A plan of Manchester and Salford', annotated by the author (red dots = institutions of coercion, blue dots = institutions of bourgeois culture).	p. 59
2.20	Plan of New Bailey Prison, Salford, 1848 (section of Old Ordnance Survey Maps, Manchester and Salford Sheet 27), Alan Godfrey Maps.	p. 62
2.21	Plan of Hulme Barracks, 1849 (section of Ordnance Survey Town Plan – Manchester and Salford Sheet 37), CC BY, National Library of Scotland.	p. 62
2.22	Quartermaster's house (one of Pooley's Houses), Hulme Barracks (Author, 2021).	p. 63

2.23	Ladysmith Barracks, Ashton-under-Lyne (Author, 2024).	p. 64
2.24	Map of radical addresses in Manchester 1789–1820 (Navickas 2016, 110, all rights reserved).	p. 65
2.25	The remains of the Round House, Ancoats (with All Souls showing in the left-hand corner) (Author, 2021).	p. 67
2.26	Map of radical and trade union processions in Manchester 1819–1842 (Navickas 2016, 181, all rights reserved).	p. 68
2.27	Plan of Manchester Infirmary and Piccadilly Square, 1850. Unknown author. Wikimedia Commons, public domain, https://commons.wikimedia.org/wiki/File:Plan_of_Manchester_Royal_Infirmary_1845.jpg	p. 70
2.28	John Rowland Fothergill, Mosley Street engraving, 1824 (showing the Portico Library, front left and St Peter). Image courtesy of Manchester City Galleries.	p. 71
2.29	Friends Meeting House, Mount Street (Author, 2009).	p. 72
2.30	Mosley Street, 1849 (section of Ordnance Survey Town Plan – Manchester and Salford Sheet 28), CC BY, National Library of Scotland.	p. 73
2.31	Portico Library, Mosley Street (with sole surviving facade of the original Georgian terraced houses that aligned Mosley Street) (Author, 2022).	p. 74
2.32	Royal Manchester Institute, Mosley Street and Athenaeum, Princess Street (Author, 2023).	p. 75
2.33	Theatre Royal, Peter Street (Author, 2022).	p. 76
2.34	Francis J. Sargent, 'Manchester Exchange', 1810 (the church of St Ann can be seen in the background). Image courtesy of the British Library.	p. 76
2.35	Blackfriars Bridge (Author, 2022).	p. 77
2.36	Manchester and Salford Savings Bank (now Pizza Express) and Bank of England, King Street (Author, 2022).	p. 78
2.37	Plan of Stevenson's estate (Taylor and Holder 2008, 19, all rights reserved).	p. 80
2.38	Georgian residential houses on Lever Street with Number 8 on the right (Author, 2025).	p. 81
2.39	Edward Baines' 1824 Map of Ashton-under-Lyne.	p. 82
2.40	Ardwick Green (Author, 2022).	p. 84

List of Illustrations   *xiii*

2.41	Higher Ardwick, 1849 (section of Ordnance Survey Town Plan – Manchester and Salford Sheet 40), CC BY, National Library of Scotland.	p. 84
2.42	Old stable block, now Apsley Cottage pub, Ardwick (Author, 2022).	p. 85
2.43	The Crescent, Salford (Author, 2023).	p. 86
2.44	Map of Manchester and Salford District, 1845 (the location of Ardwick Green is highlighted in green, The Crescent in pink, Higher Broughton in blue and Victoria Park is highlighted in yellow; annotated by the author). Ordnance Survey map Lancashire Sheet CIV, CC BY, National Library of Scotland.	p. 87
2.45	258–260 Great Clowes Street, Salford (Author, 2020).	p. 87
2.46	Buile Hill mansion, Pendleton, Salford. Photograph by Matt Ratcliffe (2014), *Manchester Evening News*.	p. 88
2.47	Ashburne House, Fallowfield (Author, 2020).	p. 89
2.48	Victoria Park, 1889 (section of Ordnance Survey map Lancashire Sheet CIV.15), CC BY, National Library of Scotland.	p. 91
2.49	Victoria Park Hotel, Rusholme (Author, 2024).	p. 91
2.50	Liverpool Road Station (showing the first- and second-class passenger entrances) (Author, 2023).	p. 93
2.51	River Irwell Railway Bridge (Author, 2023).	p. 93
2.52	Storerooms at the Arrivals Station, Water Street (Author, 2023).	p. 94
3.1	Free Trade Hall (Author, 2025).	p. 97
3.2	Municipal Borough of Manchester, 1838 (Kidd 2002, 62, all rights reserved).	p. 99
3.3	J. Mennie's 1857 Ernst and Co's illustrated plan of Manchester and Salford. Wikimedia Commons, public domain, https://commons.wikimedia.org/wiki/File:Plan_of_Manchester_and_Salford_-_Designed_%26_drawn_by_J._Mennie_-_btv1b10679888h.jpg#/media/File:Plan_of_Manchester_and_Salford_-_Designed_&_drawn_by_J._Mennie_-_btv1b10679888h.jpg	p. 102
3.4	Manchester railways c.1855 (Andy Mason in Dawson 2017, 6, all rights reserved).	p. 103
3.5	Hunts Bank Station (Victoria) (Author, 2022).	p. 104

3.6	London Road Station (Piccadilly) (Author, 2022).	p. 105
3.7	Goods Office, London Road Station (Author, 2022).	p. 105
3.8	Salford Central Station (showing columns with Egyptian-style lotus leaf capitals) (Author, 2022).	p. 106
3.9	Manchester South Junction and Altrincham Railway viaduct (Author, 2022).	p. 107
3.10	William Morton, 'Manchester Royal Infirmary', engraving, c.1853/1857, showing the Royal Infirmary and Piccadilly Esplanade. Wellcome Collection, public domain, https://wellcomecollection.org/works/qtcfufgu/images?id=c9cv6t28	p. 110
3.11	12 Charlotte Street, palazzo-style warehouse (Author, 2022).	p. 113
3.12	Watts Warehouse (Britannia Hotel), Portland Street (Author, 2022).	p. 114
3.13	3–5 Portland Street (Author, 2022).	p. 115
3.14	Benjamin Heywood's Bank, St Ann's Square (with adjoining house) (Author, 2023).	p. 115
3.15	Manchester and Salford Bank, Mosley Street (Author, 2022).	p. 116
3.16	Smithfield Meat Market Hall, 'Erected by the Corporation of this City' (Author, 2022).	p. 118
3.17	Manchester Corporation water works, reservoirs and mains (1881), public domain.	p. 119
3.18	Manchester's coat of arms, Gould Street Gas Station (Author, 2023).	p. 120
3.19	Hulme, 1922 (looking south from the city centre with towards Moss Side, with Gaythorn Gas Works visible at the bottom left). Image courtesy of Manchester Libraries.	p. 122
3.20	Hulme, 1844 (note the positioning of Chorlton-upon-Medlock Workhouse amongst the by-law terraces) (section of Ordnance Survey Town Plan – Manchester and Salford Sheet 38), CC BY, National Library of Scotland.	p. 122
3.21	Standardised by-law housing (© Michael Nevell).	p. 123
3.22	Manchester and District, 1896, showing location of public parks, baths and cemeteries, annotated by the author (yellow dots = municipal parks; blue dots = baths; and black dots = cemeteries), (section of Old Ordnance Survey Maps, England Sheet 85) Alan Godfrey Maps.	p. 124

List of Illustrations xv

3.23	Adshead's map of Queens Park and Manchester General Cemetery, Harpurhey, 1851.	p. 126
3.24	Front elevation of Greengate Baths, Salford. Artist and date unknown.	p. 128
3.25	Mechanics' Institute, Princess Street (Author, 2022).	p. 129
3.26	Mechanics' Institute, Levenshulme (Author, 2012).	p. 129
3.27	Manchester's branch library network in the 1870s (Hewitt 2000, 70, all rights reserved).	p. 130
3.28	Manchester Free Library, Deansgate (Author, 2023).	p. 131
3.29	Salford Museum and Art Gallery (Author, 2025).	p. 132
3.30	St Mary, Hulme and Sunday Schools (Author, 2021).	p. 134
3.31	Manchester and Salford map, 1913, showing distribution of extant Anglican churches by phase, annotated by the author (red dots = Phase 1, yellow dots = Phase 2, blue dots = Phase 3, green dots = Phase 4, purple dots = Phase 5).	p. 135
3.32	St Wilfred's Catholic Church, Hulme (Author, 2011).	p. 136
3.33	Cathedral of St John Evangelist (RC), Salford. Wikimedia Commons, CC BY-SA 2.0, https://commons.wikimedia.org/wiki/File:Salford_rc_Cathedral.jpg#/media/File:Salford_rc_Cathedral.jpg	p. 136
3.34	Unitarian Chapel and Sunday School, Upper Brook Street (Author, 2021).	p. 137
3.35	Lancashire Independent College, Whalley Range (Author, 2022).	p. 138
3.36	William Wyld, *Manchester from Kersal Moor*, 1852. Wikimedia Commons, public domain, https://commons.wikimedia.org/wiki/File:Wyld,_William_-_Manchester_from_Kersal_Moor,_with_rustic_figures_and_goats_-_Google_Art_Project.jpg	p. 140
3.37	Gaskell House, 84 Plymouth Grove (Author, 2025).	p. 142
3.38	The Firs, Fallowfield. Photo by Richardhandscombe (2014), Wikimedia, CC BY-SA 2.5, https://commons.wikimedia.org/wiki/File:Chcc_blue_sky_2.jpg#/media/File:Chcc_blue_sky_2.jpg	p. 143
3.39	Addison Terrace, Victoria Park (Author, 2022).	p. 143
3.40	Maryland, Victoria Park (Author, 2022).	p. 144
3.41	Semi-detached villa on 124-126 Palatine Road (Author, 2023).	p. 145

3.42	Gaskell House floor plan (Elizabeth Gaskell's House, all rights reserved).	p. 146
3.43	Abney Hall, Cheadle (Author, 2023).	p. 147
4.1	Manchester Town Hall and Albert Square. Photo by Mark Andrew (2012), Wikimedia Commons, CC BY 2.0, https://commons.wikimedia.org/wiki/File:Manchester_Town_Hall_from_Lloyd_St.jpg#/media/File:Manchester_Town_Hall_from_Lloyd_St.jpg	p. 149
4.2	Manchester Town Hall, ground floor plan, 1868 (after Crinson 2022, 106).	p. 152
4.3	South side of Albert Square (Author, 2022).	p. 153
4.4	University of Manchester, Oxford Road (Author, 2023).	p. 155
4.5	Police and Sessions Court, Minshull Street (Author, 2023).	p. 156
4.6	Rylands Library, Deansgate (Author, 2023).	p. 157
4.7	Illustration of Barlow Moor Workhouse, 1856, unknown artist, public domain.	p. 160
4.8	Barlow Moor Workhouse, main entrance and chapel (Author, 2023).	p. 161
4.9	Prestwich Union Office (next to former Cheetham Town Hall), Cheetham Hill Road (Author, 2023).	p. 162
4.10	Strangeways Prison (and Assize Courts), 1930, unknown photographer. Image courtesy of Manchester Libraries.	p. 163
4.11	Plan of Pendlebury Children's Hospital, Salford, 1873, public domain.	p. 165
4.12	Barton Arcade, Deansgate (Author, 2022).	p. 167
4.13	Hayward's Building, Deansgate (Author, 2022).	p. 168
4.14	Reform Club, King Street (Author, 2025).	p. 169
4.15	Law Library, Kennedy Street (Author, 2022).	p. 170
4.16	Victoria Double Mill, Miles Platting (Author, 2021).	p. 171
4.17	Manchester and District Map, 1896, annotated by the author (showing location of major engineering works (blue dots) in East Manchester and new church foundations (yellow dots)), (section of Old Ordnance Survey Maps, England Sheet 85), Alan Godfrey Maps.	p. 172
4.18	Gorton, 1933, showing Gorton Carriage Company, 'Gorton Tank' and Gorton Foundry (section of Ordnance Survey map, Lancashire Sheet 104.07), CC BY, National Library of Scotland.	p. 173

4.19	Gorton Foundry (Author, 2021).	p. 173
4.20	Brookfield Unitarian Chapel, Gorton (showing the Peacock Mausoleum on the left) (Author, 2023).	p. 174
4.21	St James, Gorton (Author, 2020).	p. 175
4.22	Houldsworth Mill, Reddish (Author, 2020).	p. 176
4.23	Houldsworth Working Men's Club (Author, 2020).	p. 177
4.24	Gorton, 1905 (section of Ordnance Survey map, Lancashire Sheet CIV.16), CC BY, National Library of Scotland.	p. 178
4.25	Gorton by-law housing. Photograph by John Critchley, Dreamstimes.com.	p. 179
4.26	Ardwick and Ancoats Dispensary, Mill Street. Photo by Pete Birkinshaw (2008), Wikimedia Commons, CC BY 2.0, https://commons.wikimedia.org/wiki/File:Ancoats_Hospital_(3192798312).jpg#/media/File:Ancoats_Hospital_(3192798312).jpg	p. 180
4.27	Adult Deaf and Dumb Institute, Chorlton-on-Medlock (Author, 2025).	p. 180
4.28	Northern Hospital for Women and Children, Park Place, Cheetham Hill (Author, 2023).	p. 181
4.29	Nicholls Hospital, Ardwick (Author, 2021).	p. 182
4.30	Stretford Public Hall, Chester Road (Author, 2022).	p. 183
4.31	Alexandra Park, Moss Side, plan by Alfred Darbyshire, 1869. Wikimedia Commons, public domain, https://commons.wikimedia.org/wiki/File:Plan_of_Alexandra_Park,_Manchester.jpg#/media/File:Plan_of_Alexandra_Park,_Manchester.jpg	
4.32	Map of Manchester and Salford, 1913, showing location of Manchester Board Schools, annotated by the author (yellow dots = extant schools, blue dots = demolished schools).	p. 186
4.33	Varna Street School, Openshaw (Author, 2021).	p. 187
4.34	Elliot House, School Board Office, Deansgate (Author, 2022).	p. 187
4.35	Clayton Conservative Club (Author, 2021).	p. 188
4.36	Derby Brewery Arms, Cheetham Hill (with the former Town Hall and Poor Law Union Office on the far right) (Author, 2020).	p. 189
4.37	Plymouth Grove, Chorlton-on-Medlock (Author, 2022).	p. 190

4.38	White Lion, Withington (Author, 2022).	p. 191
4.39	Newton Street Police Station, central Manchester (Author, 2022).	p. 192
4.40	Chapel Street Police Station (with a police wagon shed painted blue on the right), Salford (Author, 2021).	p. 193
4.41	A lower 'middle-class terrace' consisting of a tightly packed row of semi-detached houses, Osbourne Road, Levenshulme (Author, 2023).	p. 195
4.42	By-law terraces with front gardens and bay windows, Forest Range, Levenshulme (Author, 2023).	p. 196
4.43	Levenshulme, 1905, annotated by the author (the position of Anglican church shown as a red dot, the Methodist chapel a yellow dot and Congregationalist chapel as a blue dot) (section of Ordnance Survey map, Lancashire Sheet CIV.04), CC BY, National Library of Scotland.	p. 196
4.44	Church of St Benedict, West Gorton (Author, 2023).	p. 199
4.45	Church of the Holy Name of Jesus, Oxford Road (Author, 2023).	p. 200
4.46	Church and Friary of St Francis, Gorton (Author, 2023).	p. 201
4.47	St Bede's College, Whalley Range (Author, 2022).	p. 202
4.48	Greek Orthodox Church, Bury New Road (Author, 2020).	p. 203
4.49	Armenian Church, Upper Brook Street (Author, 2022).	p. 204
4.50	Spanish and Portuguese Synagogue, Cheetham Hill Road (Author, 2023).	p. 204
4.51	Cheetham Hill Road, 1931 (section of Ordnance Survey map, Lancashire Sheet CXI.06), CC BY, National Library of Scotland.	p. 205
4.52	Manchester New Synagogue and Cheetham Branch, Manchester Free Library (left), Cheetham Hill Road (Author, 2023).	p. 206
4.53	Jews' Burial Ground, Prestwich (Author, 2021).	p. 207
4.54	Map of Manchester and Salford, 1913, showing location of municipal cemeteries and large commercial cemeteries, annotated by the author (red dots = municipal cemeteries, yellow dots = large commercial cemeteries).	p. 208

List of Illustrations

4.55	Brotherton's funerary monument, Weaste Cemetery (Author, 2023).	p. 209
5.1	Map of Manchester Ship Canal, 1890. Wikimedia Commons, public domain, https://commons.wikimedia.org/wiki/File:Plan_of_Manchester_Ship_Canal_1890.jpg#/media/File:Plan_of_Manchester_Ship_Canal_1890.jpg	p. 213
5.2	G. W. Bacon's Plan of Manchester and Salford, c. 1900. Image provided by The John Rylands Research Institute and Library, The University of Manchester.	p. 214
5.3	Main entrance and the Dock Office, Port of Manchester, Ordsall (Author, 2013).	p. 215
5.4	Map of Trafford Park Estate, 1902. Image courtesy of Manchester Libraries.	p. 216
5.5	Adolphe Valette, *Oxford Road, Manchester*, 1910. Image courtesy of Manchester Art Galleries.	p. 220
5.6	Map of Manchester and Salford railways, 1910. Wikimedia Commons, public domain, https://commons.wikimedia.org/wiki/File:Manchester_RJD_47.JPG#/media/File:Manchester_RJD_47.JPG	p. 221
5.7	Great Northern Railway Offices, Deansgate (Author, 2023).	p. 222
5.8	Victoria Station (Author, 2025).	p. 222
5.9	Castlefield's railway viaducts (Author, 2011).	p. 223
5.10	Manchester Corporation, existing and proposed tramways in Manchester and neighbouring boroughs and districts, 1916. Image courtesy of Manchester Libraries.	p. 225
5.11	Time-zone map of tramways in Manchester and surrounding districts, 1916. Image courtesy of Manchester Libraries.	p. 226
5.12	Queens Road Tram Depot, Cheetham Hill (Author, 2021).	p. 227
5.13	Midland Hotel (Author, 2022).	p. 229
5.14	London Road Police and Fire Station (Author, 2023).	p. 230
5.15	Refuge Assurance Building, Oxford Road (Author, 2023).	p. 231
5.16	Eagle Star House, Cross Street (Author, 2022).	p. 231
5.17	Parrs Bank, Spring Gardens (Author, 2023).	p. 232

5.18	The Royal Exchange (from the corner of Cross Street and Market Street) (Author, 2022).	p. 233
5.19	The Royal Infirmary, Oxford Road (Author, 2023).	p. 234
5.20	Manchester's civic boundaries, 1931 (Kidd 2002, 202, all rights reserved).	p. 236
5.21	Gas Board Offices, Bloom Street, Salford (Author, 2023).	p. 238
5.22	Gas holder at Bradford Road Gas Works (Author, 2023).	p. 238
5.23	Manchester Corporation Water Works – Plan of line of Aqueduct from Thirlmere to Manchester, 1894, Wikipedia Commons, https://commons.wikimedia.org/wiki/File:Blacklock_%26_Co.(1894)_p73_-_Manchester_Corporation_Water_Works_-_Plan_of_Line_of_Aqueduct_from_Thirlmere_to_Manchester.jpg.	p. 239
5.24	Hydraulic Pumping Station, Water Street (Author, 2023).	p. 239
5.25	Wilburn Street Basin, Salford (Author, 2023).	p. 240
5.26	Manchester Corporation Electricity Works sub-station, Heaton Moor (Author, 2023).	p. 241
5.27	Electricity substations, Brailsford Road, Fallowfield (with a plague displaying the city's coat of arms) (Author, 2023).	p. 242
5.28	Manchester Municipal Technical School, Sackville Street (Author, 2023).	p. 243
5.29	Royal Salford Technical Institute, Chapel Street (Author, 2023).	p. 244
5.30	Manchester Central School, Whitworth Street (Author, 2022).	p. 245
5.31	Crumpsall and Cheetham District Library (Author, 2022).	p. 246
5.32	Didsbury District Library (Author, 2023).	p. 246
5.33	Manchester Central Library (Author, 2025).	p. 248
5.34	Victoria Baths, Chorlton-on-Medlock (Author, 2022).	p. 249
5.35	Harpurhey Baths, Rochdale Road (Author, 2022).	p. 250
5.36	Victoria Square apartments, Oldham Road, Ancoats (Author, 2023).	p. 251

List of Illustrations xxi

5.37	Salford Lads Club, New Barrack Estate, Ordsall (and Ragnhild Steinshamn) (Author, 2021).	p. 252
5.38	Manchester and District, 1896, showing major municipal parks in Manchester, annotated by the author (red dots = Phase 3; blue dots = Phase 4; yellow dots = Phase 5), (section of Old Ordnance Survey Maps, England Sheet 85), Alan Godfrey Maps.	p. 253
5.39	New Theatre (Opera House), Quay Street (Author, 2025).	p. 256
5.40	Picture House, Oxford Street (Author, 2023).	p. 257
5.41	Grosvenor Picture Palace, Oxford Road (Author, 2025).	p. 258
5.42	J. Gosling's map of Manchester's Theatreland, 1937. Image courtesy of Chetham Library.	p. 259
5.43	Mr Thomas's Chop House, Cross Street (Author, 2021).	p. 260
5.44	The location of the football and cricket grounds at Old Trafford, c.1922, public domain.	p. 261
5.45	The Pavilion, Old Trafford Cricket Ground. Photo by Anthony O'Neil (2013), Wikimedia Commons, CC BY-SA 2.0, https://commons.wikimedia.org/wiki/File:Enlarged_pavilion_at_Old_Trafford_geograph-3720447-by-Anthony-ONeil.jpg#/media/File:Enlarged_pavilion_at_Old_Trafford_geograph-3720447-by-Anthony-ONeil.jpg	p. 262
5.46	The Castle Irwell racecourse, c.1923, public domain.	p. 263
5.47	Manchester and Salford Tennis and Racquet Club, Blackfriars Road, Salford (Author, 2025).	p. 264
5.48	Official guide to the Belle Vue Zoological Gardens, c.1892, Wikimedia Commons, public domain https://commons.wikimedia.org/wiki/File:Belle_vue_zoological_gardens_plan_1892.jpg	p. 265
5.49	Temperance Billiard Hall, Manchester Road, Chorlton-cum-Hardy (with Chorlton District Library to the right) (Author, 2024).	p. 266
5.50	Manchester and Salford Street Children Mission, Bridge Street (Author, 2022).	p. 269
5.51	Working Men's Church, Wood Street (Author, 2022).	p. 270
5.52	Charter Street Ragged School and Working Girls Home (Author, 2012).	p. 271

5.53	Onwards Building, Deansgate (Author, 2025).	p. 272
5.54	Oddfellows Hall, Grosvenor Street (Author, 2023).	p. 273
5.55	Co-operative Wholesale Society headquarters, Corporation Street (Author, 2020).	p. 275
5.56	Pendleton Co-operative Industrial Society, Broughton Road (Author, 2021).	p. 275
5.57	Beswick Co-operative Society Assembly Hall, Northmoor Road, Longsight (Author, 2021).	p. 276
5.58	Co-operative Sundries Manufactory, Greenside Lane, Droylsden (Author, 2023).	p. 276
5.59	Tramway workers meeting during the 1926 General Strike in Albert Square, photographer unknown. Image courtesy of Manchester Libraries.	p. 279
5.60	Map used as frontispiece in T. Marr, *Housing Conditions in Manchester & Salford* (Manchester: Sherratt and Hughes, 1904), https://archive.org/details/housingcondition00marr/page/n5/mode/1up, public domain.	p. 281
5.61	Barry Parker's plan for Wythenshawe Garden City, 1928, public domain.	p. 283
5.62	Ordnance Survey Map of Wythenshawe Estate, 1951, public domain.	p. 284
C.1	L. S. Lowry, *The Lake*, 1937 (© The Lowry Collection, Salford).	p. 285
C.2	Royal Infirmary railings, Piccadilly (Author, 2023).	p. 287
C.3	Manchester University 1968, Shirley Baker (© 2025, Nan Levy for the Estate of Shirley Baker. All rights reserved).	p. 288
C.4	Statue of Friedrich Engels, Tony Wilson Place, Manchester (looking out towards 'The Engels' penthouse in 'Manc-Hatten' (Author, 2025).	p. 290

Introduction

> In my beginning is my end. In succession
> Houses rise and fall, crumble, are extended,
> Are removed, destroyed, restored, or in their place
> Is an open field, or a factory, or a by-pass.
> Old stone to new building, old timber to new fires,
> Old fires to ashes, and ashes to the earth
> Which is already flesh, fur and faeces,
> Bone of man and beast, cornstalk and leaf.
> Houses live and die: there is a time for building
> And a time for living and for generation
> And a time for the wind to break the loosened pane
> And to shake the wainscot where the field-mouse trots
> And to shake the tattered arras woven with silent motto.
>
> —T.S. Eliot, *East Coker*, 1940

I was born in Elm Road in High Barnet in a house that was demolished to make way for Barnet College. I grew up in a mid-Victorian semi-detached villa in New Barnet that was subsequently pulled down and replaced with a block of flats. And now I currently live an Edwardian redbrick by-law terrace in Levenshulme, Manchester, in a city undergoing rapid redevelopment with so many high-rise blocks going up on the skyline that it has gained the ironic nickname, Manc-hattan. The constant changing of the built environment is part of the dynamics of urbanism, an innate feature of urban life that has long fascinated me. But not everything changes with the new. The present never fully eradicates the past, as traces and fragments are left behind, with these elements of the old being transfigured within the new.

Eliot completed *East Coker*, the second poem in his famous *Four Quartets*, in early 1940 at the onset of the Second World War. The coming disorder and destruction are anticipated in the images of the poem. Yet in his self-reflective meditation on the human condition, Eliot found a measure of hope in the divine, the 'wisdom of humility', and the need for humanity to look inwards, beyond the ephemeral materialism and rationalism of the present. However, in this vision, the fragments and traces of what has gone on before lose their significance.

As an atheist and archaeologist, Eliot's idea of spiritual renewal is not for me. The vestiges of buildings and spaces, and their destruction and replacement over time provides a key for understanding both the past and our position within the present. Making sense of the material world involves a form of archaeological looking and imagination, of peeling back and examining the very human, physical environment. This is the intention of this study, to try to make sense of the material form of Manchester, my adopted home.

Manchester. It was only in the midst of depths of depression in Trondheim, Norway, when I was contemplating moving back to England, that I seriously thought about the city. I had been to Manchester for various student demonstrations, marching up Oxford Road to Whitworth Park or Platt Fields Park, and even stayed in the infamous Hulme Crescents during one New Year's Eve. However, it was the imminence of a return and relocation to the city, the abode of my oldest friend Doug Hawes (now Dee), that served to concentrate my mind on the history and architecture of Manchester. Being a Marxist, I was familiar with Friedrich Engels' association with the city and was now motivated to properly read and study *The Condition of the Working Class in England*. From the distance of Norway, Engels' Manchester seemed a strangely exotic place. I was intrigued by the names of the streets and the different locales such as Shudehill, Withy Grove, Little Ireland and Irk Town, as well as Engels' disturbing but marvellous descriptions and accounts of the squalor, poverty and class dynamics of the city. And on arriving in Manchester, Engels' book provided a way into my investigation and served as my initial guidebook for many urban walks. Manchester may not be immediately attractive to the eye, its urban geography confusing and initially hard to navigate around, but it was clearly a place imbued with historical meaning and significance. It excited me and still does. This was the city that gave birth to industrial capitalism and the modern world. The buildings, spaces and places of Manchester seemed to me pregnant with the past politics and the history of class struggle. It is through discovering and untangling this complex physical environment that I have come to identify Manchester as my home.

Although a long time in gestation, with its roots in two decades worth of tramping through the streets of the city, much of which in the company of Dee Hawes, this study emerged as a project pursued during the lonely days of the Covid-19 pandemic and lockdowns of 2020 and 2021. It is an investigation of the way in which the physical form of the city both captures and embodies social dynamics of the past. Despite the nature of urban dynamics meaning cities such as Manchester are in a constant process of change and development, the past always exerts a material influence on the present. Streets, buildings and spaces from the past still structure and shape how we move around and experience the city. It is this that makes walking through Manchester so rewarding. The place is full of 'living archaeology'. This incorporates much more than just the city's 'historic' buildings and 'heritage' sites that have been consciously restored and dressed up to be seen in a particular way, it also includes the seemingly mundane and overlooked places such as the blocked Georgian pedimented doorway in Back Pool Fold, now a back alley to a business, rather than a residential entrance way (see Fig I.1 below).

It is understanding this 'living archaeology', the extant built environment and what it reveals about the social history of Manchester, that is the focus of this study. The aim is therefore twofold: to unpack and make sense of the development of the city in its material form, as well as to explore the way these patterns of development highlight the social dynamics in the making and transformation of Manchester. But the overall goal is a more general one; to enhance an appreciation of Manchester's visible past and to encourage a social 'reading' of the city's existing but so often hidden and ignored historic physical fabric.

Fig. I.1 Back Pool Fold, off Cross Street (Author, 2021).

A Contextual and Marxist Approach

My basic approach to the study of the urban built environment is influenced by an archaeological perspective on material culture which emphasises contextual relationships. Archaeology is commonly associated with 'digging', excavating and uncovering what is below the ground, although it is an approach that can be equally applied to the study of what is above the ground. The physical elements of the built environment can be broken down into its various parts. But rather than analysed individually and in isolation from each other, the different components that make up the urban matrix—buildings, streets and spaces for instance—are explored in relation to each other. It is by identifying and examining these contextual patterns that inferences can be made about the social dynamics of urban development. As Ian Hodder, a leading theoretician of the discipline, has argued 'archaeology is defined by its concern with context' (1986, 120). Archaeologists use contextual data to build interpretations through 'reading the past' in terms of deciphering the patterns observed in material culture.

Three essential dimensions of analysis lie at the heart of an archaeological contextual approach: the material, the temporal and spatial. This is true of the micro-level of archaeological analysis of excavating and recording single layers on a site to the macro-level of the investigation of whole sites, settlements and landscapes. The different material elements need to be defined and examined relationally in time and space. Hence, an archaeological 'eye' can not only draw attention to key chronological developments, but also to changing patterns in the social use of space. It is on the basis of studying these contextual material, temporal and spatial relationships that broader historical interpretations can be made.

It must be emphasised that the present built environment is the main focus of this analysis—the tangible places and spaces of Manchester that can be visited and experienced. Despite the constant and ongoing process of urbanisation, there is still much to be seen. But while not everything has been eradicated, a lot has. These uneven patterns of survival in the physical fabric of the city are of interest in their own right. What is preserved and repurposed, and what is neglected and demolished, tells us a great deal about the dynamics of urbanism (the priority given to capital accumulation over any other consideration) and the ever-changing cultural values attached to different buildings, places and spaces. Although some of these differential patterns of survival will be highlighted, this is not an issue directly addressed in this study. Still, the physical destruction of the material past carries important implications, as it obviously produces enormous gaps in the historical and architectural record. This means that existing historic buildings are often detached from their original material and spatial contexts. So, understanding what survives also requires our appreciation of what has gone before and is no longer visible. To contextualise Manchester's present past then, we must consider urban features that have been erased or buried beneath the ground, by drawing upon a wider range of evidence and sources than just the existing architecture of the city. This will involve making use of old maps, the results of recent archaeological excavations, as well as engravings, paintings, photographs and written sources.

While this archaeological methodology provides the basic framework of analysis, the interpretations of the contextual patterns in the urban built environment will be explored within a Marxist perspective emphasising the importance of social class and class conflict. When it comes to the study of Manchester, a Marxist perspective is particularly pertinent as it was Engels' classic account of the city that helped forge the class analysis of Karl Marx himself. Further, his *The Condition of the Working Class in England* remains one of the formative texts of modern urban studies, being widely recognised as a pioneering analysis of class zoning. Engels' socio-geography of Manchester, therefore, provides the starting point. The intention is to draw upon and extend Engels' class analysis of Manchester, focusing upon the dynamics of capital and labour. The contradictions, tensions and conflicts inherent in the industrialisation process will form the lens through which to view of the contextual patterns of Manchester's present physical form.

Manchester has rightly been labelled by Asa Briggs as the 'shock city' of industrial capitalism. Much has been written about the novelty of the city's dramatic growth at the end of the eighteenth century and beginning of the nineteenth century. Manchester became the showcase for the industrial city attracting visitors from far and wide to observe, in astonishment, and often, horror, this new form of urban living dominated by the demands of capital. The basic argument, on its most abstract and simplistic level, is that Manchester's emerging physical form as an industrial city was shaped by the socio-economic logic of capitalism, which constantly transformed the built environment. At the heart of this dynamic was the configuration of new class relations between capital and labour. The interests of competing industrialists and merchants drove the expansion of the city, but importantly capital, dependent on labour, sucked in workers in increasing numbers during the 'Industrial Revolution', creating diverse and multicultural urban communities. Manchester, in a constant state of change, was consequently riven with social tensions and conflicting interests. These were primarily between capital and labour, but also within the bourgeoisie and proletariat, which were themselves internally divided by occupation, religion, ethnicity and politics. The central idea that I wish to pursue is that these class divisions in particular, and competing social identities more generally, were both constituted and mediated through the architecture and the places and spaces of Manchester. It was a class dynamic that led to the making and remaking of the built environment. These developments left distinctive physical traces. My aim is to identify and map these traces to analyse patterns of social and cultural change in the material fabric of the city.

This general perspective owes a debt to the work of Marxist geographers who have clarified and extended Engels' ideas on power, class divisions and urban space. Andy Merrifield's *Metromarxism* (2002) provides a good introductory summary of this research, but it is the work of David Harvey, in particular, that informs this study. From the publication of *Social Justice and the City* in 1973, Harvey's theoretical framework for understanding the urban experience has focused on the central role of 'the industrial city as a powerhouse of accumulation and a crucible of class struggle' (1989, 33). It is this dialectic that underpins the spatial patterning of urban land use. The city plays an active role in the process of capital accumulation and is implicated in the cycles of economic growth and crisis. Speculation in land and property, the tearing down and rebuilding of the urban fabric, 'creative destruction', is therefore part of the logic of capitalism. In particular, Harvey has stressed how investments in the built environment provide an outlet for the problems of overaccumulation. In times of economic crisis when faced with a decline of profitability in the sphere of production, capital becomes channelled into real estate—the secondary circuit of capital. The consequence of this dynamic is that the industrial city is beset with tensions and conflicts, and as such, 'an unstable configuration, both economically and politically, by virtue of the contradictory forces that produced it' (1989, 33).

Alongside Harvey's approach, this analysis of Manchester makes use of other pioneering studies in urban geography and social history that also emerged during the 1970s and 1980s, when the Victorian city was the subject of much academic discussion. This return to these earlier intellectual debates is significant as the trajectory of Postmodernism has dragged recent historical scholarship in a very different direction, one in which talk of class, capitalism and industrialisation have been virtually expunged from frames of analysis. As one American reviewer of Patrick Joyce's influential Foucauldian book, *The Rule of Freedom: Liberalism and the Modern City* (2003), commented: 'Although Manchester is one of the case studies that Joyce draws upon, an ignorant and inattentive reader might scarcely notice that it was the centre of the Industrial Revolution' (Koditschek 2006, 183). Looking back to past research is a way of moving beyond this preoccupation with language and discourse. It also takes inspiration from more contemporary studies that have returned to more materialist perspectives that consider the impact of economic and industrial processes as well as the social dynamics of class, with Katrina Navickas' *Protest and the Politics of Space and Place 1789–1848* (2017), and

Mark Crinson's *Shock City: Image and Architecture in Industrial Manchester* (2022) being two of the most noteworthy.

In terms of the geographical area of study, the focus will be the Manchester and Salford conurbation. It might seem unfair to subsume Salford into Manchester, as after all, Salford is a separate city with its own history and identity, but the two cities form one integrated urban built environment. An analysis of Manchester's physical fabric cannot be neatly disconnected from that of Salford's and vice versa; both need to be examined together.

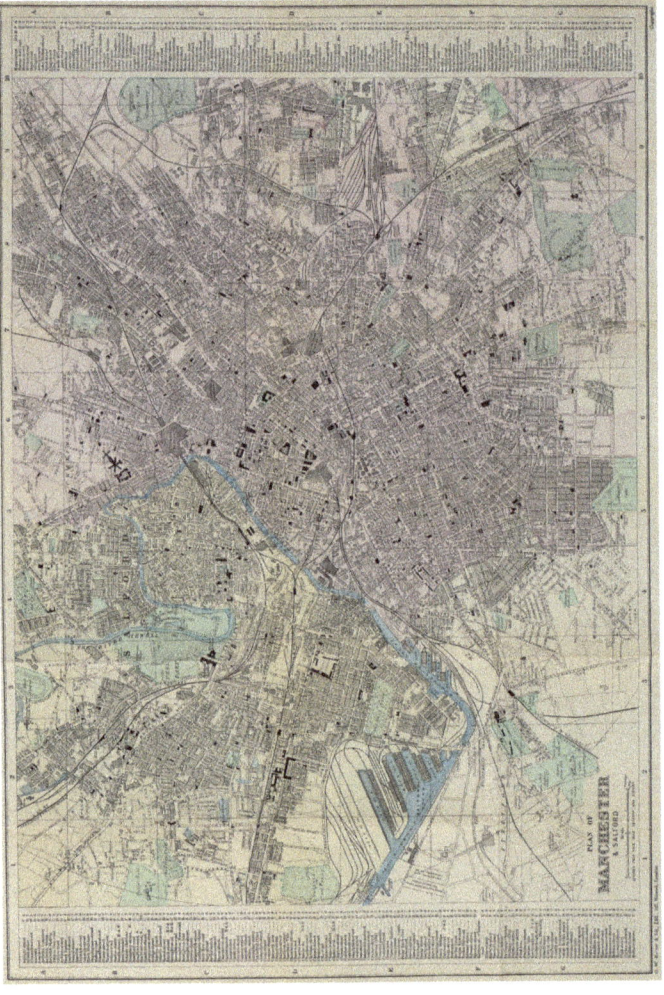

Fig. I.2 G. W. Bacon's Plan of Manchester and Salford, c.1900. Image provided by The John Rylands Research Institute and Library, The University of Manchester.

Fig. I.3 Manchester and Salford conurbation from the air (looking east with Trafford Park and Salford Quays in the foreground). Photograph by M. J. Richardson (2010). Wikimedia Commons, CC BY 2.0, https://www.geograph.org.uk/photo/2103101

When it comes to chronology, this study will cover a roughly two-hundred-year period from the beginning of the eighteenth century to the start of the twentieth century. This was a period defined by the making and transformation of industrial Manchester, hence the subtitle of the book. Obviously, it could have chronologically continued to explore the phases of decline of the industrial city and its reconfiguration as a post-industrial metropolis at the end of the twentieth century, but there are sound reasons for ending this analysis when Manchester was at its height. The post-Edwardian era was characterised by a very different form of urbanism, shaped by the development of motorised road transport, as well as by a strikingly new architectural style—Modernism.

So, in terms of the built environment, the start of the period under study will be defined by the physical expansion of the town beyond the medieval core (which was focused upon the parish church and marketplace) and a distinctive change in the urban geography and architecture. The building of the Baroque St Ann's church, which was consecrated in 1712 and the associated St Ann's Square that was completed in 1720s, in this respect can be seen as markers of modernity in Manchester's urban form.

The end point of this study is also similarly defined by the conscious expansion beyond the limits of the Victorian and Edwardian city in the form of 'garden suburbs', as in the construction of the Wythenshawe estate during the 1920s. This spatial shift corresponded with the end of the iconic by-law gridiron, redbrick terraced housing that had been such a visual feature of the industrial cityscape. When Wythenshawe was formally incorporated into the city in 1931 Manchester had reached its peak in terms of its demography and geography. These urban changes therefore serve as a useful end point for this study as they mark the start of the long decline of industrial Manchester during the twentieth century and a new form of urban living.

Fig. I.4 Manchester Royal Infirmary, Piccadilly (just before its demolition in 1910), photographer unknown. Image courtesy of Manchester Libraries.

However, there is also an important negative space that provides further chronological bookends for this research, namely the space of Piccadilly Gardens. It was on this site that Manchester Infirmary was built and opened for patients in 1755. The Infirmary delineated another geographical shift away from the old town, and the streets around it became the focus of Manchester's Georgian polite society and rising middle class. Its demolition in 1910 was part of the rationalisation of the city centre when the hospital was moved to the periphery on Oxford Road. Although there were plans to erect another monumental public building in the space, nothing was built and Piccadilly was left open, perhaps symbolising Manchester's decline as an industrial city.

Fig. I.5 Piccadilly Gardens today. Photograph by And-Rew (2007), Wikimedia Commons, CC BY-SA 3.0, https://commons.wikimedia.org/wiki/File:Piccadilly_ Grdns.jpg#/media/File:Piccadilly_Grdns.jpg

Although during this two-hundred-year period Manchester experienced a continuous process of transformation, distinctive patterns or phases of development can be identified. The boundaries between these phases are inevitably blurred (due to the fluid nature of urban expansion) but they can be defined contextually in terms of major interventions in the built environment, new building types and architectural styles, transport innovations and marked shifts in patterns of land use. These phases help capture the dynamics of Manchester's physical growth. Consequently, within this period of urban growth are five separate phases of development which relate to a broader historical narrative of the city. What is interesting to note is the degree of correlation between the materially, or archaeologically, defined phases and key events in the wider economic, political and social history of Manchester, especially in the realm of local government. As such, this study serves to illustrates how the built environment is fundamentally implicated in the making of the past.

The first two phases demarcate the making of industrial Manchester. This begins with 'The Georgian Boomtown, c.1720–c.1780' (Chapter 1) which is characterised by the eighteenth-century residential developments beyond the medieval core and the establishment of the town's two principal civic buildings, the Exchange and the Infirmary, but also by the commercial innovations that laid the ground for the later economic take-off, especially in terms of the opening of the Bridgewater Canal in in 1761. Then, at the turn of the century, Manchester was metamorphised by industrialisation; a novel phenomenon that cannot be underplayed as it becomes 'The "Shock City" of Industrial Capitalism, c.1780–c.1840' (Chapter 2). Steam-powered cotton mills come to dominate the townscape with the genesis of factory production generating an architecture of industrial discipline as exhibited in the district of Ancoats. At the same time, a peculiar geography of class polarisation emerges with institutions of coercion, such as New Bailey Prison and barracks, surrounding working-class districts, with middle-class cultural institutions such as the Portico Library and Theatre Royal centred around Mosley Street in the heart of the town. The open social conflict that this phase generates, focused on the battle of public space, is epitomised by the infamous Peterloo Massacre of 1819 and the rise of Chartism. Finding itself entrapped within urban contradictions of industrialisation, Georgian polite society then slowly retreats from the centre to form middle-class residential suburbs.

The next three phases relate to the transformation of this industrial city as it is reconfigured to accommodate rapid urban growth and mediate the resulting social conflicts through establishing new forms of urban living. Manchester is transformed from an industrial city to a bourgeois city, shaped by a rising middle class and their attempts at harnessing new economic forces through reordering the city to express and enforce their own class interests, especially in relation to emerging working-class communities—the industrial proletariat—which comprised the vast majority of the urban population. Significantly, when it comes to the built environment, these latter phases are all physically framed by the emerging railway system which exerted a strong influence on the ongoing industrial, commercial and residential expansion of the city. This network of train stations, brick and iron viaducts and bridges that was established in the nineteenth century is still very much in use today, and so probably the most obvious embodiment of the city's 'living archaeology'.

In the third phase, during the middle decades of the nineteenth century, Manchester can be seen as the 'City of Triumphant Liberalism, c.1840–c.1860' (Chapter 3) following its formal incorporation into a municipal borough in 1838. This bourgeois optimism is architecturally symbolised by Edward Walters's Renaissance palazzo-style Free Trade Hall, which was completed in 1856. This is the phase when the urban zoning observed by Engels starts to take root with the first attempts at municipal urban improvement. The central business district becomes dominated by the architecture of commerce, with grand Renaissance-style cotton warehouses replacing residential housing. Beyond this core, municipal interventions in the form of by-law housing creates solid working-class townships of gridded, redbrick terraces, with the bourgeoisie moving further afield into fine suburban and semi-rural villas.

The fourth phase encompasses major civic reordering, with the attempt at creating a 'one-nation' Manchester: the 'City of Civic Pride and Industrial Paternalism, c.1860–c.1890' (Chapter 4). There is a conscious effort to bring together and regulate social classes within the built environment in an era of emerging mass politics. Alfred Waterhouse's new Town Hall and Albert Square, opened in 1877, is emblematic of civic pride and social cohesion during this phase, with the Gothic style defining a distinctive architecture of industrial paternalism. While the city centre becomes the focus for civic ceremonies, commerce, clubs and societies, the old institutions of corporate order, workhouses, hospitals and prisons are moved to the periphery. There is also a notable expansion of Manchester's industrial base, especially on the eastern fringes, which emerges as the prime centre for engineering in the city. Accompanying these developments is a further process suburbanisation with the rise of more cosmopolitan and socially mixed townships. The prominence of middle-class religious and charitable institutions in the built environment is another feature of this phase, together with new municipal interventions in the form of parks, board schools and cemeteries.

The fifth and final phase, at the very end of the nineteenth century and the beginning of the twentieth, is the most extensive in terms of urban growth and levels of building and rebuilding around Manchester—'City of Ambition and Popular Culture, c.1890–c.1920' (Chapter 5). This phase is defined by the construction of the Manchester Ship Canal together with Salford Quays between 1887 and 1894, which represented another radical urban intervention that helped reorientate developments during the so-called 'second Industrial Revolution'. This is a phase that witnessed the formal expansion of the city's boundaries to incorporate the surrounding satellite townships, now integrated together by a new tram network, creating a 'Greater Manchester'. It is a time when the city's Corporation is most visible in the urban arena through its supply of public utilities, and in the setting up of suburban libraries, parks and swimming baths (amongst other things). In tandem with these municipal improvements is the conspicuous rise of urban leisure and popular culture in the form of theatres, cinemas, pleasure gardens and sports arenas. Lastly, this is the phase when the presence of a working class becomes more openly expressed in the architecture and physical fabric of the city; a reflection of the burgeoning power of organised labour.

While this sequence of five phases draws attention to the major chronological patterns of development, each phase will be broken down into sub-phases to highlight the main material and spatial contours of the city's history. These subdivisions capture significant patterns in the social development of the built environment and are defined in terms of different building types and associated complexes (industrial, commercial, religious, domestic, civic and so on), transport networks and infrastructure (roads, rivers, canals, railways, quays and docks) as well as built spaces and facilities (squares, parks, esplanades, cemeteries, sports arenas and grounds). These categories are discussed in each of the five phases.

The rest of this study will lay out a more detailed picture and analysis of these five phases of urban growth, drawing specific attention to the way in which the material, spatial and temporal changes in Manchester's built environment constituted and mediated class relations between capital and labour from the very beginnings of industrial capitalism. Throughout I will seek to integrate a contextual study of the physical fabric of the existing city into a broader economic, political and social history of Manchester and the long nineteenth century.

1. The Georgian Boom Town, c.1720–c.1780

In the famous travelogue of Daniel Defoe's 1724–1726 tours through the country, he described Manchester as the 'greatest mere village in England' (1971, 544) to draw attention to the contradiction of a burgeoning cloth manufacturing town without borough status or parliamentary representation. After describing the growth of the town with fine new houses and streets, Defoe came to the conclusion the Manchester would in time 'obtain some better face of government, and be incorporated, as it very well deserves to be' (1971, 546). But this did not happen until well into the next century. Manchester was not a 'typical' Georgian town, nor did its development during the eighteenth century follow more established urban trends. Defoe's rather optimistic account can be dramatically contrasted with Engels' much darker, critical analysis from the early 1840s. Cataloguing the urban squalor and the condition of the working-class district by district, Engels asserted that he had 'never seen so ill-built a city' (2009, 275); its physical fabric being totally subordinated to the pursuit of 'Mammon'. Manchester represented something new. The rapid growth of this regional centre linked to the mechanisation of the textile industry took the town in a radically different urban direction, one which was distinctively unique for the time.

This chapter will explore two features of the eighteenth century townscape. Firstly, 'Manchester and the Landed Aristocracy' looks at the aristocratic presence in the town in terms of the Georgian mansions that survive, and discusses the relative lack of direct aristocratic interest in urban developments. Secondly, 'Manchester's

Urban Modernity' examines the new interventions in the built environment (principally the church-based residential developments, the new religious and civic buildings and improvements to the urban infrastructure) and how they were driven by commercial and middle-class interests.

Manchester and the Landed Aristocracy

The lack of borough status and a local government capable of overseeing and coordinating developments carries important implications for understanding Manchester's distinctive urban trajectory, as does the relative absence of direct aristocratic involvement in the development of the town during the early modern period. Manchester was not a county town and so did not attract the interest of the local aristocracy who went to Chester to socially network and enjoy the pleasures of urban polite society. The major landowners used their property and estates in and around Manchester to primarily extract rents and fines, as well as to accumulate capital through selling-off parcels of land, rather than to actively influence urban planning decisions.

This lack of direct aristocratic interest in Manchester can be illustrated with the example of the Mosley family. Sir Nicholas Mosley purchased the Manor of Manchester in 1596, with the Mosley family holding the manor until its municipal incorporation in 1846. Despite being a wealthy woollen cloth merchant, Nicholas Mosley built his main seat of residence some distance from the town, in his estate at Chorlton-cum-Hardy, where he constructed a large, brick-built 'Elizabethan' mansion, Hough End Hall. Furthermore, it was not Manchester's parish church that the Mosley family invested in, but St James's chapel in the nearby village of Didsbury, which they rebuilt in the early seventeenth century and where Sir Nicholas is buried in an impressive family funeral monument. Consequently, Manchester was a decidedly 'bourgeois' town. It unfolded in a piecemeal and loosely regulated manner; its physical character reflecting and embodying principally middle-class economic, social and political interests, rather than those of the local aristocracy.

Fig. 1.1 Hough End Hall, Chorlton (Author, 2020).

Although the aristocracy played a limited role in the development of the town, with many selling their estates and halls during the course of the eighteenth century, a few remained and invested in their property. The mansions that were built in the immediate vicinity of Manchester were subsequently absorbed into the city during the later nineteenth century.

Fig. 1.2 Platt Hall, Rusholme (Author, 2022).

Platt Hall in Rusholme, now a museum and municipal park in south Manchester, was the home of the Worsley family since the early seventeenth century (with Charles Worsley a key Parliamentarian during the English Civil War and appointed as MP for Manchester by Oliver Cromwell in 1654 during the First Protectorate Parliament). The present redbrick Neoclassical, Palladian-style hall was built in 1761 for John and Deborah Carrill-Worsley, based upon designs of John Carr of York.

On the other side of the city, located on the higher ground to the north of Manchester, is Heaton Hall, the seat of the Egerton family since the late seventeenth century. It was Sir Thomas Egerton who commissioned James Wyatt in 1772 to design a splendid Palladian mansion, which Nikolaus Pevsner regarded as the finest house of its period in Lancashire. It was set in a landscaped estate along Brownian lines which was later incorporated as part of a municipal park. The success of Wyatt's design meant that it was copied by other local aristocrats, such as at Parrs Wood House, which formed a smaller version of Heaton Hall, complete with a similar fluted frieze with garlanded ox skulls. This is now part of Parrs Wood School.

Fig. 1.3 Heaton Hall, Heaton Hall (Author, 2023).

The Trafford family (one of the earliest recorded families in England) also had their ancestral estate near Manchester and remained living at a hall in Trafford Park right up until 1896, when it was sold, due to the encroachment of Manchester Ship Canal and transformed into Trafford Park industrial estate. But despite the close physical presence of the Traffords, Egertons and Worsleys (as well as others), these aristocratic families left little imprint on Manchester's urban built environment, apart from one notable exception, Francis Egerton, the third Duke of Bridgewater. It was Francis Egerton who was responsible for the Bridgewater Canal which played such an important role in the making of the industrial city (as will be discussed below).

Manchester's Urban Modernity

Russell Casson and John Berry's 1746 plan of Manchester provides a visual representation of the early Georgian town described by Defoe. Not only does it represent the town's first authentic street map, but it provides a prospect of Manchester, from the south-west, as well as illustrations of key buildings that frame the plan. The expansion of Manchester from its medieval and early modern core is clearly represented on this map. The focus of the old town had been the fifteenth-century collegiate church of St Mary, St Denys and St George (which later became Manchester Cathedral). It was beside this church that the old marketplace had been established and where the two principal charitable institutions of early modern Manchester were sited—the Grammar School in 1515 (rebuilt on the same spot in 1776) and Chetham's Hospital and Library in 1653. However, while the streets of the old town surround the parish church in a muddled but roughly circular pattern, Manchester's urban modernity is defined by distinctive planned developments beyond this core: namely residential squares and straight, chartered streets. St Ann's Square, set out in 1720 in association with the church of St Ann, is the most obvious example of this shift away from the medieval centre, together with King Street and Quay Street, the latter of which was laid out in 1735 to link Manchester first quay on the River Irwell to Deansgate.

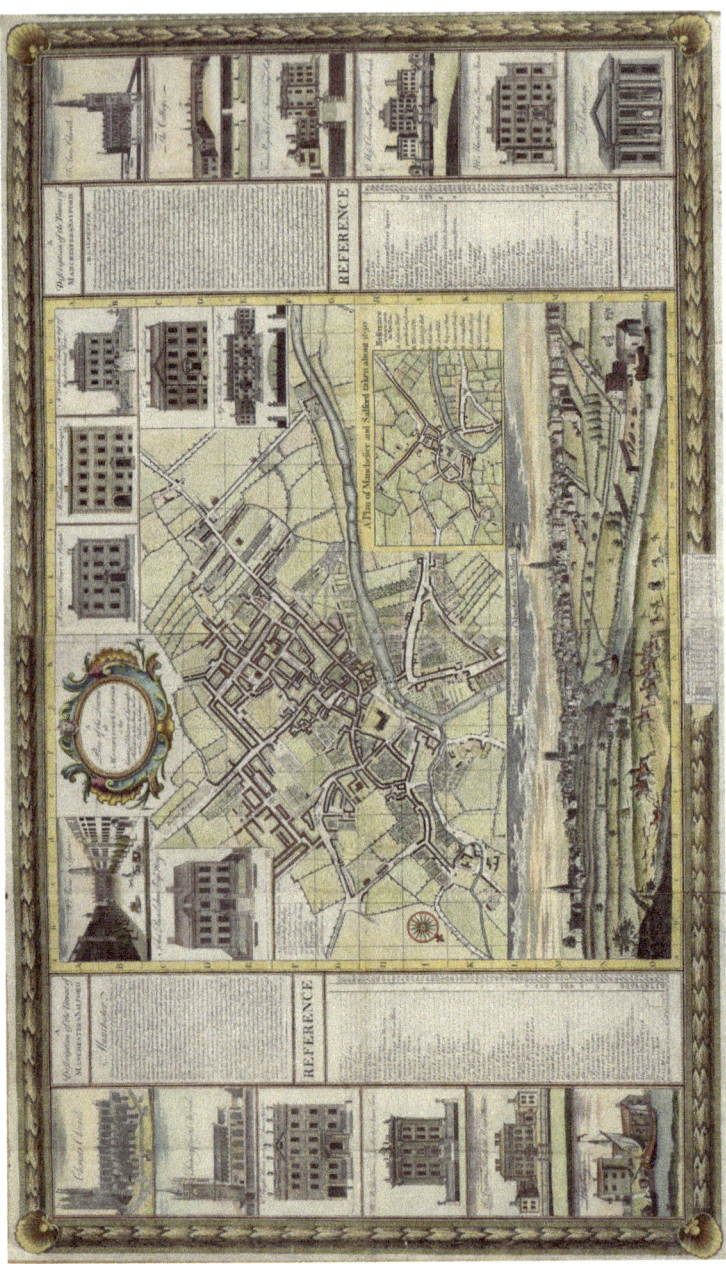

Fig. 1.4 Casson and Berry's 1746 'A plan of the towns of Manchester and Salford'. Image provided by Manchester Central Library/Bridgeman Images.

Fig. 1.5 Manchester Cathedral (Author, 2023).

These early Georgian urban innovations were driven by Manchester's middle class, and architecturally expressed their rising power, status and identity in the town. While being men of property, these people were defined by their qualified professions rather than the ownership of landed estates, being manufacturers, merchants, bankers, doctors and lawyers etc. They formed the core of Manchester's emerging bourgeoisie. Direct commercial interests clearly underpinned much of the urban developments during this phase as evidenced by Edward Byrom's construction of the quay for the Mersey and Irwell Navigation Company in 1720, and Sir Oswald Mosley's erection of the first Cotton Exchange in 1729, a Neoclassical structure positioned between the old marketplace and the new St Ann's Square. Partial canalisation made the river commercially navigable enabling the direct transport of American slave-produced cotton, which was critical for the town's economic take-off, while the Exchange became the business centre of Manchester's cotton merchants and a monumental structure symbolising the power of commerce. It was rebuilt several times during its history. However, this new built environment also gave expression to Manchester's wider polite society with its religious and political differences and conflicts.

Lady Ann Bland built the church of St Ann (1709–1712), for example, in opposition to the high church, Tory-dominated parish church—providing a place of worship for the town's middle-class Whig and anti-Jacobite factions. It is significant that its Baroque architecture stands in marked contrast to the perpendicular Gothic of the parish church, and that the formal elegance of the adjoining residential square stands out next to the adjacent irregular courts and alleys of the old urban core. Sectarian differences, therefore, were an important feature of Georgian Manchester as they were embedded within the various political and social identities of the middle class. This is reflected in the ecclesiastical geography of the town. Religion played a crucial role in forging different social groups through creating networks and establishing respectability and legitimacy. It was a complex phenomenon appealing to both the elite and subaltern groups. As Marx notoriously put it 'Religion is the sigh of the oppressed creatures, the heart of a heartless world and the soul of soulless conditions' (1974, 244). Churches and chapels and other places of worship were therefore central to all communities, and their physical presence formed a highly conspicuous component of the built environment. Consequently, a discussion of religious buildings will form a key element of this study.

Fig. 1.6 St Ann's Church and St Ann's Square (Author, 2023).

1. *The Georgian Boom Town, c.1720–c.1780*   23

Fig. 1.7 Cross Street Chapel, 1900, unknown photographer. Image courtesy of Manchester Libraries.

Protestant Nonconformity, especially Unitarianism, performed a particularly important role in Manchester's development with Cross Street Chapel, first established in 1694 on the fringes of the town, providing the early centre for Dissenter worship and for social networking amongst the social elite. Around 1761, it became a Unitarian meetinghouse which was highly influential in cultivating a civic leadership, especially amongst the more 'liberal' leaning section of Manchester's polite society. In this sense it played as similar role to Mill Hill Chapel in Leeds. It was from Cross Street Chapel that various Unitarian congregations spread out through the expanding town during the late eighteenth and early nineteenth century, nurturing the leading families of the day such as the Heywoods. Manchester's Unitarians still meet there, although the present building dates to 1997.

Fig. 1.8 Moravian Church, Fairfield, Droylsden (Author, 2023).

The importance of Nonconformity in Manchester's development is also reflected in the fact that Dissenters outnumbered Anglicans amongst the town's middle class. In contrast to the institutional unity of the Church of England, Nonconformists were affiliated to various denominations. As well as Unitarians, other Protestant groups were drawn to Manchester, such as Baptists, Quakers, Methodists, Congregationalists, and followers of the Moravian Church (which had originated in fifteenth-century Bohemia). The Moravians established a settlement at Fairfield, Droylsden in 1784. Although it lies a few miles east of the town, this site is worth mentioning for its particular significance within Greater Manchester. Remarkably, it survives almost entirely intact, with its central church, the attached Sisters' and Brethren houses, schools and other residential buildings arranged in terraces around three streets. The settlement's burial ground, known as God's Acre, also remains, with its uniform gravestones laid flat in rows. Elite members of this community formed part of the local middle class, with a number of brethren, such as the engineer John Frederick Bateman, playing notable roles in Manchester's later development.

Fig. 1.9 Sacred Trinity, Chapel Street, Salford (Author, 2020).

Fig. 1.10 35 King Street, Manchester (Author, 2020).

Fig. 1.11 Old Wellington Inn and Sinclair's Oyster Bar, Shambles Square (Author, 2022).

In the town, much of the street pattern recorded on Casson and Berry's 1746 map is still in existence and used today, but virtually nothing of the standing architecture survives, apart from three churches: the medieval parish church; Sacred Trinity in Salford, founded in 1634 and rebuilt in Baroque style in 1753 (apart from the tower); and St Ann. However, in King Street a single, early Georgian town house remains largely intact (although minus its two wings)—Number 35, built for Dr Peter Waring in 1736. This is the only physical testament to the fashionable early Georgian Manchester, described by Defoe and recorded in Casson and Berry's map, when the urban elite resided in the centre of the town. This symmetrical, redbrick structure represented a new architectural aesthetic, in contrast to the timber-framed buildings of the old town (of which the much-restored Old Wellington Inn and Sinclair's Oyster Bar by the cathedral are a pale reminder of what has been lost).

1. The Georgian Boom Town, c.1720–c.1780

Fig. 1.12 William Green's 1794 'A plan of Manchester and Salford'. Image provided by The John Rylands Research Institute and Library, The University of Manchester.

William Green's map of Manchester and Salford at the start of the industrial take-off in the late eighteenth century strikingly reveals the geographical expansion of the Georgian boom town, especially to the east and south of the old core. This physical growth was intimately linked to Manchester's rising status as the centre for the manufacture and marketing of cotton textiles with regional, national and increasingly international importance—'Manchester Goods'.

Fig. 1.13 Cobden House, 10 Quay Street (Author, 2025).

The Green map shows a continuity in the church-focused pattern of residential development, initiated first in the consecration of St Ann (and which continued into the early nineteenth century). For instance, to the west, in what is now Parsonage Croft, St Mary was founded in 1756 together with a graveyard that was surrounded on all four sides by fashionable residential housing. To the east, the church of St Paul was built at the end of Turner Street in the Northern Quarter in 1765, while Edward Byrom's residential development to the south of Quay Street was planned around St John's church and graveyard which was constructed in 1769. Not one of these three churches have survived, being demolished during the twentieth century, although the graveyards of St Mary and St John still exist as public gardens. And the only extant house associated with these mid- to late eighteenth-century developments is Cobden House (c.1770), 10 Quay Street, a large symmetrical redbrick Georgian town house with a Venetian window. However, as well as patterns of continuity, three new developments in Manchester's urban morphology can be highlighted on Green's map, as they were to exert an influence on subsequent phases of development.

Fig. 1.14 The Infirmary, Dispensary and Lunatic Asylum, Manchester, England. Line engraving by J. Davies after S. Austin (1831). Wellcome Collection, https://wellcomecollection.org/works/trrq4wes/images?id=vd63xnfr, public domain.

Firstly, there is the Infirmary, the largest and perhaps the most significant public building of Georgian Manchester. Built on a monumental scale with a classical facade, the hospital was co-founded by the physician Charles White and industrialist Joseph Bancroft, and opened in 1755 on land leased by the Mosley family in an area to the west of the town (now Piccadilly Gardens). A lunatic asylum was added to the Infirmary in 1765, public baths in 1779 and a dispensary in 1792. This complex was a charitable institution, part of a national voluntary hospital movement which provided free medical care for the deserving poor. But these voluntary hospitals were more than just medical institutions: they were equally important sites of social networking and social advance for the urban middle class, who were the subscribers and potential governors. Manchester's Infirmary, positioned on the eastern limits, along one of the main arterial routes into the town, provided a focus for fashionable residential developments that shifted the orientation of Manchester eastwards. Further, as a popular form of philanthropy, voluntary hospitals had a role in mediating social unrest and generating social cohesion between classes. It is not a coincidence, therefore, that hospital foundations tended to follow periods of disorder. As Roy Porter argues, 'the infirmary threw a cloak of charity over the bones of poverty and naked repression' (1989, 152). This is the case in Manchester. The Infirmary was founded after the Jacobite Rising of 1745 and during a period of frequent food riots, the most notable being the 'Shudehill Fight' of 1757, which resulted in multiple fatalities.

Fig. 1.15 New Cross, c.1800 painting. Unknown artist. Image courtesy of Manchester Libraries.

Secondly, is the importance of the northeastern route into the town along Oldham Road (what was then Newton Lane) and the establishment of New Cross at the junction with Great Ancoats Street. The breadth of the street indicates its use for the transport of goods and especially livestock into the town. By the late eighteenth century, Manchester had outgrown the limitations of the cramped, old medieval marketplace and so required additional space. The open land on the northern fringes of the built-up area provided such space and New Cross subsequently emerged as a new marketplace with permanent booths (as depicted in this painting dated to the early 1800s). It was adjacent to an area on top of Shudehill that became the town's main wholesale marketing district during the nineteenth century (and into the twentieth). As well as a commercial district, the New Cross area was to become an important locale of radical plebeian and working-class politics and a notable site of protests during the early nineteenth century, including the infamous food riots of April 1812, which lasted three days and left several people dead.

Fig. 1.16 Grocer's Warehouse, Castlefield (Author, 2023).

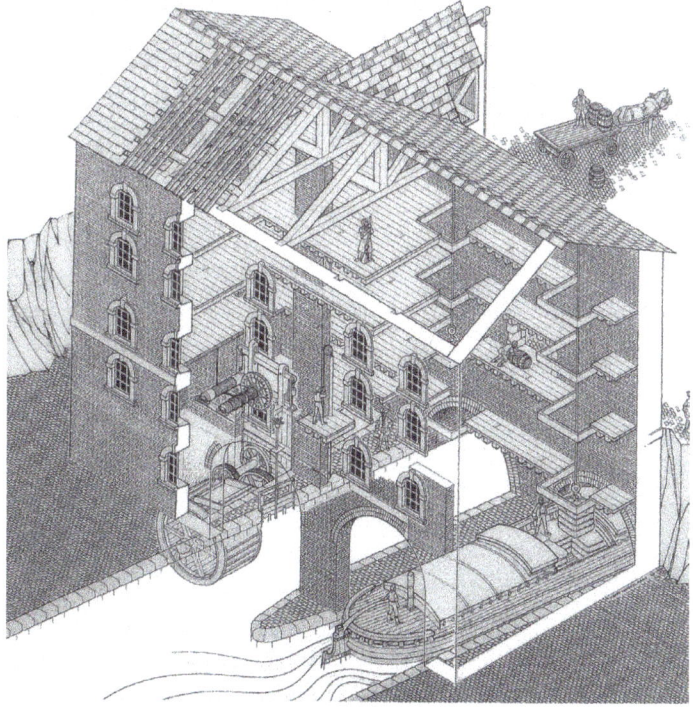

Fig. 1.17 Reconstruction of Grocer's Warehouse (© Michael Nevell).

Thirdly, the Green map records the cutting of the Bridgewater Canal with its basin on the very southern fringes of the town at Castlefield—Francis Egerton, the third Duke of Bridgewater, being unable to locate it closer to the urban centre due to opposition from Edward Byrom, who refused to allow access to his estate. Opened in 1761 to transport coal directly from the Duke's mines at Worsley into Manchester, the Bridgewater Canal was an amazing feat of advanced engineering. It was designed by James Brindley and included an aqueduct over the River Mersey and a terminal warehouse with water-powered hoist to lift coal from the canal basin to the street (now partially rebuilt as Grocer's Warehouse). The basin was fed from the River Medlock, which was culverted in an ingenious fashion to run under it, and contained a sluice, the Giant's Basin, to drain excess water back into to the river. The conserved remains of the Bridgewater Canal Basin now form part of the Castlefield 'urban heritage park', a designated conservation area since the 1980s.

The immediate success of the Bridgewater Canal initiated the wave of canal building in Manchester and around the country during the late eighteenth and early nineteenth centuries. It was a major piece of capital investment that directly influenced the growth of the city, drawing attention to the way Manchester's built environment was decisively shaped by improvements in its transport infrastructure. In particular, the Bridgewater Canal reduced the price of coal and so helped facilitate the industrial take-off of Manchester in terms of fuelling the proliferation of coal-fired, steam-powered cotton mills.

The entrances to Duke's mines at Worsley are impressive, with the original canal tunnels that took coal barges underground directly into the colliery still visible at Worsley Delph. It was during the second half of the eighteenth century that the Manchester Coalfield became more intensely exploited, with the remains of early coal mines and workings also observable along the Irwell Valley at Clifton, Salford, where James Brindley helped solve water management problems at Wet Earth Colliery, and at Park Bridge in the Medlock Valley near Ashton-under-Lyne, where the remains of the engine 'pumping' house of Rocher New Pit can be visited, along with the related ironworks.

By 1780, the end of this phase, Manchester had emerged as a manufacturing town of some note based on the manufacture and trade of cotton textiles. The corresponding growth of the built environment had been driven in an uneven and unregulated manner by a middle class that was largely unrestrained by local aristocratic interests. They could boast of possessing a prestigious voluntary hospital and a developing townscape based around new church foundations, together with fashionable Georgian houses along chartered streets. At this point, Manchester might have progressed like many other urban centres of the era into a typical late eighteenth-century town, complete with all the social and architectural trappings of Georgian polite society. But this did not happen. The dramatic industrial take-off at the end of the century took Manchester in a very different urban direction, as it was made into a city of capital and labour.

2. The 'Shock City' of Industrial Capitalism, c.1780–c.1840

In 1782, Richard Arkwright opened his mill on the northern outskirts of Manchester along Miller Street. This was the first mill to use steam-power (albeit just to raise water to work the wheel rather than to drive spinning machines themselves) and is often cited as marking the start of the city's industrial take-off and its transformation into 'Cottonopolis'. The introduction of the Boulton and Watt patented steam engines may have been initially slow, with water-power generally favoured rather than expensive coal-fired steam-power, but significantly it facilitated the movement and expansion of textile production within the urban arena. By the turn of the century, there were over a hundred separate mills in the immediate vicinity of the town, and by the 1830s the spinning and weaving of cotton was mostly driven by steam-powered machines—Sharp, Roberts and Company's self-acting mule (the 'Iron-Man') and the power-loom.

However, Manchester was never just a mill town. It was the commercial capital of the cotton industry. The spinning, weaving, processing and distributing of cotton textiles generated a diverse industrial base including chemical dye works, foundries and engineering plants, as well as whole commercial districts of warehouses, banks and financial institutions. This produced an architecture of industry: mills, factories and chimneys belching smoke—a Dickensian 'Coketown'. Conversely, this industrial townscape was closely connected to the architecture of discipline which included the building of a prison, workhouse and two barracks. This is not commonly commented upon in discussions of Manchester's built environment, but I think it is important to draw attention to it. Industrialisation cannot be separated from the disciplining of labour. As Andreas Malm eloquently argues in his masterful book, *Fossil Capital*, there was an intimate relationship between steam-power and social power, the use of coal-fired steam engines to drive spinning, and weaving machines and the exploitation of an urban workforce to generate surplus value—profits. The sharp class polarisation of urban society which accompanied the industrial take-off, and that was such a concern for many contemporary writers, was embedded in the physical fabric of the city (as Engels observed). Manchester was a town of brutal capitalist exploitation, and this produced an urban geography unseen before. Despite the enormous amount of wealth that was generated, the town was conspicuously poor in terms of Georgian 'polite' architecture. In the words of General Charles Napier, who wrote in his diary in 1839 after being appointed to command the armed forces in the north of England to suppress the Chartists: 'Manchester is the chimney of the world. Rich rascals, poor rogues, drunken ragamuffins and prostitutes form the moral; soot made into paste by rain, the physique; and the only view is a long chimney; what a place! The entrance to Hell realised' (cited in Bradshaw 1987, 5). Clearly capital was being invested in Manchester's productive economy, rather than being consumed in prestigious private and civic building projects, which had generally been the case in Britain at this time. However, Manchester's middle class did begin to adopt a new form of urban living during this initial phase of industrialisation. This involved a change in domestic arrangements and the movement away from the city centre to residing in the suburbs and beyond. With this development the distinctive pattern of the suburban, 'bourgeois' villa was born.

To make sense of these developments, this phase will be broken down into five separate sub-phases. Firstly, 'Steam-Power and the Industrial Take-Off' looks at the surviving material evidence for industrialisation in terms of the early mills (textile factories) that used steam-power to spin cotton, the weavers' workshop dwellings where this thread was woven into cloth, and the new road and canal network that helped facilitate Manchester's economic growth, together with the associated warehouses. Secondly, 'Urban Expansion and Working-Class "Slums"' examines the indirect evidence for working-class districts by discussing the results of recent archaeological excavations and through plotting the spread of new religious buildings and foundations, especially the Commissioners' churches. Thirdly, 'Power and Resistance in Industrial Manchester' explores how the built environment of the town was implicated in the disciplining of the emerging industrial working class. It considers the distribution of the institutions of coercion (workhouse, prison and barracks) that were established at the same time as Manchester's economic take-off, as well as the places and spaces of working-class radicalism. Fourthly, '"Polite Society" and the Transformations of the Central District' turns analysis towards Manchester's social elite and explores how a middle-class locale was created around Mosley Street, associated with institutions of bourgeois culture. This development was notably short-lived, due to the transformation of the residential centre as businesses took over previously fashionable streets. Manchester's Georgian architecture is consequently relatively impoverished due to the impact of industrialisation, and this is also reflected in the failure of the planned residential developments to take-off. The final subsection of this phase will move on to explore the middle-class residential movement beyond the centre in the form of suburban developments, such as Victoria Park. It ends by describing Liverpool Road Station, which was opened in 1830 and marked the all-important start of the age of the railway.

Steam-Power and the Industrial Take-Off

The introduction of steam-power allowed the movement of mechanised textile production from the countryside, where water-power had been utilised to drive spinning machines, to the town. While the cost of coal was a financial burden on industrialists, an urban base for manufacturing was desirable primarily because of the availability of labour. Water may have been free to use, but a rural location meant that it was hard to attract enough workers, and the cost of accommodating them in purpose-built colonies, like Arkwright's Cromford (Derbyshire) and Samuel Greg's Styal (Cheshire), was an expensive investment. Towns like Manchester, however, were increasingly full of migrants seeking work, and therefore there was a ready supply of labour that did not need to be housed and nurtured by the employer. Mill hands in the city were cheap and disposable.

James Pigot's 1838 printed map of the Manchester district, when compared with Green's earlier map of 1794, visually illustrates how the town grew in all directions over this forty-odd-year period. The speed of the growth is striking. Manchester doubled its physical extent, with the population increasing from a figure of 76,788, recorded in the first national census of 1801, to 242,983 in the census of 1841 (so, more than trebling in total). Such a dramatic expansion of the population over so short a period of time was a consequence of Manchester's Industrial Revolution, as mechanisation absorbed urban labour and encouraged more workers to migrate to the town. This in turn promoted further industrialisation and population growth. Manchester, following the industrial take-off, was a city of migrants. Thousands upon thousands of people moved into the town from the immediate hinterlands of Lancashire and Cheshire, and further afield from North Wales, Scotland, and above all Ireland. These migrants formed the organic heart of the city.

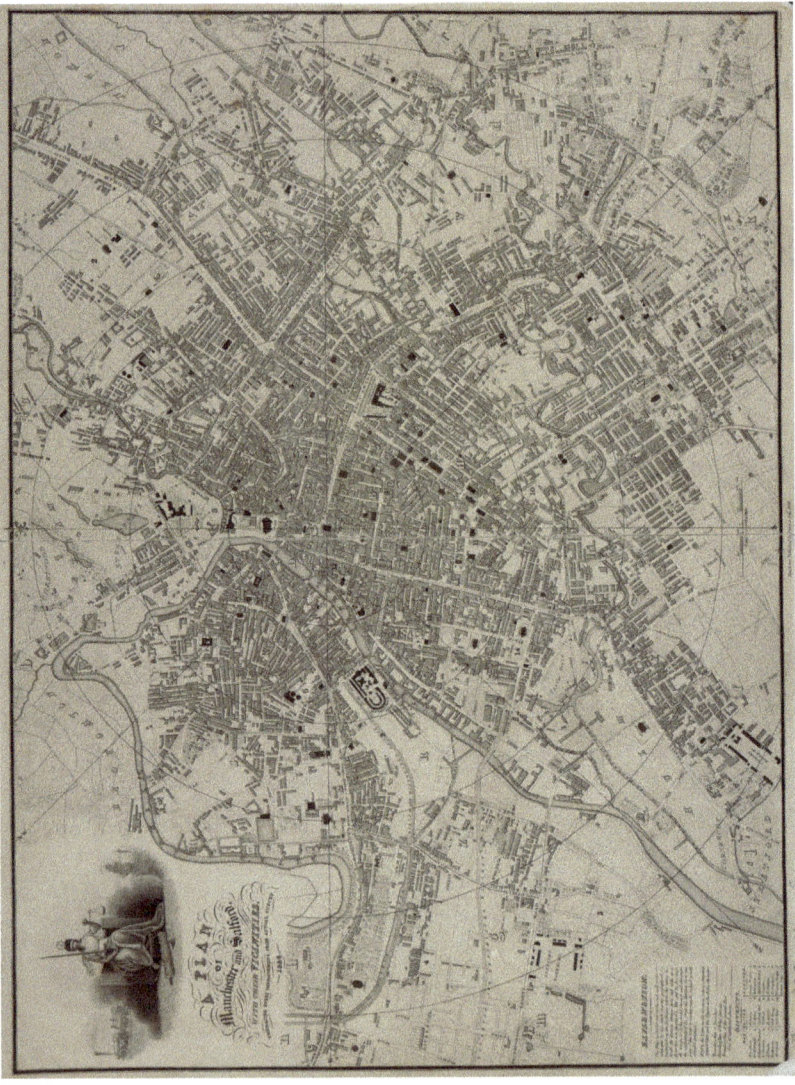

Fig. 2.1 James Pigot 'A plan of Manchester and Salford', 1836. Image courtesy of Manchester Libraries.

Murrays' Mills and Early Textile Factories

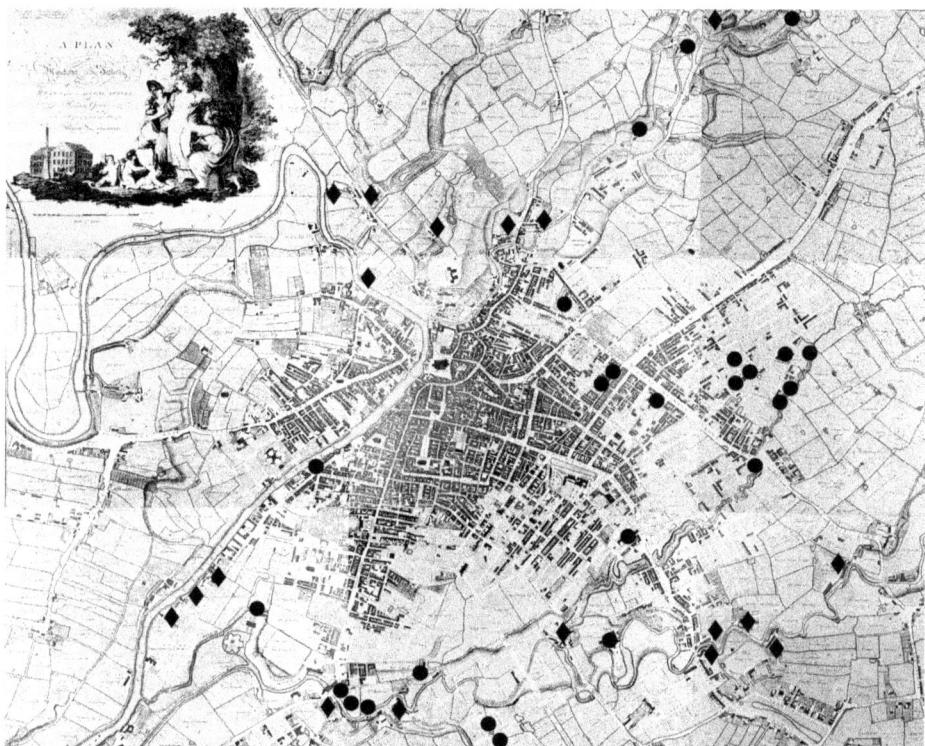

Fig. 2.2 The distribution of Manchester's textile factories by 1800. The base map is Green's map of Manchester published in 1794. Key: dots = cotton spinning factories; diamonds = finishing works (© Michael Nevell).

Michael Nevell's annotated map, which uses Green's map of 1794 as its basis, shows the location of the first factories and how they were initially concentrated around the edges of the built-up area, along the rivers Irwell, Medlock and Irk where they could make use of the water-power available. However, it also reveals another focus of mills fronting the arms of the Ashton and Rochdale canals (which were cut between 1792–1796 and 1794–1806, respectively) in the area of Manchester known as Ancoats. This concentration of textile factories in Ancoats meant that this district became an informal industrial suburb which incorporated foundries, glass works and other industries amongst the mills. It is in this area, especially along Jersey Street, Redhill Street and Pollard Street, that some of these early mills survive and provide the best examples of the architecture of industrial discipline.

Fig. 2.3 Murrays' Mills, Redhill Street, Ancoats (showing the blocked entrance of the arm of the Rochdale which led to a basin within the mill complex), Photograph by Clem Rutter (2010), Wikimedia Commons, CC BY-SA 3.0, https://commons.wikimedia.org/wiki/File:Ancoats_Redhill_Street-_4557.JPG#/media/File:Ancoats_Redhill_Street-_4557.JPG

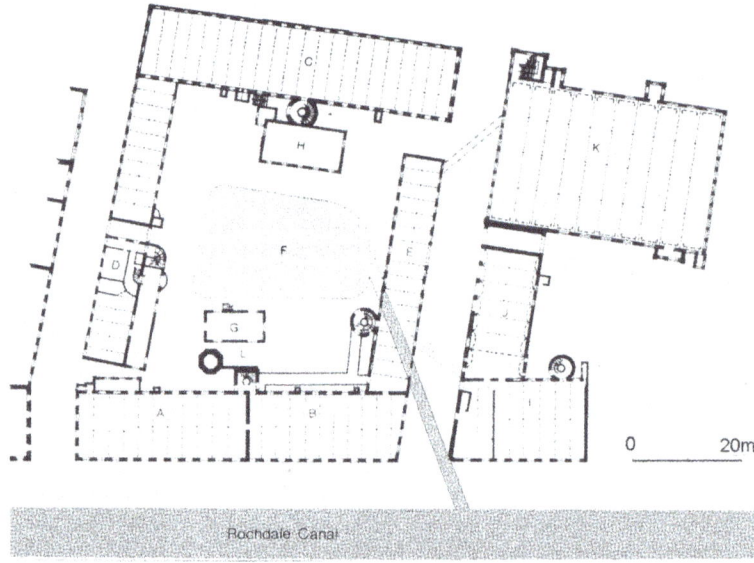

Fig. 2.4 Plan of Murrays' Mills complex, Redhill Street, Ancoats (© Michael Nevell/Historic England Archive).

The Scottish entrepreneurs James McConnel and John Kennedy, and brothers Adam and George Murray, were the first to apply Boulton and Watt's rotary beam steam engine to drive the spinning mule. They had migrated to Manchester from Kirkcudbrightshire and became the biggest employers in the local cotton industry, building some of the largest mills in the town. These were located together in Ancoats on Redhill Street fronting the Rochdale Canal and still form an important collection of industrial buildings which retain their imposing presence. McConnel and Kennedy erected their first cotton-spinning factory in 1798, the Old Mill, on a site now occupied by Royal Mill. However, their Sedwick Mill, constructed between 1818 and 1820, still stands. This is an eight-storey, fireproof structure with an impressive seventeen-bay canal range. Immediately adjacent to it is Murrays' Mills, the earliest surviving and most complete cotton mill complex in Manchester. This was built in three stages, between 1798 and 1806, with the five different mills arranged around a canal basin with an arm linking it to the Rochdale Canal. The overall plan of Murrays' Mills shows the compact, redoubt-like military appearance of the first mills. These were all purpose-built in fireproof construction and subsequently equipped with gas lighting to enable work to be continued during the mornings and evenings of the dark winter months. Together the Old Mill (1798) and Decker Mill (1802) formed an enormous twenty-two-bay canal range in eight storeys with regularly spaced windows along each floor. On visiting Manchester in 1826, the German architect Karl Friedrich Schinkel was shocked by these industrial structures, disclaiming them as 'monstrous shapeless buildings [...] without architecture' (cited in Crinson 2022, 21). Looking up at the facade facing the canal today, it is hard to appreciate the novelty of this industrial architectural complex and how it would have been experienced by those that worked within the building. Complexes such as Murrays' Mills could accommodate hundreds of workers and were Manchester's largest employers, with the biggest firm, McConnel and Kennedy, employing more than 1,500 mill hands by 1836. The austere uniformity of the facades of mills like McConnel and Kennedy's and Murrays' Mills expressed the logic of work discipline associated with factory production and the regularity of clock-time that was imposed upon the workforce. In the words of the architectural historian Mark Crinson, 'Ancoats was a kind of Petri dish for industrial modernity' (2022, 22). It was a type of architecture that consequently became a template for industrial buildings and offices more generally. Work space, along with the productive process itself, became highly regulated and controlled through architectural design. Entrances to mills, for instance, were tightly restricted, usually with just one prominent gateway that could be closed and secured against riot (as illustrated in the adjacent Beehive Mill on Jersey Street with its military-like, large stone-arched entrance, with a plaque dating to 1824). Ancoats mills were indeed attacked; the working-class threat was real. During the industrial disturbances of 1826, a mill on Jersey Street was burnt down with similar attempts made on several others.

Fig. 2.5 Entrance to Beehive Mill, Jersey Street, Ancoats (Author, 2012).

Of the other early mills and factories that survive in Ancoats, a number are worth noting. Located along the adjacent Pollard Street is Hope Mill. This was built in 1824 for Joseph Clarke and Sons, textile spinners and fustian weavers, and is similar in design to the other examples, consisting of a seven-storey, redbrick rectangular block, with regular spaced windows and direct access to Ashton Canal. It is now a theatre. Nearby, on Great Ancoats Street, is the well-preserved Brownsfield Mill, dated to around 1825. This was L-shaped, with blocks of six and seven storeys including an unusual circular external stair tower. There is also a shipping hole with the mill purposely aligned with an arm of the Rochdale Canal.

Fig. 2.6 Marsland's Mill, Chester Street, Chorlton-on-Medlock (Author, 2021).

Fig. 2.7 Chorlton Old Mill and Chorlton New Mills (far-left building with chimney), Cambridge Street, Chorlton-on-Medlock (Author, 2021).

As the 'shock city' of industrial capitalism, Manchester's industrial heritage is indeed impressive, despite the scale of subsequent destruction and dereliction. It is not just in the suburb of Ancoats that several have been preserved—there is also an important concentration of restored early mills in the Chorlton-on-Medlock district, along Cambridge Street by the River Medlock. These include those owned by the Marsland and Birley families, two leading and contrasting industrialists. Marsland's Mill originated in 1795 and was rebuilt in 1813, while Chorlton Old Mill, built for Robert Owen in 1795, was purchased by the Birley family in 1809, who then constructed Chorlton New Mills on Hulme Street between 1813 and 1815. The Marslands were prominent Unitarians, Samuel Marsland being a member of the Cross Street Chapel, while the Birleys were Tory Anglicans, with Hugh Hornby Birley a leading political figure in Manchester—the man responsible for charging the yeomanry into the Peterloo crowds in 1819.

The surviving factories at Chorlton-on-Medlock also attest to the fact that Manchester's industrial manufacturing was not simply based on the spinning of cotton. Opposite the mills on Cambridge Street, the Birleys built a factory to produce waterproof fabric—the Macintosh Works, of which the second building completed by 1838 still stands as a visually prominent monument in Manchester's cityscape.

Other surviving mills from this initial phase of industrial take-off in the Manchester conurbation include Islington Mill on James Street in Salford. This was a six-storey, cast-iron-framed fireproof mill for cotton-spinning, built in 1823. Infamously, Islington Mill partially collapsed immediately following its construction due to the failure of the cast-iron beams. This resulted in the deaths of eighteen mill workers and a delay in the further introduction of this type of fireproofing. A little further afield is the Silk Mill in Newton Heath constructed in 1826 and enlarged in 1832 with a stone dating plaque on its front. At the time of its construction, this was one of the largest silk mills in the country, built for the industrialist James Taylor who lived nearby in Brookdale Hall (now Brookdale Park). All these mills took on a similar and identifiable form in the urban environment that came to symbolise the rise of industrial society and the subjugation of the working class through steam-powered technology—William Blake's 'dark satanic mills'.

Weavers' Workshop Dwellings

Fig. 2.8 47–53 Tib Street, Northern Quarter (showing workshop attic with windows and 'taking-in' door) (Author, 2022).

However, what is fascinating in any study of Manchester's industrial heritage is how it reveals the uneven nature of industrialisation. While both the spinning and weaving of cotton yarn was open to steam-power, it was only spinning that was initially mechanised. Although the power-loom was first patented by Edward Cartwright in 1785, it was not until the 1830s that it was used for the weaving of cloth on a mass scale. Before then, weaving was carried out by hand-loom weavers operating through the well-established 'putting out' system. This remained the preferred method of production as the availability of labour to weave cloth remained so cheap. Consequently, the establishment of the first spinning mills in Manchester stimulated a boom in hand-loom weaving. Alongside steam-powered factories that employed hundreds of 'hands', therefore, were numerous individual family-based weaving enterprises. These left physical traces in the form of workshop dwellings with their characteristic long attic windows, most dating from the late eighteenth and early nineteenth centuries. Manchester has one of the finest collections of these workshop dwellings and examples can be seen throughout the central district. But a particularly important group can be found in the Northern Quarter, especially in Thomas Street and Tib Street. Workshop dwellings were purpose built, multifunctional buildings which potentially combined warehouse, dwelling, commercial and workshop facilities. They typically consisted of three-storey houses arranged in terraces, with cellars and workshop attics with distinctive long garret windows. It was also common for these buildings to have 'taking-in' doors at the gable end, where materials could be hoisted directly into and out of the attic workshop, as can be seen at 47–53 Tib Street. Another good collection can be found in Liverpool Street in the Castlefield area of Manchester, several of which have been recently restored.

These buildings are an important part of our social history, and deserve greater acknowledgement. They are a 'living' material record of a constituency of artisans whose labour Manchester's prosperity was based on, but whose fortunes were locked into the dynamics of the cotton industry which, with the adoption of the power-loom, inevitably led to the destruction of their livelihoods. During the first major economic crisis of the cotton industry in the 1820s, power-looms became a means to intensify exploitation and for disciplining labour in a way that was not possible in the traditional 'putting out' system. As this system became obsolete, the position of hand-loom weavers was fatally undermined and they became pushed into unemployment and dire poverty. It is not surprising, therefore, to find hand-loom weavers at the forefront of radical politics and militancy during this era of technological transition. Although Manchester was not a key centre of Luddism, there were Luddite incidents. When the industrialist Robert Grimshaw of Gorton tried to set up a steam-powered weaving factory at Knott Mill in 1790, he received a threatening letter. A week later, his mill was burnt down and this action delayed the further introduction of steam-power for many years. The remains of the Knott Mill factory have long gone, but Grimshaw's house in Debdale Park, Gorton, is still just about standing.

Fig. 2.9 Cutaway reconstruction of a weaver's workshop dwelling (based on 1–5 Kelvin Street, Northern Quarter) (Taylor and Holder 2008, 16, all rights reserved).

Road and Canal Network

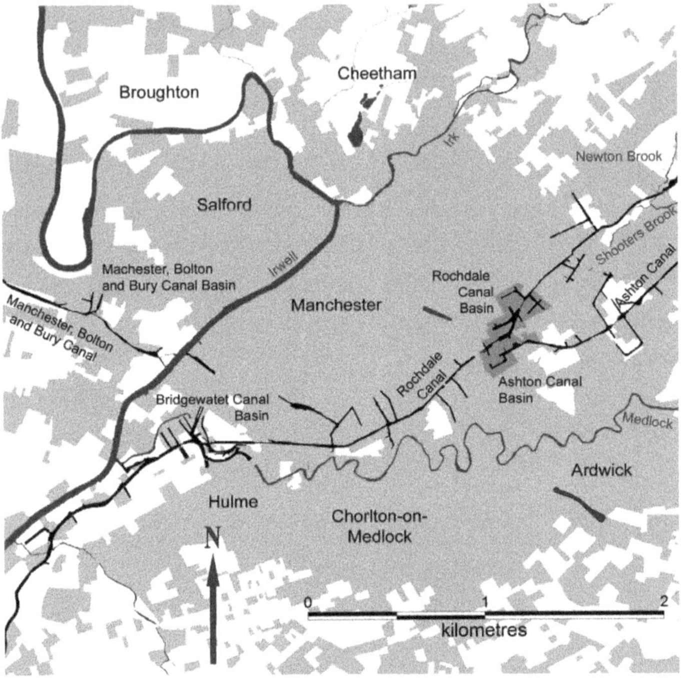

Fig. 2.10 The canal network in the Manchester and Salford conurbation (© Michael Nevell).

Manchester was more than just than a centre of textile and industrial production. The consolidation and improvement of transports links to the surrounding towns meant that the city became the nodal point of an expanding commercial network. The main atrial roads that radiate out from the centre of the town, like spokes of a wheel, shaped Manchester's physical expansion as suburban townships grew up along these major thoroughfares. They are highlighted on Pigot's 1838 map through colour coding (see Fig. 2.1). As well as the older routes into the town such as Oldham Road, Ashton Old Road, London Road, Oxford Road and Chester Road that had been steadily improved through the turnpike system during the eighteenth century, which widened and straightened them, completely new roads were also chartered. Regent Road–Eccles New Road was laid out in 1808, Cheetham Hill Road (originally York Road) in 1820, Bury New Road in 1831, Stretford New Road in 1832, which linked Oxford Road to Old Trafford, and then Hyde Road and

Ashton New Road around the same time. All of these new roads were characteristically and distinctively straight.

The canal system also expanded during this phase, and like the new roads, had a crucial impact on Manchester's evolution. The Manchester, Bolton and Bury Canal was cut between 1791 and 1808, while Ashton Canal was constructed between 1792 and 1796 (with an arm to Stockport completed in 1797), and the Rochdale Canal between 1794 and 1806. This emerging network of canals therefore intensified the links between Manchester and the satellite towns in its immediate hinterland, and created a new spatial logic that shifted the built environment away from the old town and the River Irwell. Four canal basins were established on the fringes of the central built-up area: one at Castlefield and another two at Dale Street and Ducie Street (now truncated) which provided a terminus for the Rochdale and Ashton canals respectively; and a fourth in Salford at New Windsor, now filled in. These basins subsequently became foci for warehousing and other commercial facilities. An arm of the Rochdale Canal then connected Dale Street basin with the one at Castlefield, and a little later, between 1836 and 1839, the Manchester and Salford Junction Canal, running mostly underground, linked the Rochdale Canal to the Irwell, and from there to the Bolton and Bury Canal. This integrated canal network established a new transport infrastructure that was pivotal in Manchester's transformation into the capital of the cotton industry. In particular, the extension of the Bridgewater Canal to Runcorn and the Mersey in 1773, and the Rochdale Canal to Sowerby Bridge in 1804, where river navigation gave access to the Humber and then Hull, facilitated direct commercial connections to both the west and east coasts of England. Manchester's role as a key marketing centre for the storage and distribution of wholesale goods consequently grew exponentially both nationally and internationally. This meant that it was as much a 'warehouse town' as it was a 'factory town'. As a result, a considerable amount of space was taken over by commercial warehousing, especially around the growing marketing district on Shudehill. Although much has been destroyed, individual examples of these early carriers' warehouses can still be found in the city, especially in and around the canal basins.

Warehouses

Fig. 2.11 Dale Street Warehouse (Author, 2012).

Dale Street Warehouse in the Rochdale Canal Basin, constructed out of blocks of millstone grit and dated to 1806, is the oldest surviving one, complete with shipping holes for unloading merchandise from internal wet docks. Of the other surviving warehouses in the basin is Jackson's Warehouse of 1836 on Tariff Street, a large, six-storey, brick-built structure. At the Castlefield Canal Basin, the Merchants' Warehouse (1825) and the Middle Warehouse (1831) are also well preserved—both with the distinctive shipping holes of canal warehouses. Interestingly, despite being monumental structures reflecting the wealth and status of the canal companies that built them, these early warehouses are relatively plain, solid and functional, without the architectural elaboration of the later 'showcase' warehouses of the mid-nineteenth century.

Fig. 2.12 Merchants' Warehouse (left) and the Middle Warehouse, Castlefield (Author, 2023).

Urban Expansion and Working-Class 'Slums'

Capital investment in mills, factories, canals and warehouses depended on the labour of workers who migrated into Manchester in ever greater numbers during this phase of economic take-off: industrialisation and urbanisation being intimately related. The territorial expansion of the town recorded on Pigot's 1838 map, therefore, was as much to do with the need to house this new labour force as it was to do with industrial innovation and commercial development. But there was very little investment in working-class housing. The residential needs of migrant workers were not a priority for local capitalists. Although there were notable exceptions, such as the banker Benjamin Heywood's improvements to a block of working-class houses he acquired in Miles Platting during the early 1830s, which included establishing a school, mechanics institute and public baths, such philanthropic projects were not the norm and very limited in scale. So, it is unsurprising that Manchester became known for its shoddy housing, built by speculative developers at the minimum of costs. Densely packed residential districts consequently emerged close to places of work in an unplanned and unregulated fashion. This resulted in an urban geography consisting of a mix of back-to-back terraces, blind-backs, 'rookeries', courts, blind alleys and cellar dwellings. The abject squalor and deprivation of these working-class districts was frequently commented upon by middle-class reformers and visitors to the town, such as the Utilitarian minister at Cross Street Chapel, William Gaskell, the physician, Dr James Kay, and the German revolutionary, Friedrich Engels. These contemporary accounts provide quite detailed descriptions of notorious working-class slums such as Ancoats, Angel Meadow (the district surrounding St Michael's church and the New Burial Ground for paupers) and Little Ireland (the confined area of extreme poverty near the mills at Chorlton-on-Medlock). Engels' horrifying and much quoted account of Little Ireland can serve as an illustration.

> In a rather deep hole, in a curve of the Medlock and surrounded on all four sides by tall factories and high embankments, covered with buildings, stand two groups of about two hundred cottages, built chiefly back to back, in which live about 4,000 human beings, most of them Irish. The cottages are old, dirty, and of the smallest sort, the street uneven, fallen into ruts and in part without drains or pavement; masses of refuse, offal and sickening filth lie among standing pools in all directions; the atmosphere is poised by the effluvia from these, and laden and darkened by the smoke of a dozen tall factory chimneys. A horde of ragged women and children swarm about here, as filthy as the swine that thrive upon the garbage heaps and in the puddles. (2009, 98)

In the absence of any standing remains, these writers offer valuable insights into domestic living conditions of workers at the start of the nineteenth century. Poor housing was ephemeral, quickly put up and just as quickly pulled down. However, over the last few decades archaeologists have excavated and recorded the foundations of several examples of workers' dwellings, especially in the Ancoats district. They have noted a marked decline in the quality and standard of housing, being smaller, more cramped and poorly built when compared to earlier artisan housing (like the workshop dwellings of the hand-loom weavers). It is an archaeological pattern that can be associated with the historical evidence of the rise of small-scale landowners and renters, which led to minor speculative developments in new housing and the subdivision of existing properties, resulting in overcrowding.

A good example illustrating how the quality of housing deteriorated with the impact of industrialisation is found in Manchester's Northern Quarter, in Lever Street and Bradley Street. During the 1780s, a range of five, three-storey and cellared workshop dwellings were constructed at the northern end of Lever Street as a speculative development by a plasterer, William Bradley. These then became subdivided for tenement housing, with one-up, one-down 'cottages' added at the rear, facing Bradley Street during the 1790s, a striking example of the cramped conditions that Mancunian labourers had to endure. Archaeological excavations have revealed the plans of a number of back-to-back housing blocks, such as at Jersey Street in Ancoats which also uncovered a set of eight dwellings built in a single phase between 1794 and 1800. The foundations of the outer walls of these back-to-backs were just one brick thick. Other excavations in Ancoats have exposed the basements of early nineteenth-century cellar dwellings. At Loom Street, these were tiny, measuring around four metres by four metres, accessed via ladders leading from trap doors.

The large-scale Ordnance Survey maps drawn up in the 1840s also provide detailed spatial information on the nature of Manchester's residential working-class districts and the character of the pre-Victorian townscape, with its irregular alleys, courts and winding, narrow lanes. Much of this street pattern has been swept away by Victorian urban 'improvements' and through twentieth-century slum clearances. But there are several surviving examples such as Bradleys Court, off Bridge Street, as well as Back Pool Fold and Bow Lane off Cross Street, that give us a contemporary glimpse of how much of the centre of Manchester must have appeared during the early nineteenth century.

Fig. 2.13 One-up, one-down houses at Bradley Street, Northern Quarter (Author, 2012).

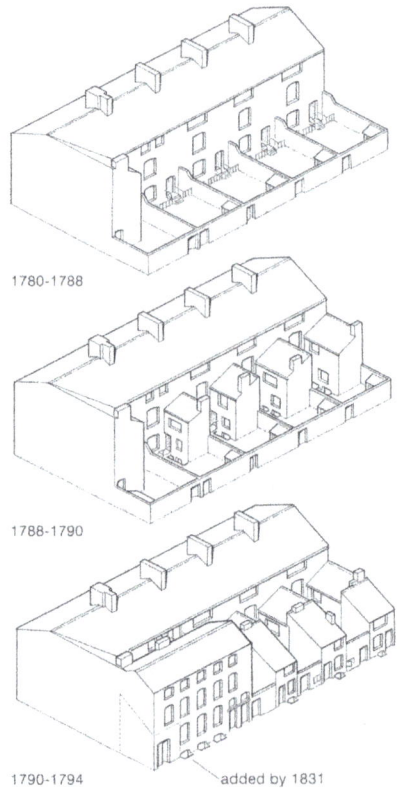

Fig. 2.14 Development of urban housing at Bradley Street (Taylor and Holder 2008, 24, all rights reserved).

Religious Buildings

Fig. 2.15 Distribution of Manchester's religious buildings by 1838, shown on James Pigot's 1838 'A plan of Manchester and Salford', annotated by the author (blue dots = Anglican churches; yellow dots = Commissioners' churches; green dotes = Catholic churches; red dots = Nonconformist chapels; pink dot = synagogue).

Fig. 2.16 Independent Chapel, Chapel Street, Salford (Author, 2023).

The near total demolition of all the working-class housing from this period in the centre of Manchester is indicative of the poor quality of their construction and the lack of concern, to the point of contempt, for working-class lives amongst the town's middle class. Working-class housing, like labour, was used and disposed of according to the will of capital accumulation. However, there is a class of monument that does tend to survive better and thus provides a way of tracking the spread of working-class residential districts during this phase—church buildings and other sites of religious worship. The annotated Pigot map shows the distribution of churches and chapels in Manchester, including Anglican, Nonconformist and Catholic foundations. It captures the way the town expanded outwards in practically all directions, and also the extent of religious diversity. Nonconformist chapels (those shown as red dots) vastly outnumber Anglican churches (shown as blue dots). The proliferation of chapels reflected the diversity of the migrant groups coming into Manchester, as they arrived with their own religious traditions. Workers from North Wales established various Welsh-speaking Methodist congregations, while those from Scotland set up Presbyterian churches. The native Catholic community was reinforced during the early nineteenth century with the massive influx of Irish labourers (and later by Italian arrivals) who established Catholic institutions around the city (indicated by green dots). There are only a few Nonconformist and Catholic institutions from this phase still present. These include the Independent Chapel in Chapel Street in Salford which was built in 1819, the Neoclassical facade of the Quakers Friends Meeting House on Mount Street that was completed in 1831, as well as the Independent Chapel on Cheetham Hill Road, also constructed with a Classical portico with an 1840 date. The prominent locations of these chapels, sited along major thoroughfares, as well as their architectural pretensions, are an indication of the growing strengths and ambitions of Nonconformist religious communities. Further, Manchester was also home to a small but growing Jewish community in the late eighteenth and early nineteenth century, with a purpose-built synagogue located in the old town in Halliwell Street in 1826 (pink dot). The remains of the oldest Jewish burial ground serving this community, dating from 1794, can still be found at Brindle Heath in Pendleton, Salford—the Old Hebrew Congregation Cemetery.

Fig. 2.17 St Philip, Salford (Author, 2023).

Another point to note when looking at the map is the distribution of Commissioners' churches (those indicated by a yellow dot). Confronted with the population growth of industrial cities, where ecclesiastical provisions were inadequate, and competition from the rise of Nonconformity, the British state promoted a wave of new Anglican church building. The 1818 Church Building Act released funds for the provision of new churches. These were part of a conscious attempt by parliament to instil discipline and morality into the emerging industrial working class. They were deliberately located in new areas of residential growth to give them an air of respectability. In Manchester, Commissioners' churches were positioned on the outer limits of town, in expanding urban districts: St Philip, Salford (1824), St Matthew, Campfield (1825), St George, Hulme (1826) and All Souls, Ancoats (1840). There are also two other foundations located beyond the limits of Pigot's map: St Thomas, Pendleton (1831) and St Luke, Cheetham Hill (1838). All these Commissioners' churches had a degree of architectural pretension, being designed by some of the leading architects of the day such as Robert Smirke and his Greek Revivalist St Philip, and Charles Barry's Gothic St Matthew. The latter even had a Sunday school attached to it, St Matthew's Sunday School (1827), which still stands, unlike the associated church.

Fig. 2.18 St Thomas, Pendleton, Salford (Author, 2021).

At Pendleton in Salford, St Thomas can be used as an example to illustrate the impact of Commissioners' churches on the built environment. It was designed by the local architect Richard Lane, and completed in 1831, replacing the chapel of ease on Brindle Heath. Lane, whose architectural presence in the town is considerable, placed his austere Gothic church on a prominent position at the top of the hill overlooking Salford and Manchester. Its tower forms a landmark that can be visually linked to other church towers and spires in the Irwell valley (such as Lane's St John in Higher Broughton). Pendleton, in the early nineteenth century, was an expanding working-class district and the commissioning of St Thomas was an attempt to impose some order on the area by creating a hub of respectability. It is significant, therefore, that immediately adjacent to the church, along Broad Street, is a row of late Georgian town houses which would have shielded from view the much poorer working-class dwellings behind.

A similar spatial pattern can be observed at St Luke on Cheetham Hill Road, which occupies a site on top of the hill so that the tower of this Commissioners' church (completed in 1839) forms a visual landmark that can be seen from miles around. Immediately next to the church on Smedley Lane is a row of fine Georgian houses, with the grandest, Temple Bank, taking the form of a classical villa.

On this note, a more general point can be made about the spatial arrangement of these new residential districts in relation to the other urban components. Working-class housing tended to form discrete blocks around workplaces that were separated from each other and from the other elements of the town by major thoroughfares. These streets, which were lined with shops and prosperous houses, effectively caged, or shut out, the working class from the more respectable areas. This pattern of residential social segregation was first identified by Friedrich Engels in his pioneer study of the industrial city. Engels read Manchester's topography through the lens of class. In particular, he drew attention to the way that class power was embedded in urban geography. For Engels, this was the hidden logic behind the apparent randomness of Manchester's development. Class polarisation explained the urban zoning that led to the exclusion of the working class from some areas and its confinement in others. This was the geography of 'two-nation' Britain. 'I have never seen so systematic a shutting out of the working class from the thoroughfares, so tender a concealment of everything which might affront the eye and the nerves of the bourgeoisie, as in Manchester' (Engels 2009, 87). Engels' approach provides a powerful tool for making sense of the spatial configurations of Manchester in the first half of the nineteenth century.

Power and Resistance in Industrial Manchester

Fig. 2.19 Distribution of institutions of coercion and institutions of culture, shown on James Pigot's 1838 'A plan of Manchester and Salford', annotated by the author (red dots = institutions of coercion, blue dots = institutions of bourgeois culture).

Returning to Pigot's 1838 map, another important dimension of class power can be noted—the conspicuous presence of institutions of coercion. The urban arena may have been the favoured location for industrial production due to the availability of cheap and disposable labour, but there was also a clear disadvantage. Concentrated in great numbers in towns, working together in large enterprises while living together in crowded courts and rookeries, the urban proletarians gained a class consciousness through collectively resisting the rigours of industrialisation. The imposition of the factory system was constantly challenged, and the urban environment enhanced the potential of collective agency due to the centralisation of both capital and labour in industrial towns. Organised labour and its impact on business is what manufacturers feared most. Combating it legally, politically and culturally therefore preoccupied the minds of the bourgeoisie, as the process of industrialisation was marked and shaped by fierce class struggle.

The design, architecture and organisation of the factory was one way of instilling work discipline at the point of production, as has been discussed. But beyond the factory gates, other mechanisms were required to maintain order. At the start of industrialisation these mechanisms were quite crude, as they drew upon open forms of penal and military power to exert extra economic means of coercion. This is where urban morphology played a crucial role. Surrounding the western side of the Manchester–Salford conurbation are four new institutions that were strategically placed to visually dominate the built environment and to regulate and control access into it: a workhouse, a prison and two military barracks. These institutions represent the iron fist of work discipline—the way in which industrialisation was accompanied with brutal repression. They were a necessary component in the entrenchment of factory production, based as it was on the naked exploitation of labour. Institutions of coercion, therefore, were established at exactly the same time as the construction of the first steam-powered cotton mills. The threat of physical incarceration and military force were conspicuously stamped on the urban environment as a continual reminder to the working class of the constant presence of state power. To use a phrase borrowed from Mark Neocleous, a Marxist theorist of police power, these institutions of coercion were part of the 'fabrication of social order', the imposition of wage labour and disciplinary logic of industrial capitalism.

Institutions of Coercion

The Bridge Street Workhouse was erected in 1792 on the high ground above the confluence of the rivers Irk and Irwell (where Manchester Arena stands now). It was solidly built, in classical design with pavilion wings, and sat within a walled precinct overlooking the old town and the poor district of Angel Meadow. It became known as the 'Poor-Law Bastille', forming the main workhouse of the Manchester Poor Law Union and was recorded as holding over a thousand paupers in 1840. Its visual prominence in the town meant that it was a constant reminder of the fate of the poor who were unable to work, or those who could find no employment. Workhouses were there to instil work discipline through fear of being incarcerated in them.

To the south-east of Bridge Street Workhouse, on the Salford bank of the Irwell was New Bailey Prison. This was completed in the same year as the workhouse in 1792. It was a huge sprawling site with the main prison building towering over the poor, working-class districts on the Salford and Manchester sides of the River Irwell (as revealed in the 1848 large-scale Ordnance Survey map). It was in New Bailey that Manchester's radicals were imprisoned after arrests on political protests such as the Blanketeers of 1817 and in the aftermath of the Peterloo Massacre. The prison building has long since gone, but its foundations were excavated in 2015 exposing a complex plan of different phases and structures, including individual cells and treadmills.

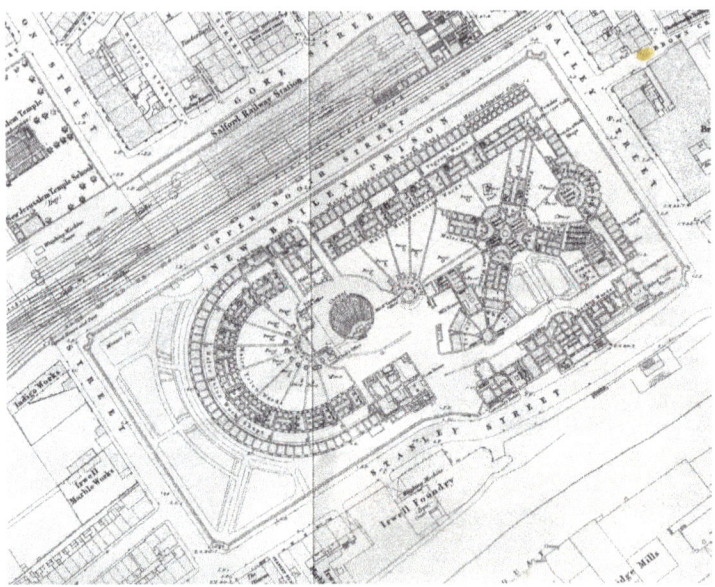

Fig. 2.20 Plan of New Bailey Prison, Salford, 1848 (section of Old Ordnance Survey Maps, Manchester and Salford Sheet 27), Alan Godfrey Maps.

Fig. 2.21 Plan of Hulme Barracks, 1849 (section of Ordnance Survey Town Plan – Manchester and Salford Sheet 37), CC BY, National Library of Scotland.

Further to the south-east, on either side of the River Irwell, were two barracks. Hulme Barracks, on the Manchester side was built between 1802 and 1804 within the emerging working-class district of Hulme, as illustrated in the 1849 Ordnance Survey map. It was a cavalry barracks, the home of the 1,500 strong 15th King's Hussars, which was the unit that charged the protesters during Peterloo. The area of the barracks survives today as an open park (St George's Park) with a few original houses, including the Quartermaster's house (marked as Pooley's Houses on the 1849 map). Salford Barracks, however, was built in 1819 immediately after the Peterloo Massacre, on top of the bank overlooking the Irwell. This was an infantry barracks and positioned strategically beside the newly constructed Regent Road (1808) which crossed the river at Regent Bridge (1808) facilitating the swift movement of troops into both Manchester and Salford. It is now New Barrack Estate.

Fig. 2.22 Quartermaster's house (one of Pooley's Houses), Hulme Barracks (Author, 2021).

Fig. 2.23 Ladysmith Barracks, Ashton-under-Lyne (Author, 2024).

The use of military installations to intimidate the working class continued throughout the first half of the nineteenth century. When General Charles Napier was appointed commander of the Northern District of the British Army between 1838 and 1841, he was commissioned to write a report on how the Chartist movement could be militarily contained. This led to the construction of new barracks in the region which were placed in key textile towns near railway stations to aid the swift deployment of troops. Napier Barracks were constructed in Bury (Wellington Barracks), Preston (Fulford Barracks) and Ashton-under-Lyne (Wellington, later Ladysmith Barracks) all in response to the threat posed by the militancy of the industrial working class. The barracks at Ashton, on the edge of the Manchester-Salford conurbation, was linked to the two in the urban centre in Manchester. Construction started in 1841 with the barracks positioned strategically on the high ground overlooking the mill towns of both Ashton and Stalybridge in the Tame Valley, the urban starting point of the 1842 General Strike (the so-called 'plug plot riots'). It initially accommodated a cavalry unit before housing an infantry regiment. Although decommissioned in 1958, the entrance and part of the perimeter wall still stands, complete with gun loops.

Places and Spaces of Working-Class Radicalism

The strategic positioning of these institutions of coercion around Manchester was indicative of the fact that industrialisation generated intense social conflict. Manchester gained a reputation for political radicalism and industrial unrest. The focus of much agitation was the call for reform and the fight for universal suffrage which initially combined radical sections of the middle class with working-class militants. This led to a politics of public space and the right to collective assembly to raise and debate political demands (what has become known as 'platform politics'). The reaction against this reform movement led to the 'Church and King' riots of 1792 (when the Cross Street Chapel and the house of the radical leader, Thomas Walker, were physically attacked), the mass arrests of the Blanketeers, along with the infamous Peterloo Massacre. The historian Katrina Navickas has explored in detail the politics of space and place in Manchester between 1789 and 1848, highlighting the way public space was contested, and how radicalism was forged in particular urban places. For instance, she has plotted the addresses of those Blanketeers arrested in 1817, as well as the victims of Peterloo in 1819, to define an important radical locale in the area of New Cross, especially Ancoats.

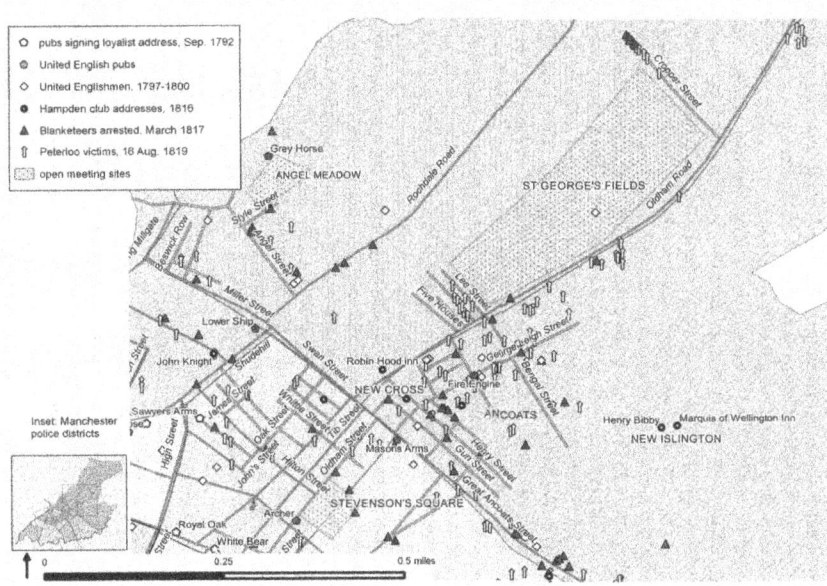

Fig. 2.24 Map of radical addresses in Manchester 1789–1820 (Navickas 2016, 110, all rights reserved).

As well as public spaces and radical addresses, Navickas' map also draws attention to the political importance of public houses which served as meeting places. Pubs were crucial in establishing and maintaining working-class political networks. Like churches and chapels, pubs have survived better than working-class housing, and there are many examples of late eighteenth-century and early nineteenth-century pubs still selling beer today, such as the Briton's Protection on Great Bridgewater Street, Sir Ralph Abercrombie, in Bootle Street, which served as a temporary mortuary after the Peterloo Massacre, and the City (originally the Prince of Orange) in Oldham Street, with its plaster panel depicting William and Mary's arrival in England during the Glorious Revolution.Other Georgian pubs in the city centre worth visiting include the Hare and Hounds and Lower Turks Head, both on Shudehill. Taverns and public houses were one of the few elements of traditional plebeian culture that survived the impact of the 'Industrial Revolution'; the imposition of industrial clock-time and the rapid process of urbanisation having severely reduced the time and space for traditional pastimes. The pub was a place of escape from the discipline of the factory and the cramped conditions of industrial housing, at least for the male section of the working population. But as well as places for relaxation and recreation, the public house was a place where radicals could meet, discuss and organise. The connection between pubs and early trade societies and unions can often be identified in terms of the names, such as Carpenters Arms. In Manchester, for example, the Sawyers Arms on Deansgate was the original meeting place of the sawyers' trade society. It was within the confines of a public house that political movements were born and spread. In particular, there was a clear link between Chartism and pubs. The National Charter Association of the Chartist movement, for instance, emerged from a meeting held at the Griffin Inn on Great Ancoats Street in 1838 (the building is now a Brazilian restaurant rather than a pub).

Fig. 2.25 The remains of the Round House, Ancoats (with All Souls showing in the left-hand corner) (Author, 2021).

There were a number of other important radical spaces in Manchester linked to this phase, such as the trade unionist John Doherty's Coffee House and Bookshop (1832) at 37 Withy Grove, and the Owenite Hall of Science (1840) in Campfield, which was demolished in 1877. Another, that partially survives today, is the Round House on Every Street in Ancoats, first erected in 1821. This was established by the militant Swedenborgian minister, James Scholefield, and served as a Nonconformist chapel and burial ground, as well as a political meeting place for Manchester's radicals, especially during the era of Chartism. There was no coincidence, therefore, that one of Manchester's Commissioners' churches, All Souls, built in 1840, was positioned almost next to the Round House; this spatial juxtaposition being an attempt to curtail or temper the radicalism of the area.

These struggles over places and spaces meant Manchester's built environment was a crucial arena of conflict. This was a pattern that was to continue with the rise of Chartism and resulted in political processions or marches and mass open-air meetings in Manchester's urban 'fields': St Peter's Fields, Campfield, St George's Fields and Granby Row Fields (a defining feature of 'platform politics'). The largest and one of the most famous open-air meetings was held at Kersal Moor, 'the *Mons Sacre* of Manchester' according to Engels. It was on Kersal Moor that the Chartists held two 'monster' meetings, the first one of which took place in September 1838, was attended by over 300,000 people.

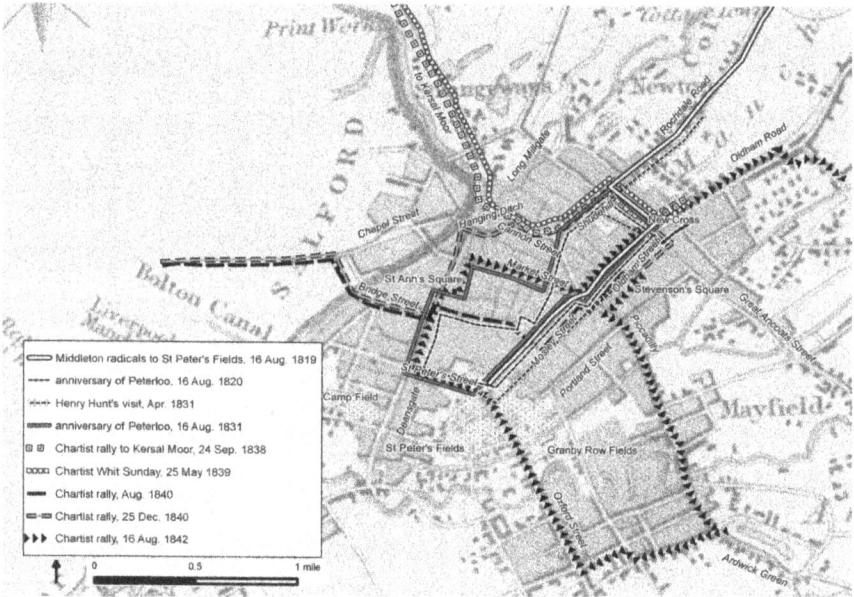

Fig. 2.26 Map of radical and trade union processions in Manchester 1819–1842 (Navickas 2016, 181, all rights reserved).

'Polite Society' and the Transformations of the Central District

While the twin processes of industrialisation and urbanisation created and shaped the newly emerging industrial working class in Manchester, the same forces were at work transforming Georgian polite society into an industrial middle class or bourgeoisie. This development was likewise embedded in the changing spatial arrangements of the built environment. Manchester's urban elite of merchants, mill owners, bankers, doctors, lawyers and other professionals may have been internally divided by wealth, religion and political allegiance, but in relation to the working class, they formed a coherent social grouping. This is reflected in the patterns of urban geography. Traditionally, a prominent central residential location was favoured by the early modern social elite, and this was true of Manchester with the old town around the parish church (now cathedral) being where high-status property was located. However, with the rapid urban expansion accompanying industrialisation, the elite moved out and formed new locales, first around the church of St Ann and square and along King Street, and then focusing upon new church foundations such as St Mary and St John (as described in Chapter 1). But by the end of the eighteenth century, a new centre of polite society had been established along Mosley Street in the shadow of the Infirmary in Piccadilly Gardens. It was here that Manchester's key cultural institutions became relocated and concentrated in striking contrast to the distribution pattern of the institutions of coercion. While the workhouse, prison and military barracks are roughly equally spaced around the western side of the town to oversee and dominate working-class districts, Manchester's Assembly Room, literary clubs, library, art gallery, museum, concert hall and theatre were all focused together on or near Mosley Street, which now formed a new middle-class locale. There was clearly a different spatial logic at work, embodying the pursuit of Mammon and the clash between capital and labour.

Significantly, however, the dynamics of industrial urbanisation in Manchester meant that the transformation of the central district was not fixed, but subject to ongoing change. The establishment of a new middle-class residential zone around Mosley Street was relatively short-lived. Manchester's dramatic industrial take-off led to the commercialisation of the centre and the subsequent residential movement of the middle class into the suburbs. This resulted in the new and distinct urban form. The centre of Manchester, therefore, was not characterised by the accumulation of prestigious Georgian polite architecture, as was the case in the majority of contemporary British towns and cities. In contrast, it was defined by the relative poverty of its public buildings and public spaces as Manchester's built environment was subsumed under the commercial dynamics of industrial capitalism.

Mosley Street Locale

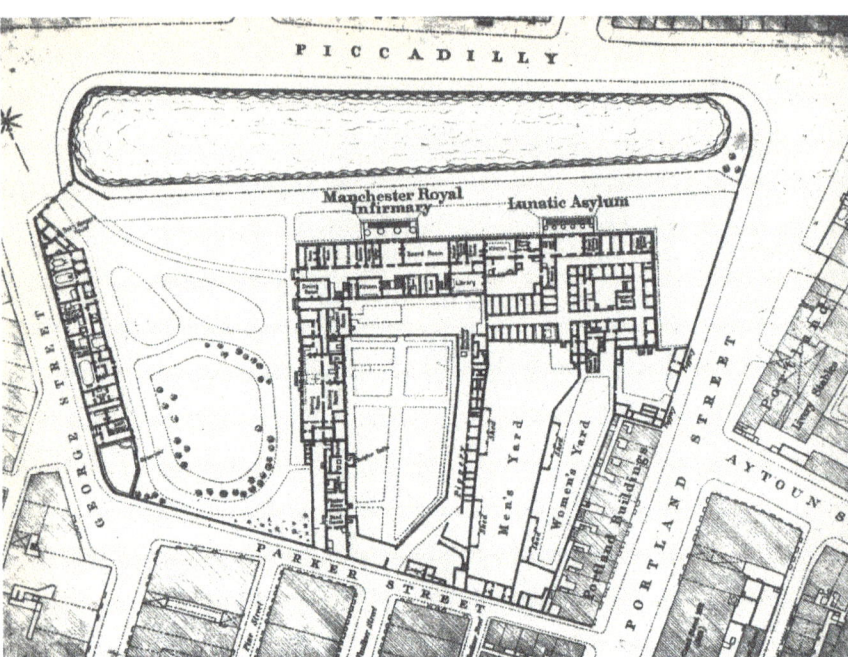

Fig. 2.27 Plan of Manchester Infirmary and Piccadilly Square, 1850. Unknown author. Wikimedia Commons, public domain, https://commons.wikimedia.org/wiki/File:Plan_of_Manchester_Royal_Infirmary_1845.jpg

Manchester Infirmary was established in 1755, with the hospital being steadily enlarged during the eighteenth century with the addition of a lunatic asylum (1765), public baths (1779) and dispensary (1792). It was then refurbished by the local architect Richard Lane in the 1820s and 1830s, who added two classical porticos making it the town's pre-eminent civic building. The Infirmary was surrounded with gardens (Piccadilly Square), including a linear pond along its frontage making it one of the few green spaces in Manchester. Consequently, it became a new focus for urban development to the east of the old town, with the streets surrounding it forming the heart of late Georgian Manchester. As well as a district of fine residential housing, this is where the civic institutions of polite society were located and formed an important middle-class locale.

Fig. 2.28 John Rowland Fothergill, Mosley Street engraving, 1824 (showing the Portico Library, front left and St Peter). Image courtesy of Manchester City Galleries.

Mosley Street, the principal street of this locale, was laid out in the 1780s. It ran perpendicular from the junction of Market Street at Piccadilly, in a straight line to St Peter. This church was consecrated in 1794, and was the planned focal point of the vista from Piccadilly (as depicted in contemporary engravings). Mosley Street, and those streets around it, subsequently became the most fashionable part of the town in the early nineteenth century. Leading middle-class figures had their residences there. It was the home of German businessman and later famous banker, Nathan Mayer Rothschild, the cotton manufacturers Samuel Brooks and Hugh Hornby Birley, who was buried in a family vault at the church of St Peter. The demonstrations on the anniversaries of the Peterloo Massacre would pass along Mosley Street and pause at Birley's house to 'moan and groan' in symbolic protest. The Quaker scientist, John Dalton had his home in the neighbouring George Street, Number 36, which became the meeting place of Manchester's prestigious Literary and Philosophical Society. Dalton worshipped at the Quaker Meeting House (1831) nearby on Mount Street, which was designed by Richard Lane, a fellow Quaker, in the style of a Greek temple.

Fig. 2.29 Friends Meeting House, Mount Street (Author, 2009).

The residential importance of the locale is therefore reflected in the number of places of worship in the immediate vicinity. The Anglican community was served with the church of St James (1788) as well as St Peter, while for the Dissenters there was the Unitarian Mosley Street Chapel (1787), a Methodist George Street Chapel, the Presbyterian 'Scotch Church' in St Peter's Square (1833), New Jerusalem Church (1793) on Peter Street, and the Quaker Friends Meeting House, which is the only one of these establishments still standing and functioning.

Institutions of Bourgeois Culture

Fig. 2.30 Mosley Street, 1849 (section of Ordnance Survey Town Plan – Manchester and Salford Sheet 28), CC BY, National Library of Scotland.

Fig. 2.31 Portico Library, Mosley Street (with sole surviving facade of the original Georgian terraced houses that aligned Mosley Street) (Author, 2022).

Interspersed with residential housing and places of worship were institutions that also helped to promote and integrate Georgian polite society. As the historian Martin Hewitt has argued, 'The Concert Hall and the Manchester Assembly Rooms were central to the social constitution of the city's middle class' (1996, 86). Even though later urban transformations have removed most of these original buildings, there are three survivors that formed part of this middle-class area. At the corner of Mosley Street and Charlotte Street, directly opposite the site of Manchester's Assembly Rooms is the Portico Library and Reading Room, a subscription library established by two businessmen. Designed by Thomas Harrison in his typical Greek Revivalist style, it was completed in 1806 and forms Manchester's earliest Neoclassical structure. The Portico Library was supposedly modelled on the Temple of Athena Polias at Priene (although Harrison himself never managed to visit Greece). This is Harrison's only surviving building in the town as he was also responsible for the rebuilding of the Exchange (1809) and the construction of a Theatre Royal (1807). Harrison was a prolific Neoclassical architect in Lancashire and Chesire and excellent examples of his work can be found in Chester and Liverpool. He also built the villa of the local industrialist Peter Marsland in Greek Revivalist style, Woodbank (1814), that can be visited in Woodbank Memorial Park, Stockport. In this phase of development, Neoclassical and in particular

Greek Revivalist designs were the most favoured style of Manchester's rising middle class, as it provided them with architectural legitimacy by linking them to Britain's wider social elites. In this sense, Manchester was simply following the national trends in architecture.

Further down Mosley Street is another good example of a monumental public building constructed in Greek Revivalist style. This is Charles Barry's Royal Manchester Institute for the Promotion of Science Literature and the Arts, completed in 1835, and the original base for Manchester's School of Art, now the City Art Gallery. Behind it, along Princess Street, Barry also built the Athenaeum (1839), the premises of a club promoting adult education. Despite its name, the Athenaeum was not built as a Greek Revivalist structure, but as a Renaissance palazzo. It was this style that became the architectural signature of Manchester's elite during the next phase of the triumph of Liberalism.

Fig. 2.32 Royal Manchester Institute, Mosley Street and Athenaeum, Princess Street (Author, 2023).

The middle-class cultural institutions of Mosley Street spread out beyond the church of St Peter into Peter Street. It was here that the Theatre Royal was rebuilt, as the former theatre, designed by Thomas Harrison, had burnt down. The new Theatre Royal, completed in 1845 was also another classical composition with a giant portico with Corinthian columns and pilasters.

Fig. 2.33 Theatre Royal, Peter Street (Author, 2022).

The Transformation of the Residential Centre

Fig. 2.34 Francis J. Sargent, 'Manchester Exchange', 1810 (the church of St Ann can be seen in the background). Image courtesy of the British Library.

At the same time that the Mosley Street area was being established as a middle-class locale, there were attempts to reconfigure the old town into a new financial, commercial and administrative district. Significant urban improvements took place. The rebuilding and enlargement of the Exchange has already been mentioned. Thomas Harrison designed a distinctive Neoclassical structure with a curving facade as depicted in Francis J. Sargent's 1810 etching. Access to the Exchange was enhanced by the rebuilding of Blackfriars Bridge (1820) in stone (its Neoclassical form perhaps making it the most handsome of Manchester's bridges across the Irwell), and by the straightening and widening of Market Street in 1822. It was in the same year that Smithfield formally became the new market place on Shudehill for the sale of meat, fish, fruit and vegetables. Later, in 1837, Richard Lane built the Corn and Produce Exchange near the parish church in his austere classical style. Rather than being a focus of elite housing, the previous fashionable residential streets in the centre, such as King Street, became a focus for finance and business.

Fig. 2.35 Blackfriars Bridge (Author, 2022).

A good example of this transition is Dr Waring's house at Number 35 which became a bank that sat alongside other purpose-built banks. For instance, it was on King Street that Richard Lane built the Manchester and Salford Savings Bank (1842), and this is also where the Bank of England constructed their branch in Manchester, employing Charles Cockerell to design another Neoclassical structure in 1846. It was on the corner of King Street and Cross Street, on the plot that had been occupied by Dr Charles White's grand town house (the co-founder of the Infirmary), that a new town hall was erected in 1825. This was designed by Francis Goodwin in Neoclassical style with a portico that is said to echo the Erectheion temple on the Acropolis in Athens. Although subsequently pulled down, the facade was reconstructed as an architectural feature in Heaton Park in the later nineteenth century.

Fig. 2.36 Manchester and Salford Savings Bank (now Pizza Express) and Bank of England, King Street (Author, 2022).

The change of land use in King Street, from residential to commercial and administrative, is significant as it is indicative of a transformation of the centre during this phase of industrial take-off. As well as banks, Georgian houses were being converted into or replaced by warehouses by the 1830s, as landed property assets rapidly increased in value. This was the fate of fashionable Mosley Street, as noted by the manufacturer and free trade campaigner, Richard Cobden, when he purchased a house in the street in order to convert it into a warehouse. As he explained in a letter to his brother in September 1832:

> My next-door neighbour Brooks, of the firm Cunliffe and Brooks, bankers, has sold his house to be converted into a warehouse. The owner of the house on the other side has given his tenant notice for the same purpose. The house immediately opposite me has been announced for sale, and

my architect is commissioned by George Hole, the calico printer, to bid six thousand guineas for it; but they want eight thousand for what they paid only four thousand five hundred for only five years ago. (cited in Parkinson-Bailey 2000, 31)

Planned Residential Developments

Manchester may have had examples of fine, monumental civic and commercial buildings that were expressive of Georgian polite society, but what was apparent to contemporary observers was the relative poverty of the architecture. For a boom town that was generating a phenomenal amount of wealth and riches, the built environment was remarkably impoverished and debased. As Engels declared in *The Condition of the Working Class*, he had 'never seen so badly built a town in my life' (2009, 274). This peculiarity is one of the reasons why Manchester is regarded as the 'shock city' of industrial capitalism. It was a feature that clearly struck contemporary visitors. In the French economist Leon Faucher's account of Manchester, which was published in English in 1844 (a year before Engels' more famous work), he describes the appearance of the town, capturing the distinctiveness of Manchester's physical form:

> There are no great boulevards or heights to aid the eye in measuring the vast extent of surface which it occupies. It is distinguished neither by those contrasting features which mark the cities of the middle ages, nor by that regularity which characterizes the capitals of recent formation. All the houses, all the streets, resemble each other; and yet this uniformity is in the midst of confusion. (1844, 16)

Faucher goes on to comment on the 'want of public squares, fountains, trees, promenades and well-ventilated buildings' (1844, 18). It is still striking how Manchester's Georgian architecture pales in significance when compared to the buildings of Nash's Regency London, or Edinburgh's New Town. The ports of Bristol and Liverpool both have far superior planned residential Georgian developments. Manchester does not even have the equivalent of Leeds's Park Square, Sheffield's Paradise Square or Preston's Winkley Square. Thomas Harrison's Portico Library may be a first-rate Greek Revival structure, yet it is modest and unassuming when compared to the size of Harrison's earlier commission in Liverpool—the Lyceum Library, News Room and Gentlemen's Club (1802).

Overall, therefore, what was built in Manchester was on a small scale, piecemeal and largely uncoordinated. This can be further illustrated by considering the two most ambitious residential projects of this phase: Stevenson's estate in the Northern Quarter and Chorlton-on-Medlock.

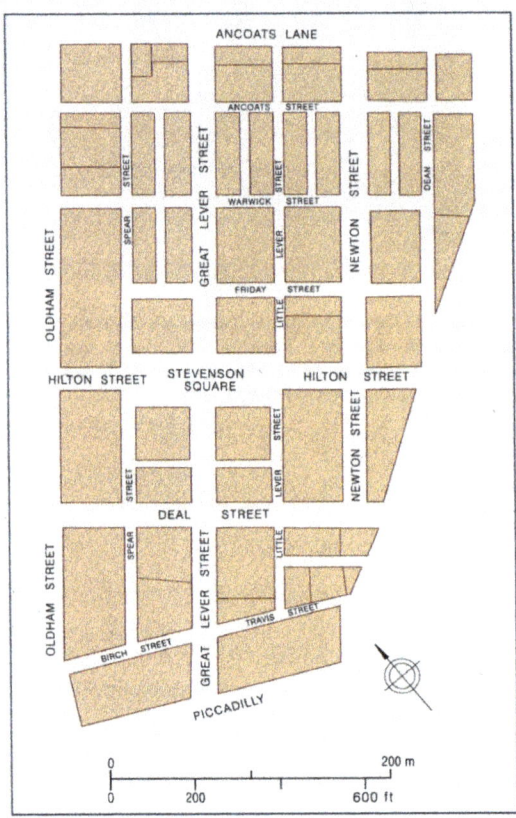

Fig. 2.37 Plan of Stevenson's estate (Taylor and Holder 2008, 19, all rights reserved).

Buying up a ten-hectare parcel of land from Sir Ashton Lever, the speculator William Stevenson laid out a grid of streets around Great Lever Street, centring on Stevenson Square and the church of St Clement in the 1780s. The plan was to develop the estate as a high-end residential suburb. There are a number of surviving Georgian houses which attest to this, as in the five-bay, double-fronted house at 8 Lever Street (built between 1780 and 1793).

Fig. 2.38 Georgian residential houses on Lever Street with Number 8 on the right (Author, 2025).

But Stevenson's speculative development never took off and rather than affluent residences, the area became filled with cheaper tenement housing, some with top-floor loom shops, as already noted in the previous discussion of the terrace at 69–77 Lever Street. The accelerating nature of Manchester's economic growth meant that the Stevenson's residential estate was quickly swallowed up and the area taken over by industrial and commercial enterprises.

Chorlton-on-Medlock, on the other hand, was originally planned as a separate new town. In 1792 a group of industrialists, including Samuel and Peter Marsland, purchased Chorlton Hall Estate with the intention of developing a complete residential suburb with the church and graveyard of All Saints forming a central square—Grosvenor Square (modelled on those of London). Samuel Marsland built a family mansion on the square and Richard Lane constructed a Neoclassical town hall (1831). A Dissenters' cemetery was opened in 1821, Rusholme Road Cemetery, and purported to be the first modern, private cemetery in Britain. It was funded by a joint-stock company and gained income from burial fees with the sale of different types of memorials, from vaults to gravestones, primarily to the more affluent members of the community. Its success led to its demise, as once full, there was no commercial incentive to continue with its maintenance. The cemetery subsequently declined and is now a local park with no indication of its former use and what lies under the ground! However, the Chorlton-on-Medlock development failed to take off due to the proximity of the cotton mills off Oxford Road. Rather than a fashionable residential area, it became a district of mixed housing. Behind the fine, early nineteenth-century Georgian terraces and villas on Grosvenor Street and Oxford Street were poor, substandard, working-class dwellings.

A similar pattern occurred at Cheetham Hill to the north of the centre where a fashionable residential township was planned in conjunction with the laying out of Cheetham Hill Road (originally York Road) in 1820. By the mid-nineteenth century, this area had degenerated into a poor, working-class district (see discussion of Cheetham Hill in Chapter 5).

Fig. 2.39 Edward Baines' 1824 Map of Ashton-under-Lyne.

The limited nature of Manchester's planned Georgian developments can be drawn sharply in relief when contrasted with the satellite, mill town of Ashton-under-Lyne. At the same time, the Stevenson's estate and Chorlton-on-Medlock were being laid out, the fifth and sixth Earls of Stamford planned and completed a far more ambitious urban development. This was a whole new town with an extensive grid of streets around the axis of Stamford Street, which linked the old square to the new Commissioners' church of St Peter (1824), a distance of over a kilometre. This contrast with Ashton illustrates how the lack of direct aristocratic interest in Manchester affected the development of the built environment. As the landowner, the Earls of Stamford possessed the opportunity to think 'big' and instigate wholesale change. Manchester, however, was a middle-class town. Without any centralised coordination, Manchester developed in a fragmented and piecemeal manner according to the competing interests of different sections of the middle class.

So, Manchester's bourgeoisie soon found that the Frankenstein's monster that they had created threatened to devour them. Industry was physically surrounding and encroaching upon their homes, while the emerging working class politically challenged their very existence. The response to this crisis was an escape to the suburbs.

Middle-Class Residential and Suburban Developments

H. J. Dyos and D. A. Reeder have eloquently explored the dialectic at work between 'slums and suburbs': 'The fact of the suburb influenced the environment of the slum; the threat of the slum entered the consciousness of the suburb' (1973, 360). An escape to the suburbs was the way the middle class could detach and shelter themselves from the hazards of the city and find a safe haven. But the investment of capital in house building in middle-class suburbs diverted resources away from the city centre. Earlier housing was subdivided to maximise rent collection, leading to degraded properties and inner city slums. This general pattern of development was evidently at work in nineteenth-century Manchester.

Ardwick, immediately south-east of the centre on Stockport Road, was a small village prior the industrial take-off. St Thomas was built as a chapel of ease in 1741 and became a parish church with an Italianate tower added in 1836. Ardwick was to become Manchester's first suburb, with smart Georgian houses and terraces arranged along Ardwick Green with its serpentine pond (as depicted on the Pigot 1838 map, see Fig. 2.1). Some of these houses are still present, such as on the corner of Ardwick Green North and Manor Street where there is a terrace named Ardwick Grove, and 31 Ardwick Green North, a symmetrical two-storey house with a central pedimented doorway, which is recorded in Green's 1794 map (see Fig. 1.12).

Fig. 2.40 Ardwick Green (Author, 2022).

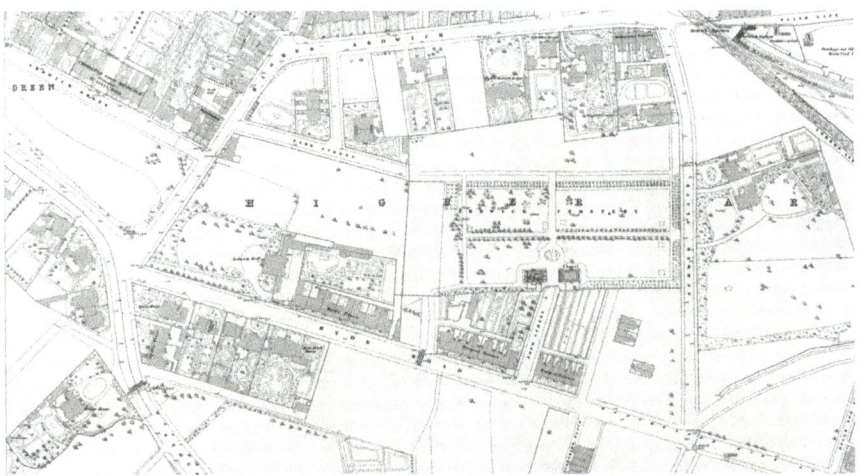

Fig. 2.41 Higher Ardwick, 1849 (section of Ordnance Survey Town Plan – Manchester and Salford Sheet 40), CC BY, National Library of Scotland.

Unfortunately, time has not been kind to Ardwick and it is a shadow of its former glory. But in the early nineteenth century, Ardwick was home to many famous Mancunians, as it became one of the most prestigious addresses to reside in, with the 1849 large-scale Ordnance Survey maps depicting the area around the green filled with large villas with walled gardens. James McConnel lived in a property at Polygon in Ardwick Green, while his partner John Kennedy purchased Ardwick Hall, and

George Murray bought the nearby Ancoats Hall in 1813, which had been a family seat of the Mosley family. Further, Ardwick, like Chorlton-on-Medlock, also possessed its own private cemetery, funded by a joint-stock company, that was opened in 1838. This was a Dissenter's cemetery and built to appeal to the middle classes, with a fine Neoclassical mortuary chapel. It became a fashionable place to establish family vaults and was the resting place of some of Manchester's 'great and good', with prestigious memorials including for the scientist John Dalton, Thomas Potter (Manchester's first major) and the Chartist, Ernest Jones (there were also plots for the poor, including unmarked common graves). With the changing status of Ardwick, however, the cemetery declined and the gravestones were eventually removed to transform the area into college playing field. The only physical echo of Ardwick's once handsome villas is the stable block for a house fronting Hyde Road, which is now the Apsley Cottage pub.

Fig. 2.42 Old stable block, now Apsley Cottage pub, Ardwick (Author, 2022).

Another early suburb that emerged in the late eighteenth and early nineteenth century was the Crescent in Salford; an attractive row of Georgian terraced housing arranged at the top of the riverbank overlooking a tight loop in the River Irwell. This still forms an unbroken row and captures some of elegance of this early suburb. These were erected around the 1820s in three phases. More well-known residents included the local architect Thomas Worthington, who was born in a house on the Crescent in 1824.

Fig. 2.43 The Crescent, Salford (Author, 2023).

The mid-nineteenth-century district map of the Manchester and Salford conurbation can be used to illustrate suburban development in the first half of the century. While Ardwick Green and the Crescent were located near to the central district, the construction of new roads in the 1820s and 1830s facilitated middle-class movement into the countryside. The laying out of Bury New Road in 1831 (a turnpike road still with its toll house), for instance, promoted villa building in Upper Broughton, Salford. This was overseen by the Clowes family that encouraged wealthy merchants and industrialists to erect villas around their estate at Broughton Park. These residents would commute to work in the city using a horse-drawn omnibus service, set up for precisely this purpose. Some of these early nineteenth-century houses still survive, especially on The Cliff at the top of Lower Broughton Road, with vistas overlooking another picturesque loop in the River Irwell. This was probably the most upmarket location for bourgeois residences during this phase. Other examples of middle-class residences can be found along the upper reaches of Great Clowes

Street, such as the 1830s range at Numbers 258–260, with its large Ionic porticos.

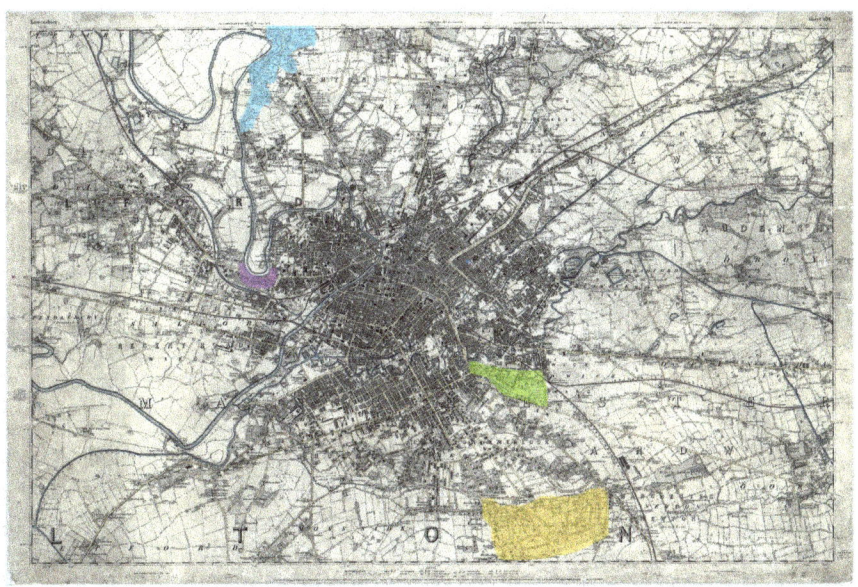

Fig. 2.44 Map of Manchester and Salford District, 1845 (the location of Ardwick Green is highlighted in green, The Crescent in pink, Higher Broughton in blue and Victoria Park is highlighted in yellow; annotated by the author). Ordnance Survey map Lancashire Sheet CIV, CC BY, National Library of Scotland.

Fig. 2.45 258–260 Great Clowes Street, Salford (Author, 2020).

Fig. 2.46 Buile Hill mansion, Pendleton, Salford. Photograph by Matt Ratcliffe (2014), *Manchester Evening News*.

Alongside distinct suburbs, the wealthiest sections of Manchester's middle class also built mansions in their park estates, directly copying the lifestyles of the aristocracy. For instance, Mark Philips, one of the first two MPs for Manchester was born in his family estate in Philips Park in the Irwell Valley at Whitefield. The Philips family were prosperous merchants who bought the estate in 1798 and built a Neoclassical mansion and landscaped the gardens and park. Unfortunately, the house was demolished when the city council took over the park. However, there are other examples of early nineteenth-century middle-class mansions that still are present. One of these is Buile Hill in Pendleton, Salford. The mansion was the home of Utilitarian industrialist and first mayor of Manchester, Thomas Potter, who commissioned Charles Barry to design him a Greek Revivalist building in 1826 (which was enlarged by Edward Walters, who built a third storey). Neoclassical, especially Greek style, was the preferred aesthetic for Georgian civic and private architecture during this phase. The popularity of this trend means that there are many other examples in the Manchester and Salford district worth visiting, such as Ashburne House in Fallowfield which is regarded as one of Manchester's best Greek villas. Didsbury, to the south of Manchester, also has a concentration of villas and mansions, as the village was transformed into a fashionable middle-class suburb during the nineteenth century, including Richard Lane's Neoclassical The Elms.

Fig. 2.47 Ashburne House, Fallowfield (Author, 2020).

These middle-class, suburban mansion and villa residential developments represented an important trend, encompassing a radically new way of living and of relating to an urban environment. In contrast to eighteenth-century polite society, in which profession, workplaces and residencies were closely spatially related, these developments physically separated the middle class from the commerce and politics of the city. While occupation and wealth continued to be focused on the urban arena, residing in the leafy suburbs allowed the middle classes to imagine themselves as rural dwellers removed from the morally corrupting influence of the industrial city where they could pursue 'aristocratic' fantasies about traditional, morally uplifting, country life. The spatial segregation between work and home was central for creating a division between public and private spheres, which was so crucial for the establishment of bourgeois values, such as the Victorian 'domestic ideology' and the primacy of the family.

Residential 'Parks'

Investments in suburban, domestic architecture subsequently drove further and grander speculative residential developments, and a conscious break from Georgian terraces with the construction of villas and villa estates in semi-rural settings. Although such developments had been initiated in London, Manchester was a pioneer in the suburbanisation of the industrial city. This took the form of planned, residential 'parks'. The cotton manufacturer and banker, Samuel Brooks, initiated the trend in 1834 by buying land in an area to the south of the city centre to develop it into a wealthy residential estate, Whalley Range. This consisted of a grid of planned streets, guarded by toll bars with 'gentlemen's' villas and landscaped gardens, including Brook's own residence, Whalley House. Unfortunately, very few of the original buildings now stand. However, the most ambitious and best surviving of these suburban park developments was Richard Lane and Partner's Victoria Park, also located to the south of the city centre (between Rusholme and Longsight, as depicted on the c.1850 map of the Manchester and Salford district, see Fig. 2.44). This venture took off in 1837 and involved a planned 140 acres, including a walled and gated enclave with large houses in generous plots, aligned to curving tree-lined avenues. This basic arrangement was inspired by John Nash's Park Village beside Regents Park in London and drew upon the Georgian concept of the picturesque. Lane also designed the first buildings in Victoria Park as semi-detached houses in stripped down Tudor Gothic style (as illustrated in the photograph of Victoria Park Hotel at the main entrance to this residential enclave at Park Crescent in Rusholme, see Fig. 2.49). But, as building proceeded on a speculative basis by different builders, Victoria Park came to possess a diversity of nineteenth-century house designs (as will be discussed in the following chapter).

Fig. 2.48 Victoria Park, 1889 (section of Ordnance Survey map Lancashire Sheet CIV.15), CC BY, National Library of Scotland.

Fig. 2.49 Victoria Park Hotel, Rusholme (Author, 2024).

As the American urban historian Robert Fishman argues in his insightful book, *Bourgeois Utopias*, 'Suburbanisation in Manchester was not simply a flight from the industrial city. The decision of the middle class to break with their tradition of living in the urban core decisively altered the form of city' (1989, 76–77). It created a divided environment which spatially separated bourgeois work and residence, and consolidated the tendency towards class segregation. Further, living in suburban 'parks' in mansions and villas was also a means of legitimising the rising middle classes through the appropriation of aristocratic symbolism. In the words of Fishman again, 'Suburbia proved the perfect setting in which the older symbolism of aristocratic power could be appropriated by the middle classes. Insecure in its new status, the bourgeoisie grasped eagerly at the well established symbolism of the traditional elite' (1989, 95).

Liverpool Road Station

The final intervention in the built environment in this phase of development, although really representing the start of the next phase, was the opening of the Liverpool and Manchester Railway in 1830, designed and built by George Stephenson. This was the first intercity passenger railway in the world and started a transport revolution that was one of the defining developments of the nineteenth century. In Manchester, the railways were to have a dramatic impact on the spatial arrangement of the city, reorientating the axis of urban development. The novelty of this innovation can be seen in the way the design of the station building in Manchester, without any architectural precedent to follow, was modelled on a Georgian town house. The Liverpool Road Station, with its first- and second-class entrances with separate booking offices, has a classical front, faced with stone and stucco. It now forms part of the Science and Industry Museum, together with the station agent's house, the associated 1830 warehouse and Stephenson's magnificent River Irwell Railway Bridge (Princes Bridge).

Fig. 2.50 Liverpool Road Station (showing the first- and second-class passenger entrances) (Author, 2023).

Fig. 2.51 River Irwell Railway Bridge (Author, 2023).

The Liverpool Road Station complex included the Arrivals Station on Water Street, built in 1837 and integrated into Stephenson's bridge. The now partially blocked entrance facade of this station survives, as does some of the storage and stable rooms with brick ventilated windows, along with the ramp to the platform to facilitate the movement of animals transported by rail.

Fig. 2.52 Storerooms at the Arrivals Station, Water Street (Author, 2023).

Manchester, around 1840, was a remarkable urban phenomenon, representing the emergence of a new industrial society. It was at the cutting edge of technological progress, with steam-powered machinery driving manufacturing and a centre for innovations in transport with the development of the canal network (and later with a railway infrastructure). As a result, the city sat at the heart of an expanding regional, national and international web of production and exchange. But while the cotton mills and factories may have attracted considerable attention, the rapid process of change in Manchester also generated fear and horror. Industrial capitalism opened gilded opportunities for a select few, but entailed the immiseration and pauperisation of the majority, as the accumulation of wealth was based on the wholesale exploitation of an urban working class whose very growth seemed to threaten the entire system. This contradiction played out in the transformations of the built environment. It can be seen in the spread of mills and working-class slums, and it underpinned the imposition of institutions of coercion and the commercialisation of the central district, which led to the middle-class diaspora to the suburbs and contributed to the debased nature of Manchester's 'polite' architecture. It was a contradiction that came to a head with the rise of Chartism and the 1842 so-called 'Plug plot riots', the first general strike in history, with Manchester and its satellite towns at the centre of this social movement. Yet Chartism and the general strike was defeated, and this carried significant consequences for the subsequent development of Manchester. The crushing of working-class resistance led to an era of bourgeois triumphalism in which the middle class attempted to address some of the problems of industrial capitalism in defiantly liberal terms. Freed from the fear of revolution, the middle class conspicuously reconfigured the built environment to project liberal values and to help nurture a new type of urban citizen. Once the industrial city had been firmly established, it was soon transformed into a bourgeois city.

3. City of Triumphant Liberalism, c.1840–c.1860

Free Trade Hall

Fig. 3.1 Free Trade Hall (Author, 2025).

Between 1853 and 1856, Manchester's Free Trade Hall was built, fronting Peter Street on what had been St Peter's Fields. This monumental palazzo-style building, designed by Edward Walters, symbolised the triumph of bourgeoise liberalism. As A. J. P. Taylor commented, 'Other great halls in England are called after a royal patron, or figure of traditional religion. Only the Free Trade Hall is dedicated to a proposition' (cited in Glinert 2008, 29). This new civic building, which functioned as a public speaking hall and concert hall, was erected to celebrate the repeal of the Corn Laws in 1846, on land given by Richard Cobden, the great advocator of free trade, and a key leader of the Anti-Corn Law League. Its construction, paid for by public subscription, was intimately connected to the building of what the historian Simon Gunn has described as a 'new industrial civilisation'.

Located on the site of the Peterloo Massacre, the positioning of the Free Trade Hall was significant as it spatially appropriated Manchester's radicalism in the name of liberalism. The ornate Italianate facade, modelled on Gran Guardia Vecchia in Verona, was a proclamation of 'Manchester Economics'. It is rich in architectural sculpture. The tympani of the upper arches on the first floor contain figures representing Free Trade, flanked by Art, Commerce, Manufacture and Agriculture and the four continents, while the lower reliefs in the spandrels of the ground floor arcade display the badges of the Lancastrian towns associated with the Anti-Corn Law movement (Rochdale even being symbolised with a relief of a textile mill).

With this iconography, the building was a physical expression of bourgeois optimism that industry and free trade could deliver progress and prosperity to Manchester, Lancashire, Britain and the world. The palazzo-style became the architectural signature of bourgeois power, with Manchester's industrialists, merchants and bankers presenting themselves as modern-day Renaissance princes.

3. City of Triumphant Liberalism, c.1840–c.1860

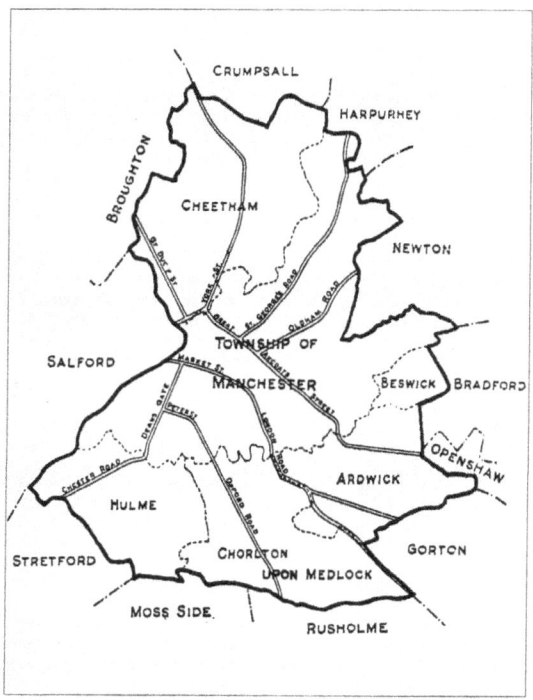

Fig. 3.2 Municipal Borough of Manchester, 1838 (Kidd 2002, 62, all rights reserved).

The transformation of Manchester as an industrial city during the second half of the nineteenth century was consequently a feature of middle-class empowerment following the Great Reform Act of 1832 and the Municipal Corporation Act of 1835. Manchester gained parliamentary representation and was incorporated in 1838 (and then awarded city status in 1853). Salford gained borough status slightly later in 1844. After the challenge of labour in the storm of Chartism had been weathered, middle-class confidence and social aspiration was further boosted. This ushered in an era of liberal political dominance in which the middle class saw themselves as builders of an 'Industrial Jerusalem' (to use the historian Tristram Hunt's phrase), forging a civic culture linked to the values of free trade, individualism, self-help and self-improvement. The built environment of Manchester was reconfigured in terms of liberal governmentality. It was transformed to accommodate new phases of industrialisation and capital accumulation, but also to establish civic spaces and institutions in which the 'Manchester Man' could take shape. Urban improvements were therefore being consciously linked to the development of a public culture focusing on nurturing rational, self-regulating behaviour. It was one of the great ironies and contradictions of the times that such liberal 'freedoms' were intrinsically associated with the paternalistic control and policing of labour. Behind the liberal triumphalism of what has been called the 'age of equipoise', was a deep-seated concern about the activities of the working class, not only at work but also increasingly at home and at leisure as well. This tension was worked out in the streets, buildings and public spaces of the city.

To analyse these developments this phase will be divided into six sub-phases. It starts with 'The Railways and Their Impact on Urban Developments', which discusses Manchester's expanded railway network that exerted such a profound influence on the built environment, looking specifically at the surviving railway stations and viaducts. The next section, 'The Central Business District and the Architecture of Commerce', then considers the way in which the centre of the city was reconfigured during the middle decades of the nineteenth century. Piccadilly Esplanade is established as the principle civic space and what was previously a middle-class residential locale becomes filled with grand, palazzo-style warehouses and banks. The third sub-phase, 'Municipal Interventions in the Built Environment' looks at how Manchester Corporation becomes actively involved in the urban arena through rationalising Smithfield Market, the construction of new roads and bridges, and by directly taking control of the city's water and gas supplies. Fourthly, 'Liberal Governmentality and Working-Class Communities' widens discussion out to examine middle-class civic reforms more generally and how they were directed towards managing the built environment in order to 'police' the industrial working class. This is the time that by-law housing, arranged into grids of redbrick terraces became a feature of Manchester's working-class residential districts. The Corporation was also the moving force behind the first municipal parks and public baths, as well as encouraging the establishment of mechanic institutions and free libraries to nurture the moral character of labour. The next subphase, 'Townships, Church Building and Religious Pluralism', then explores the growth of suburban townships around the centre through the mapping of new church foundations. It explores the spread of Anglican, Catholic and Nonconformist institutions in terms of the city's religious pluralism and the growing confidence of different communities. The final section, 'Bourgeois Housing and the Age of the Suburban Villa' then turns attention to Manchester's middle class and how there was an exodus to semi-rural locations where numerous large suburban villas were built, many of which are still in use today.

The Railways and Their Impact on Urban Developments

The Ernst and Co's map of Manchester was produced for Art Treasures Exhibition of 1857: an event that advertised the city as being more than just a 'Coketown' or 'cottonopolis'. Manchester's industrial middle class asserted their social status by refashioning the place as a city of culture and not a backwater. Art and architecture were a means to demonstrate this, and so Manchester followed the example of London's Great Exhibition of 1851. The street plan of Ernst and Co's illustrated map, published to help visitors to the exhibition navigate the city, is surrounded by images of prestigious buildings, churches and chapels, cultural institutions and civic buildings, as well as commercial entities, such as banks and warehouses. This built environment was becoming an integral part of the city's new identity. When compared to Pigot's map of 1838 (see Fig. 2.1), however, the most important intervention depicted on Ernst and Co's map, is the establishment of Manchester's railway network, shown as thin black lines leading into and surrounding the city. This railway infrastructure of track lines, stations, viaducts and bridges, as well as associated goods warehouses and marshalling yards, was probably the most important single influence on the spatial arrangement of the city in the second half of the nineteenth century. Its presence is still very much felt today, with the current railway network being one of the most obvious elements of Manchester's 'living archaeology'.

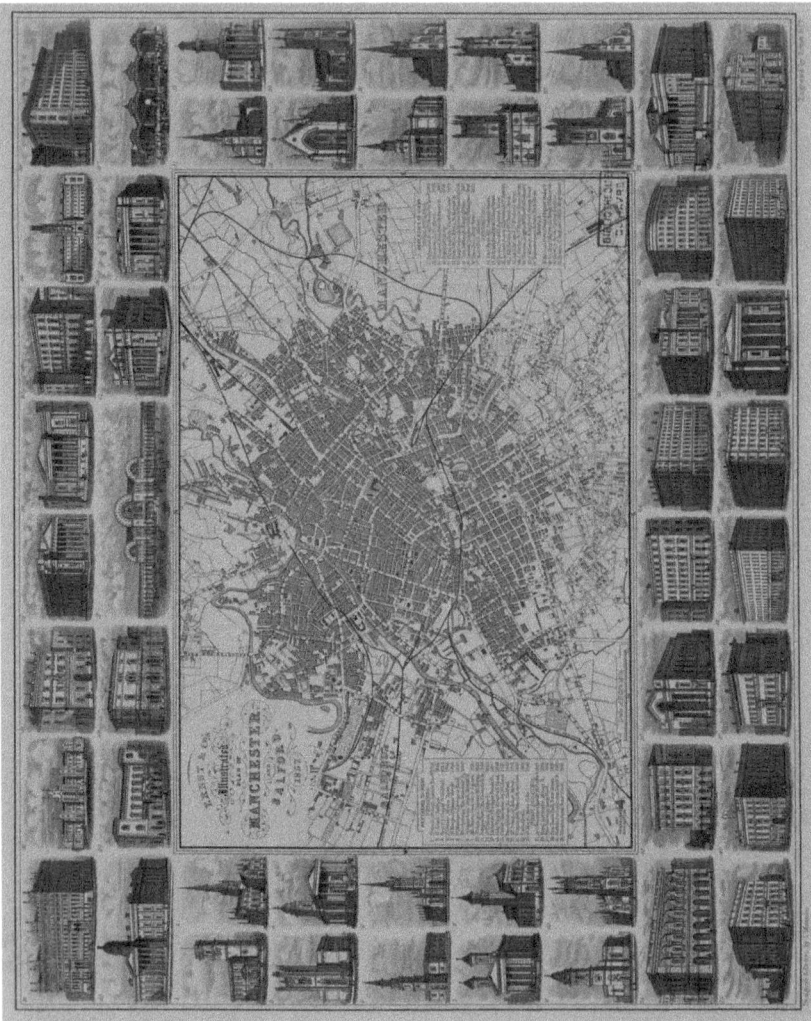

Fig. 3.3 J. Mennie's 1857 Ernst and Co's illustrated plan of Manchester and Salford. Wikimedia Commons, public domain, https://commons.wikimedia.org/wiki/File:Plan_of_Manchester_and_Salford_-_Designed_%26_drawn_by_J._Mennie_-_btv1b10679888h.jpg#/media/File:Plan_of_Manchester_and_Salford_-_Designed_&_drawn_by_J._Mennie_-_btv1b10679888h.jpg

3. City of Triumphant Liberalism, c.1840–c.1860   103

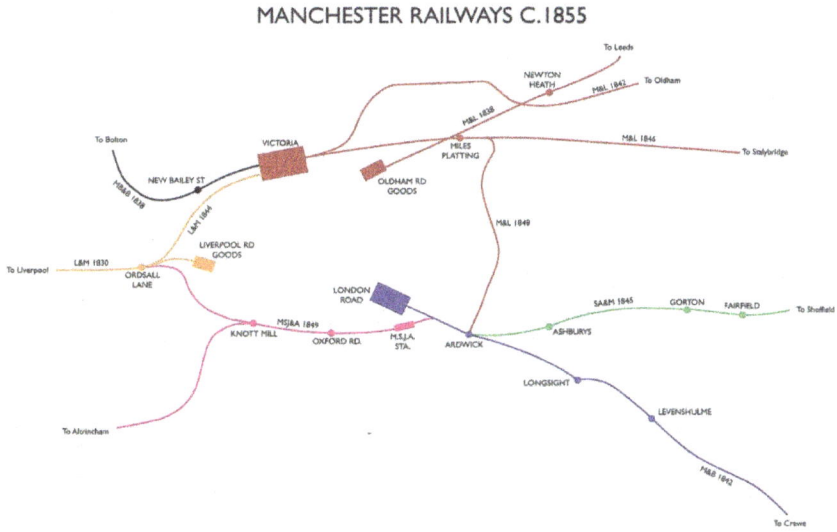

Fig. 3.4 Manchester railways c.1855 (Andy Mason in Dawson 2017, 6, all rights reserved).

The commercial success of the Liverpool and Manchester Railway of 1830 soon inspired other entrepreneurs to build their own lines and stations in an around the city, as is clear from the schematic railway map of the network around 1855. Investments in railway building was a way to absorb the enormous amount of surplus of capital that had been generated by the initial phase of the industrialisation of the cotton industry. But speculation in railway construction created a new transport infrastructure that was critical for the subsequent waves of capital accumulation. These developments were very much private endeavours, without much direct involvement from either local or central government. It was this that led to the proliferation of railway tracks, viaducts and stations around the city, which was a peculiar feature of Britain's private railways in contrast to the state-instigated systems of continental Europe. Investment in railway infrastructure during the late 1830s and 1840 also provided an outlet for surplus capital during the downturn in the cotton industry. Liverpool Road Station was followed by Salford (Central) Station in 1838, initially the terminus for the Manchester and Bolton Railway (originally named New Bailey

Street Station). The Manchester and Leeds Railway built Oldham Road Station, which was transformed into a goods station when the company built Hunts Bank (Victoria) Station in 1844. London Road Station, or today's Piccadilly, was the terminus for the Manchester and Birmingham Railway in 1841, while the Manchester South Junction and Altrincham Railway opened Oxford Road and Deansgate stations in 1849. By the end of this phase, Manchester had three main railway termini surrounding the centre (Liverpool Street, Victoria and Piccadilly). A fourth, Central Station, was to open in 1880.

Railway Stations and Viaducts

Significantly, the coming of the railways introduced new architectural forms into the built environment: an architecture of iron and brick and the distinctive linear arrangements of viaducts linked to the station termini surrounding the city centre. In this sense, the railways exhibited the importance of these new materials, with locally sourced and fired bricks dominating the built environment. In particular, the station termini were the showcases for the companies that invested in the railways. They were not simply functional, utilitarian structures. They were designed to establish a corporate identity and to attract customers to this new, revolutionary form of transport.

Fig. 3.5 Hunts Bank Station (Victoria) (Author, 2022).

3. City of Triumphant Liberalism, c.1840–c.1860   105

Fig. 3.6 London Road Station (Piccadilly) (Author, 2022).

Fig. 3.7 Goods Office, London Road Station (Author, 2022).

Along with Liverpool Road Station, the original 1844 terminus at Hunts Bank partially survives, now integrated into the later Victoria Station. It was built in Italianate style with an upper storey added later. At London Road Station, the colossal iron viaduct bearing the weight of the platform is also still in use. This was designed by George W. Buck for the Manchester and Birmingham Railway with cast iron columns with Roman Doric capitals ingeniously underpinning the whole station. Although the original terminal building constructed in an Italianate style has long gone, the ornate Renaissance-inspired Goods Office still survives on London Road. It was Buck who took the line of the Manchester and Birmingham Railway south along viaducts and embankments towards Stockport, where it traversed the Mersey Valley via the twenty-seven-arched, brick-built Stockport Viaduct. At the time of its completion in 1841, this was the largest brick-built viaduct in the world, and it remains an iconic monument in the Greater Manchester landscape.

Fig. 3.8 Salford Central Station (showing columns with Egyptian-style lotus leaf capitals) (Author, 2022).

There are many other examples of this architecture of iron linked to the early railways, such as the original 1844 bridge running out of Victoria Station that spans Ducie Street, or the two iron bridges of the Manchester South Junction and Altrincham Railway at the junction of Deansgate and Whitworth Street. But of particular note is the viaduct and colonnade at Salford Central Station, designed by John Hawkshaw for the Liverpool and Manchester Railway in 1844. It has an elegant cast-iron parapet supported by cast-iron columns decorated with Egyptian lotus leaf capitals, further illustrating the way that railway companies were quick to embrace architectural historicism to create distinctive corporate identities for themselves.

The general impact of this new railway infrastructure on the wider physical environment was profound. Although Manchester's termini were placed on the edge of the built-up area of the city, the establishment of the railway network influenced and shaped subsequent patterns of urban development. Driving rail lines into the city certainly disrupted existing residential areas, especially working-class ones, as described by Engels. Standing on Ducie Bridge he famously describes how the viaduct of an extension to the Manchester and Leeds Railway 'swept away' many of the courts and alleys of the notorious slum district of Angel Meadow while 'laying others completely open for view' (2009, 90). Similar intrusions into the existing built environment are evident elsewhere. For example, in Salford the viaducts running west out of Victoria Station (and later Exchange Station) cut through the heart of old town, passing very close to the tower of Sacred Trinity chapel. Consequently, these viaducts led to the demise of Salford's old centre, forcing a shift in development west, along Chapel Street to a new focus around Richard Lane's town hall. Likewise, at Ardwick the viaducts of the London and Birmingham Railway, as well as Mayfield Goods Station, pass through what had been, until then, an upmarket suburb, causing a marked change in the social character of this district as the affluent middle class moved away to more tranquil areas.

Fig. 3.9 Manchester South Junction and Altrincham Railway viaduct (Author, 2022).

These imposing brick-built and iron viaducts and bridges were and remain prominent features of the cityscape (although, despite their presence, they are seldom commented on by architectural historians). However, viaducts formed physical barriers and boundaries that, once established, delineated subsequent patterns of land use, thus influencing different urban zones. For instance, the viaduct built for the Manchester South Junction and Altrincham Railway in 1845, to connect Piccadilly to the Irwell crossing at Castlefield, surrounded the southern and western edges of the city centre like a medieval wall (and was used as such in 1931 to stop a demonstration of the unemployed from entering the city centre). This viaduct, together with those of the other railway companies, defined inner and outer urban zones and formed a physical boundary of the central business district of Manchester, separated from the industrial and residential districts beyond.

John Kellet (1969) has been the leading British scholar exploring the physical effects of railways on Victorian cities and how they were agents of internal change. In particular, he has examined how railways influenced the location of industry, driving the tendency for industry to be dispersed to the outer suburbs. This is certainly evidenced in Manchester where the axial railway lines that radiate out from the centre formed linear corridors attracted industry, especially where the railways ran parallel to the Rochdale, Ashton and Bolton canals and the rivers Irwell and Irk. This trend can be seen in the siting of engineering and carriage works. Ashbury Carriage and Iron Company, originally located near Castlefield, for instance, moved their works to Openshaw in 1847, by the railway line running east out of the town. The Ashbury site encouraged the construction of further carriage works in the area, such as the Gorton Carriage Company that opened a works depot in 1848, known as 'Gorton Tank'. As a result, the eastern side of Manchester became the focus of engineering works and foundries during the second half of the nineteenth century. Similar developments took place along the railway line to the north of Manchester with carriage, wagon and engineering works established at Newton Heath for Lancashire and Yorkshire Railway (although slightly later during the nineteenth century in 1877). The famous engineering company Mather and Platt formed in 1845, moved to Newton Heath from Salford to become one of the major employers of the township.

The expansion of engineering works associated with the development of the railway industry highlights the way in which this revolution in transport underpinned the expansion and diversification of Manchester's productive base. Trains facilitated the movement of goods and people on an unprecedented scale that dramatically reduced the constraints of time and space on commercial transactions. This enhanced the wealth and self-confidence of Manchester's bourgeois elite, and encouraged further investments which found expression in a new architecture of commerce.

The Central Business District and the Architecture of Commerce

In terms of urban morphology, the impact of the railways helped intensify the transformation of the heart of Manchester. This phase of development was, therefore, a formative one in the making of the central business district. It was Friedrich Engels, having lived through and experienced these changes, who perceptively observed the formation of concentric urban zones around the city. He commented on how the town centre was becoming deserted of inhabitants and no longer a place for dwelling.

> Manchester contains, at its heart, a rather extended commercial district, perhaps half a mile long and about as broad, consisting almost wholly of offices and warehouses. Nearly the whole district is abandoned, and is lonely and deserted at night; only watchmen and policemen traverse its narrow lanes with their dark lanterns. (2009, 85–86)

The surrounding area outside the centre comprised working-class districts, with bourgeois housing beyond in an outer suburban zone. This innovative, first-hand analysis forms the basic framework for understanding the overall development of Manchester during this phase, as will be shown. However, the central business district was not simply characterised by the replacement of residential buildings by commercial ones. It was also defined by the way in which distinct zones of activity began to emerge within it.

The 'old town' was centred around the medieval church, whose status was enhanced into a cathedral in 1847 when Manchester became a city. As a consequence, the exterior of the building as well as the nave arcades and the tower were extensively repaired and rebuilt between the 1850s and 1870s (see Fig. 1.5), with the Gothic architecture serving as a reference point for the later more general Gothic Revival in the city (to be discussed in the next chapter). Manchester Cathedral therefore remained an important ecclesiastical and cultural focus, although the marketing functions of the 'old town' were transferred to Smithfield Market at the top of Shudehill and to the south of Swann Street in 1822. The two main eighteenth-century foundations, the Exchange and the Infirmary, also continued to be important focal points for the city. First established in 1729, the Exchange had been rebuilt and repositioned by Thomas Harrison as a Neoclassical building in 1809 and enlarged in the late 1840s and then rebuilt again at the end of the 1860s when it was renamed the Royal Exchange. This was the heart of operations for Manchester's cotton merchants and business elites. It was directly connected to the Infirmary by the widened and straightened Market Street which stood at Piccadilly. This now formed the main civic space of Manchester.

Piccadilly Esplanade

Fig. 3.10 William Morton, 'Manchester Royal Infirmary', engraving, c.1853/1857, showing the Royal Infirmary and Piccadilly Esplanade. Wellcome Collection, public domain, https://wellcomecollection.org/works/qtcfufgu/images?id=c9cv6t28

As has been described, the Infirmary, Manchester's largest public building, had been refurbished by Richard Lane in the 1830s, who added two porticos. At the same time there were plans to turn Piccadilly Square into a classical piazza with the engineer William Fairbairn's grand scheme of 1836 to reposition the Exchange as a pantheon-style building at the Piccadilly end of Market Street with a large residential crescent to the north of the Infirmary. While this plan was never realised, during the 1850s the area was transformed into monumental gateway into the city. The hospital was renamed the Royal Infirmary (after the monarch's visit in 1851) and a domed clock tower was added over the main portico, but most importantly a promenade with fountains and gardens was laid out to form Piccadilly Esplanade following a plan by Joseph Paxton (the designer of Crystal Palace). This became lined with statues to the 'great and good': the politician Robert Peel (unveiled by Gladstone in 1853); the engineer James Watt (1857); the scientist John Dalton (now moved to another location); and the general and former prime minister, the Duke of Wellington (1856). Piccadilly Esplanade therefore became a defined civic space which was used as the focal point of ceremonial processions, such as the royal visits to Manchester by Queen Victoria and Prince Albert in 1851 and in 1857 (as captured in contemporary paintings and etchings). Interestingly, the processional routes of these events were carefully planned so that the royal couple avoided the unsightliness and potential dangers of working-class districts on their way to Piccadilly (thus reinforcing Engels' observation about the class nature of the street geography of Manchester).

The Royal Infirmary and Esplanade formed a unit directly connected to the middle-class locale along Mosley Street and Peter Street with its complex of civic institutions (the Portico Library, Royal Manchester Institute, Athenaeum, Theatre Royal and the Free Trade Hall). Yet it was during this phase that this locale ceased to be a desirable residential area. The emigration of the middle class to the suburbs meant the fashionable streets around Mosley Street became lined with commercial premises rather than domestic houses. Georgian terraces were replaced with textile warehouses, banks and offices, as this central area was steadily transformed into a warehouse and financial zone. The streets to the north of Mosley Street became dominated by textile warehouses, while in those to the south there was a concentration of local and national banks, especially along King Street. However, these new commercial buildings were not prosaic in form. Like the railway termini, they were consciously constructed with a high degree of architectural pretension. The monumentalising of commercial structures was a means of display that advertised individual businesses. At the same time, the adoption of a shared architectural style provided the bourgeois with a collective, material and visual identity.

Palazzo-Style Warehouses

The shift in the land use of the central district of Manchester was therefore also linked to a marked change in architectural fashion. The Greek Revival and Neoclassicism fell out of favour, as Italianate styles began to dominate, especially the Renaissance palazzo. Buildings styled on the grand houses and palaces of Italian Renaissance nobleman became the architectural signature of Manchester's commercial elite. In this, Manchester was following national trends. Charles Barry had popularised this style with his Reform Club in Pall Mall in London and introduced it in Manchester with his Athenaeum. But the palazzo was taken up with particular relish by Manchester's cotton barons, especially for their commercial warehouses, with rows of palazzi aligning many streets to form a warehouse quarter in the central business district concentrated between Mosley Street and Portland Street. The number and density of surviving mid-nineteenth-century palazzo warehouses in this area of Manchester are an impressive feature of the city's industrial heritage, although something often overlooked (amongst the restaurants and shops of Manchester's contemporary 'Chinatown'). They form part of the finest textile warehouse quarter in the country, surpassing those, also of note, in Bradford (woollens) and Nottingham (lace).

Fig. 3.11 12 Charlotte Street, palazzo-style warehouse (Author, 2022).

Along the south side of Charlotte Street there is an almost complete range of palazzo warehouses all designed and built by Edward Walters between c.1850 and c.1860. Walters, like Richard Lane, in the previous chapter, was the dominant architect in the decades of the mid-nineteenth century whose presence can still be felt today. These were purpose-built textile, showcase warehouses with grand exteriors and interiors to impress clientele. They were places where large quantities of cloth could be pressed, packaged, labelled and stored for sale and export. Each has a similar arrangement, occupying a whole block with access to loading bays from the side streets. Although Charlotte Street has the most complete range, similar examples can be found in the neighbouring Princess Street and Portland Street. The cohesiveness and unity of the architecture of palazzo warehouses served to project a collective identity for Manchester's industrial bourgeois. As Mark Crinson argues, 'Walters's skill was not so much to vaguely "gentrify" Manchester businessmen as to pointedly reinforce their self-perception as the only properly urban elite' (2022, 65). The importance of these buildings, therefore, does not simply lie in the architectural pretensions of individual structures, but in how, taken together, their shared Renaissance style formed a common aesthetic representing middle-class dominance.

Fig. 3.12 Watts Warehouse (Britannia Hotel), Portland Street (Author, 2022).

As one of the main thoroughfares of the central business district, running parallel to Mosley Street, Portland Street is home to the grandest warehouses that visually dominated the approach into the city from London Road Station. These were 'palaces of commerce' *par excellence*, as exhibited by the sheer scale and architectural flamboyancy of Watts Warehouse (what is now the Britannia Hotel) and the group at Numbers 3–7 Portland Street. Watts Warehouse was built for the local businessman James Watts, between 1851 and 1856, who owned the largest drapery firm in Manchester and was the mayor of the city between 1855 and 1857. His wealth and ambition found expression in an architectural historicism in which each of the six floors is decorated with different styles from the Italian Renaissance, to Elizabethan, to French Renaissance and French Gothic. Inside, the original grand central staircase, with its ornate cast-iron columns, survives, rising through the entire height of the building. Further along Portland Street at Numbers 3 to 7 are more examples. This imposing group of three warehouses was designed by Edward Walters in 1858 in his Italian Renaissance style. This is where the cotton produced in Murrays' Mills in Ancoats was stored. These 'palaces of commerce' became an integral part of the city's identity, several of which, including those just discussed, are depicted surrounding Ernst and Co's illustrated plan of Manchester and Salford (see Fig. 3.3).

Fig. 3.13 3–5 Portland Street (Author, 2022).

Banks

Fig. 3.14 Benjamin Heywood's Bank, St Ann's Square (with adjoining house) (Author, 2023).

Fig. 3.15 Manchester and Salford Bank, Mosley Street (Author, 2022).

The monumentalising of both commercial and public buildings utilising Italianate Renaissance styles, and especially the palazzo, was a distinctive feature of this phase of liberal triumphalism, and architecturally connected the Free Trade Hall, station termini and textile warehouses together. It was a style also shared by the many banks that multiplied with Manchester's economic growth. One of the best survivors is Benjamin Heywood's bank. This was located in a prominent position at the south-east corner of St Ann's Square, immediately adjacent the church. It has an attached manager's house on St Ann Street. Built by J. E. Gregan in 1848, it is regarded as one of the finest of the palazzo-inspired buildings in the city. The Heywoods were a prominent banking family in Manchester, having initially made their wealth through involvement in the trans-Atlantic slave trade. But Benjamin was a philanthropist and liberal reformer, being one of the founders of Manchester's Mechanics Institution, as well as a politician, having been elected as a Whig MP in 1832. Other noteworthy banks from the phase include Edward Walters's 1862 palazzo for Manchester and Salford Bank in Mosley Street, which is regarded as his last great work.

Municipal Interventions in the Built Environment

The incorporation of Manchester in 1838, following the Municipal Incorporation Act, led to the reform of local government and the election of a council. It was through the Corporation that middle-class social forces could coalesce and push for municipal improvements in the urban environment. This was the start of the reconfiguration of Manchester from the 'shock city' of industrial capitalism, as the reform of local government opened up the opportunity for new civic developments. However, faced with entrenched opposition from the 'old guard', it was not until the early 1840s that the Corporation was able to fully exercise its power and make its mark in the management of the built environment. But these municipal interventions were circumscribed by the liberal philosophy and politics that came to dominate local government thinking at the time. Prefaced by deep-seated assumptions about the sanctity of the individual, private property and free trade, the liberal politicians that were elected favoured indirect rather than direct means to transform the city. Liberal governmentality required the nurturing of social conditions so that a new industrial civilisation could build itself through the actions of autonomous individuals, rather than being driven, in a top-down manner, by government and politicians. Nevertheless, Manchester Corporation was directly involved in a several initiatives which began to rationally transform the urban environment. Three important interventions can be highlighted.

Smithfield Market

Firstly, in 1846 the Corporation bought the manorial rights to Smithfield Market from the Mosley family and started the rationalisation of the area. It was under the city council's ownership that the market was expanded and developed. In particular, a purpose-built meat market hall was erected facing Swann Street in 1858. Although Neoclassical (Roman) in design rather than Renaissance, this monumentalising of a commercial building improved the market facilities and raised the profile of the city council. The front facade, decorated with a bull's heads, prominently declares that the building had been 'Erected by the Corporation of this City'. The slightly later Wholesale Fish Market hall, with its friezes depicting the marketing of fish, and Market Offices at the corner of Thomas Street, also survive and are a testament to the council's direct involvement in Shudehill Market (which was to grow into one of the biggest wholesale market complexes in Britain).

Fig. 3.16 Smithfield Meat Market Hall, 'Erected by the Corporation of this City' (Author, 2022).

Road and Bridge Building

Secondly, Manchester Corporation was concerned with road developments and circulation around the city. Street widening and straightening, as well laying down of new roads and bridges, had been a feature of the previous phase of urban improvement. Now local government became directly involved. For instance, Corporation Street (the name is the giveaway) was built in 1846 linking the Royal Exchange, at the end of Market Street, in a straight line to Victoria Station and Ducie Street and bridge. In the same year, New Bailey Bridge was replaced by Albert Bridge and linked to Bridge Street and John Dalton Street, easing access to the centre of Manchester from Salford Central station. Developments, such as these, were also associated with Victorian notions of sanitary reform and the liberal desire to cleanse the city centre of inhabitants. Opening up new spaces through street renovation facilitated slum clearances, as well as the free movement of traffic around the city. One of the desired consequences of these measures was that thousands of workers and their families were displaced from the city centre, making the area more amenable for the projection of liberal values through the monumentalising of commercial and public buildings.

Water and Gas Infrastructure

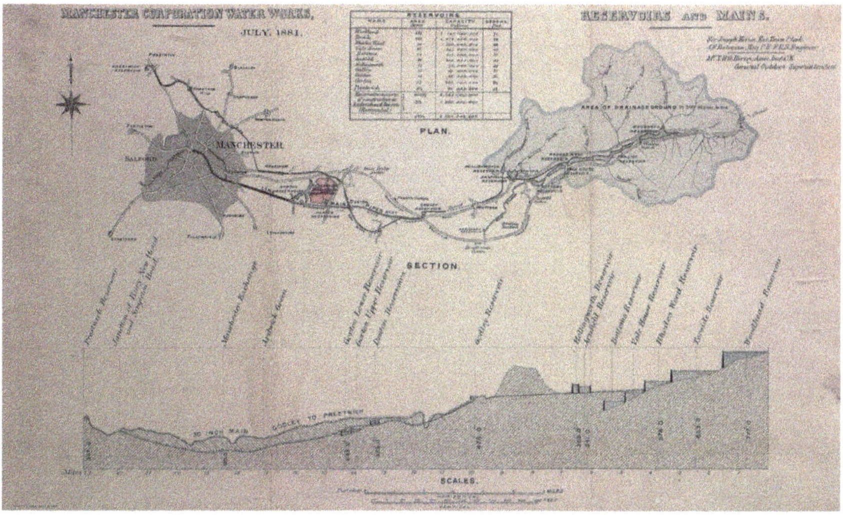

Fig. 3.17 Manchester Corporation water works, reservoirs and mains (1881), public domain.

Thirdly, and perhaps most dramatically, the Corporation became directly involved in the city's water and gas supply. In terms of water, maintaining adequate supplies had always been an issue, and the problem only intensified with the growth and expansion of Manchester. The town had been supplied by the Manchester and Salford Waterworks Company who had built reservoirs at Gorton (in what is now Debdale Park). But the limitations and inadequacies of private ownership meant that the company was bought out by Manchester Corporation in 1847, who set about initiating more ambitious long-term projects that the private company had resisted. The Corporation employed the engineer, John Frederic Bateman, who planned and built a chain of reservoirs, along the Longdendale Valley in the Pennines, connected to the city via an eighteen-mile aqueduct. This was an amazing piece of civil engineering which took thirty-eight years to be fully completed and is still in use today. Later, at the end of the nineteenth century, the Corporation commenced an even more audacious project of tapping water from the lake at Thirlmere in the Lake District.

Even before incorporation, the municipal authorities in Manchester and Salford had direct control over both the production and supply of gas with several gas works established within the conurbation at Bridge Street, Gaythorn, Clowes Street and Bloom Street. After incorporation, this municipal interest in gas intensified with profits from gas being used to subsidise other forms of urban improvements. Gould Street Gas Works, for example, was taken over and expanded by Manchester Corporation. Although now demolished with the site used as a car park, there are still remains of this sprawling complex including the city's coat of arms displayed within the pediment of one of the ruined buildings, illustrating the municipal pride in the civic control of this utility. With urban expansion, new gas works were constructed such as Salford's Regent Road Gas Works which begun in 1858.

Fig. 3.18 Manchester's coat of arms, Gould Street Gas Station (Author, 2023).

Liberal Governmentality and Working-Class Communities

The civic reforms that were associated with the rise of Manchester Corporation were linked to novel forms of knowledge about the built environment and a desire to open up the closed courts, alley ways and 'rookeries' for observation and control. Recording, listing and categorising people and property brought new knowledge and with it a degree of control that facilitated urban renewal in the middle decades of the nineteenth century. The first statistical society in Britain was born in Manchester in 1833, with many of the members holding key positions within the municipal authority. The liberal industrialist Thomas Potter, the first mayor of the town, for instance, was a leading member of Manchester Statistical Society. Further, it was also during this phase that highly detailed, large-scale Ordnance Survey maps of Manchester were drawn-up and published during the 1840s, which even depicted the internal arrangements of public buildings. Scrutinising urban space at this level of detail was a means to assert control over the built environment and a way to identify areas for improvement, especially in relation to the lives of the working class. However, although statistics and cartography underpinned urban reforms in Manchester, the philosophy of liberal governmentality that dominated municipal thinking required indirect rather direct forms of intervention. By-laws were introduced to encourage and shape reforms by individuals, societies and businesses, rather than being directly led by the Corporation itself. This can be seen, in particular, in terms of working-class housing and amenities.

By-Law Housing and Redbrick Terraces

The horror of slum dwellings, recorded by Engels and others during the initial phase of industrial take-off, was a cause of concern that began to be addressed following the triumph of liberalism. Minimum building standards on working-class housing were imposed by local by-laws. Three, in particular, are worth mentioning: the 1844 Manchester Borough Police Act, which effectively ended the building of back-to-backs; the 1852 ban on cellar dwellings; and the 1867 Manchester Improvement Act, which imposed tighter regulation on the width of streets, the sizes of rooms and window space as well as the provision of back yards. Together these by-laws led to the construction of the iconic redbrick terraces, planned in rows in a typical gridiron pattern (as depicted in the 1844 map, Fig. 3.20, and the 1922 photograph of Hulme, Fig. 3.19). The section of large-scale Ordnance Survey map of Hulme is interesting as it records the ongoing development of the area. Hulme had initially developed around the Commissioners' church of St George and the south side of Chester Road, but in 1832 Streford New Road was laid out and new streets with by-law houses aligned beside it. The 1844 map shows earlier terraces to the north of Stretford New Road, including rows of back-to-backs, while new roads and terraces were being plotted and built to the south. These uniform 'by-law houses' became a prominent feature of Manchester as well as other industrial cities. As Engels noted,

> With the exception of this commercial district, all Manchester proper, all Salford and Hulme, a great part of Pendleton and Chorlton, two-thirds of Ardwick, and single stretches of Cheetham Hill and Broughton, are all

unmixed working people's quarters, stretching like a girdle, averaging a mile and a half in breadth, around the commercial district. (2009, 86)

Fig. 3.19 Hulme, 1922 (looking south from the city centre with towards Moss Side, with Gaythorn Gas Works visible at the bottom left). Image courtesy of Manchester Libraries.

Fig. 3.20 Hulme, 1844 (note the positioning of Chorlton-on-Medlock Workhouse amongst the by-law terraces) (section of Ordnance Survey Town Plan – Manchester and Salford Sheet 38), CC BY, National Library of Scotland.

In time, almost all of this inner suburban zone was filled with by-law housing. Unfortunately, there are no surviving examples of these early redbrick terraces as they were all swept away in twentieth-century slum clearances, especially during the extensive post-war urban redevelopments. Later blocks of these by-law housing still exist and can be found further out in Manchester's suburban ring (as will be discussed in Chapter 4).

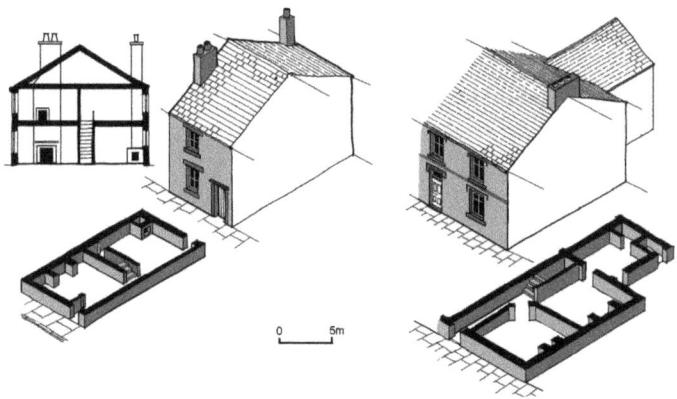

Fig. 3.21 Standardised by-law housing (© Michael Nevell).

These districts of gridiron by-law terraces represented a significant change in the physical fabric which embodied new ideas about controlling the working class. The military-like arrangement of the rows of terraces appears to be designed to instil the work discipline needed for the smooth running of industrial capitalism. The regularity and uniformity of these gridded blocks is striking. Houses were standardised, typically two-storeys (two-up and two-down) with 'tunnel backs' adding an additional room at the rear. The previous *ad hoc* working-class residential pattern of self-contained, enclosed courts and dead-end alleys were now opened up to view and observation. This new, regularly ordered, but open layout of 'through' terraces involved drawing a sharper distinction between public and private spheres, which facilitated a greater control of the public space of the street. It is therefore significant that this shift in the spatial arrangement of working-class residential districts occurred at the same time as the introduction of new policing methods. The fall out of the Peterloo Massacre and Chartist disturbances had highlighted to the ruling class the need for police reform. No longer was it feasible or desirable to enforce public order simply through the sabre of the yeomanry and the musket of the militia. A more intermediatory and less overtly militarised force was required to discipline the working class, and so consequently there was a move towards the professionalising of policing. The Manchester Borough Police was formed in the late 1830s and Salford Borough Police in 1844, which represented a new development (following national trends).

Even though the 'New Police' took time to embed itself against much opposition from sections of both the middle class and working class, these reforms encouraged the patrolling of the streets and the surveillance and regulation of public spaces, especially those connected to working-class recreational activities. This was all part of the fabrication of a liberal social order, based upon the exploitation of wage labour. The working class at both work and home needed to be disciplined. There was therefore a connection between the detailed Ordnance Survey mapping of the built environment, the establishment of the 'New Police' and the new gridiron arrangement of by-law housing.

Fig. 3.22 Manchester and District, 1896, showing location of public parks, baths and cemeteries, annotated by the author (yellow dots = municipal parks; blue dots = baths; and black dots = cemeteries), (section of Old Ordnance Survey Maps, England Sheet 85) Alan Godfrey Maps.

The liberal, middle-class desire to address and attempt to rectify social and environmental problems generated by rapid industrialisation and urbanisation was thus closely tied up with a concern about 'policing' working-class lives. Poor relief and public health policies were linked to measures to mould individual behaviour, with a perceived connection between physical hygiene and moral hygiene. The built environment of Manchester became an important arena where these middle-class anxieties about the working class were expressed. Two specific developments are worth highlighting in this respect: the construction of the first municipal parks and the building of public baths and laundries which were distributed within and around the 'girdle' of the inner suburban zone of working-class terraces (as illustrated in the annotated c.1870 map of Manchester and Salford).

Municipal Parks

A number of private parks and pleasure gardens had been established around Manchester by societies and individuals, such as the botanical gardens at Old Trafford built by the Botanical and Horticultural Society (1830), Pomona Gardens (originally Strawberry Gardens) close to the Bridgewater Canal by Chester Road (1845), and John Jennison's famous Belle Vue Zoological Gardens on Hyde Road to the east of the city (1836). But in 1846, three public parks were opened: Peel Park to the west in Salford; Queens Park to the north in Harpurhey; and Philips Park to the east in Bradford (named after the Manchester MP Mark Philips, who led the local campaign for public parks). These were paid for by public subscription and a government grant, rather than the local authority, but were run and supervised by the council. Municipal parks were defined spaces for rational recreation, where the working class could take the air and exercise away from the corrupting influence of the pub. Manchester, like other industrial cities, was notorious for its lack of greenery, with nothing but bricks, cobbles, paving stones and mud, without a tree, bush or grass lawn in sight in the inner district, let alone flowers. These parks were therefore regarded as the city's lungs. However, they were bounded and regulated spaces, with walls and iron railings, entrance lodges and park keepers who could oversee and maintain responsible social behaviour. Parks were places designed to improve the moral, as well as the physical, well-being of the working class. In terms of this moral dimension, it is interesting that two of these parks are linked to public cemeteries. Queens Park was built immediately adjoining Manchester General Cemetery that had opened in 1838 (as a commercial, private cemetery), while Philips Park Cemetery, Manchester's first municipal cemetery was planned to the north of the park along the River Irk, which divided the two places (opening for interments in 1866). Both these parks and cemeteries were landscaped, being inspired by the ideas of the influential cemetery designer, John Claudius Loudon, and purposely used for walking and strolling around; a spatial arrangement that symbolically drew the connection between life and death. Religious and social divisions were also reinforced in the spatial arrangement of these cemeteries, with separate areas for Anglicans and Nonconformists and clear divisions between more affluent plots with individual memorials and the communal, 'guinea graves' with shared headstones and unmarked pauper burials.

Fig. 3.23 Adshead's map of Queens Park and Manchester General Cemetery, Harpurhey, 1851.

There is no coincidence that these public parks were being laid out at the same time that the open spaces in the centre of the town were being encroached upon and filled in. Manchester's urban 'fields': St George's Fields, Granby Row Fields and, above all, St Peter's Fields had been used for mass meetings during recurrent phases of radical agitation throughout the early nineteenth century. These expressions of working-class 'platform politics' were deliberately constrained by changes in the built environment so that politics could be channelled into areas where the middle class had a greater measure of control. The previous venues for open-air meetings were built upon during the 1830s and 1840s, and by early 1850 even Kersal Moor was enclosed. As these outdoor spaces for 'platform politics' disappeared, working-class radicalism was pushed indoors where it could be more easily supervised and made respectable. As Martin Hewitt has argued 'As the municipal authorities became ever more efficient, they began to impose their own authority on the streets, squares and fields within which radicalism had previously thrived unmolested' (1996, 280). The municipal parks provided open space for recreation and relaxation, but could not be used as political venues. The gates and fences allowed access to be regulated and restricted, thus greatly aiding the policing of these public spaces.

Public Baths

The Manchester and Salford Baths and Laundries Company was formed in 1855 as a philanthropic association designed to promote public health and sanitary reform amongst the working class by investing in the construction of public baths and laundries. Three were built, all designed by the local architect Thomas Worthington, in the heart of Manchester's working-class districts (as can be seen in the c.1870 district map, Fig. 3.22). The first was Greengate Baths in Collier Street, Salford, opening in 1855, with the second in New Store Street, Mayfield, near Piccadilly station in 1858, and the third completed in 1860, Leaf Street Baths in Hulme. All three shared a similar architectural design, but only the Italianate facade of Greengate Baths survives (just), although the tiled swimming pool of Mayfield Baths has recently been exposed by redevelopment in this area.

Fig. 3.24 Front elevation of Greengate Baths, Salford. Artist and date unknown.

The illustration of the front elevation of Greengate Baths draws attention to the fact that these bath houses were buildings of some substance. The size and monumental nature of the architecture would mean that these baths would stand out within the poor, working-class districts of Salford, Mayfield and Hulme, helping to promote and legitimate cleanliness, hygiene and health (as well as the authority of the Corporation).

Mechanics' Institutions

Nurturing the moral character of the working class by 'self-improvement' through 'rational recreation' was a preoccupation of Manchester's liberal middle class. In the hope of instilling liberal values of self-help, institutions of self-improvement were established. In particular, a culture of learning was promoted through the founding of mechanic institutions, free libraries and museums. Local businessmen William Fairbairn, Joseph Brotherton and Benjamin Heywood set up Manchester's Mechanics Institute in 1824, initially housed in a building on Cooper Street within the Mosley Street complex of bourgeois institutions. It was aimed at providing mechanics, and other skilled workers and artisans, with a library and various forms of adult education. However, it was relocated to its present location on Princess Street in 1855, with a purpose-built structure, designed as a Renaissance palazzo by J. E.

Gregan. This was the main headquarters of the mechanics movement, and was where the first meeting of the Trades Union Congress (TUC) took place in 1868. Smaller institutions were established in the suburbs, some of which still survive. There is one in Levenshulme (dated to 1853), which is now a 'Pound Shop', and another in Longsight, also facing Stockport Road, which was opened in the 1850s and later became a public hall and library.

Fig. 3.25 Mechanics' Institute, Princess Street (Author, 2022).

Fig. 3.26 Mechanics' Institute, Levenshulme (Author, 2012).

Free Libraries

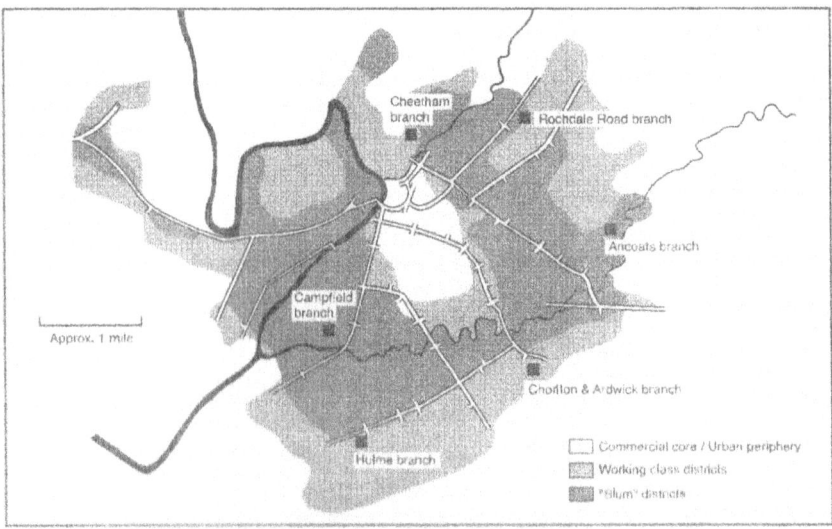

Fig. 3.27 Manchester's branch library network in the 1870s (Hewitt 2000, 70, all rights reserved).

Manchester was also the city that built the first free library after the passing of the Public Libraries Act in 1850, which granted local authorities permission to raise money for this specific purposes. The movement to establish public libraries was largely driven by a middle-class concern over the reading habits of the working class and their consumption of radical print: political broadsheets, tracts, journals and newspapers (that could be purchased in bookshops such as Abel Heywood's on Oldham Street). The promotion of 'safe' literature was therefore seen as a way to encourage self-improvement and respectability. As the Salford MP, Joseph Brotherton, quipped, public libraries were 'the cheapest form of police' (cited in Loftus 2015, 127). Manchester Free Library was opened in 1852 and initially housed in the Hall of Science in Campfield, which had been a key meeting room for the city's Owenite socialists and Chartists. The conscious subversion of this previous radical space was directly noted in the speeches given at the opening. The MP Richard Monckton Miles argued that guided by the books of the library, the working man would be 'transformed into an intelligent, clear, and sensible philanthropist, instead of becoming a blind and ferocious fanatic. This is what books could do; and this was the difference between the present building being a Socialist Hall and a Free Public Library' (cited in Loftus 2015, 127). The library was later moved to a purpose-built structure at the corner of Deansgate and London Road in 1882 (an ornate Renaissance-style building which is still standing and proudly displaying the city's coat of arms in the pediment above the main entrance). A network of branch libraries was subsequently established within working-class districts around the centre, first in Hulme and Ancoats in 1857, followed by one in Rochdale Road in 1860, Chorlton and Ardwick in 1866 and then Cheetham in 1873. These were important investments, and leading architects were commissioned to designed them such as Alfred Waterhouse who built Ancoats Free Library in Every Street. But apart from the one on Cheetham Hill Road, a fine Renaissance-style structure, this whole first wave of branch libraries has long since been demolished.

Fig. 3.28 Manchester Free Library, Deansgate (Author, 2023).

Fig. 3.29 Salford Museum and Art Gallery (Author, 2025).

The drive to encourage rational recreation also saw the founding of new museums and art galleries alongside libraries to promote self-improvement. The best example of this was the building of the Royal Museum and Public Library in Salford, what is now Salford Museum and Art Gallery. This prestigious, monumental structure, in Italian Renaissance style, was opened in 1850 and located at the entrance of Peel Park; a spatial arrangement facilitating both physical and intellectual recreational pursuits. It was a pattern replicated in later park developments (within and outside Manchester), as can be seen in the placing a museum and art gallery as a centrepiece of Queens Park in 1884.

Townships, Church Building and Religious Pluralism

The 'girdle' of working-class housing that formed a concentric ring around the central district emerged out of the growth of townships along the main arterial routes out of the city. However, it was during the middle decades of the nineteenth century that further townships connected to Manchester grew up beyond this inner zone: Collyhurst, Harpurhey, Miles Platting and Newton Heath in the north-east; Bradford, Gorton, Openshaw, Longsight and in the south-east. While these townships may not have been formerly part of the borough, they were integrated into and part of industrial Manchester. Physically little remains of these original districts. As has already been noted, buildings and spaces that were directly related to the working class from the early and mid-nineteenth century seldom survive today. This is a testament to the low quality and ephemeral nature of the structures that were put up, as well as a reflection of the ingrained disregard and disdain of working-class culture. Churches and chapels, on the other hand, which served both the working and middle classes, have a far better rate of survival. In many places they are the only nineteenth-century buildings still standing. These monuments provide evidence of the rapid expansion of Manchester and the formation of these suburban townships beyond the central business district. They are also an expression of religious pluralism and the growing confidence of different Christian denominations which manifested itself in the increasing importance of a shared Gothic architectural style for ecclesiastical buildings.

Anglican Churches

The post-Second World War slum clearances of Hulme levelled all the by-law terraces but left a number of churches standing. One of the most elegant, with its soaring 73.5-metre spire that forms one of Manchester's major landmarks, is the church of St Mary. Spires and steeples became a conspicuous feature of church architecture in the second half of the nineteenth century, with the city's level terrain emphasising their prominence so that they were visually connected with each other. St Mary is a good example of this. It was designed by J. S. Crowther and opened in 1858. Built in Geometric Decorated Gothic style, the church is associated with a Sunday school, school house and parsonage which all survive at the south-east end, with another school added across Parsonage Street in 1873. The close spatial relationship between church and schools is indicative of the fact that primary education for working-class children was monopolised almost exclusively by the church until the 1870 Education Act. The location of St Mary, at the southern edge of Hulme, is also significant as it draws attention to the physical growth of this working-class district. St George on Chester Road, just outside the central business district, completed in 1828, represented Hulme's first church. Thirty years later, with the construction of St Mary, Hulme had expanded over a mile southward.

Fig. 3.30 St Mary, Hulme and Sunday Schools (Author, 2021).

Similar patterns of urban growth can be traced through chronologically plotting the Anglican church foundations that still stand along the atrial roads radiating from the centre. These institutions helped forge local communities and were crucial for the consolidation of surrounding suburban townships of Manchester. For instance, to the south-east, Stockport Road leads from Ardwick to Longsight where in 1846 the church of St John was completed. It then continues further south into Levenshulme where St Peter was built in 1860. Likewise, in north Manchester, Rochdale Road leads from Ancoats to Collyhurst and Harpurhey where Christ Church was established in 1838. The road continues north into Blackley where the Commissioners' church of St Peter was constructed in 1844. In Salford, the tower of St George built in 1858 on Whit Lane is all that is left of the mid-nineteenth-century working-class township of Charlestown which grew up along the line of the Bolton railway and canal.

Anglican church foundations also attest to the establishment of more middle-class suburbs especially along the route of Oxford Road–Wilmslow Road to the south and Bury New Road to the north. St Paul at Withington was completed in 1841, Holy Trinity in Rusholme in 1846 and St Paul at Kersal Moor in 1852.

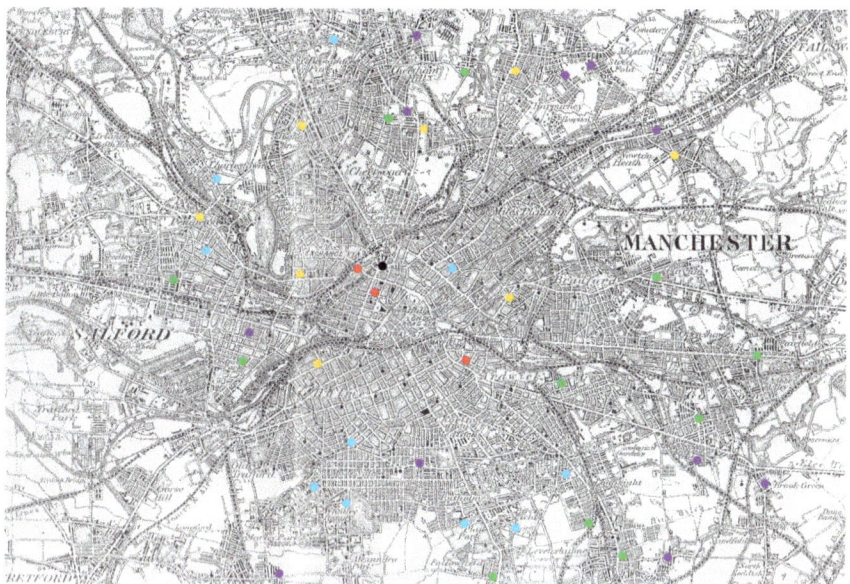

Fig. 3.31 Manchester and Salford map, 1913, showing distribution of extant Anglican churches by phase, annotated by the author (red dots = Phase 1, yellow dots = Phase 2, blue dots = Phase 3, green dots = Phase 4, purple dots = Phase 5).

Catholic Churches

Catholic church foundations can also be used in the same way to map urban growth. However, they are also emblematic of the religion of the migrants that were sucked into Manchester and the rising confidence of the Catholic community. Hulme originally had numerous churches and chapels of different denominations serving the working class. Most of these have since gone, but there is one important survivor. Alongside St George and St Mary, there is A. W. M. Pugin's Roman Catholic church of St Wilfrid, on Bedford Street. This was completed in 1842 and was one of Pugin's first commissions. It was built in Early English style in redbrick, although not fully completed due to financial restrictions, so the planned tower was never constructed.

Fig. 3.32 St Wilfred's Catholic Church, Hulme (Author, 2011).

Fig. 3.33 Cathedral of St John Evangelist (RC), Salford. Wikimedia Commons, CC BY-SA 2.0, https://commons.wikimedia.org/wiki/File:Salford_rc_Cathedral.jpg#/media/File:Salford_rc_Cathedral.jpg

After the Catholic Emancipation Act of 1829, the growing Catholic community in Manchester became more confident and conspicuous in architectural terms. The Roman Catholic chapel of St Mary in Mulberry Street in the city centre, first erected in 1794, was rebuilt and enlarged as a Romanesque church in 1848. Further, Catholic churches were sited in both working-class and middle-class residential districts, many of which survive today. As well as St Wilfred in Hulme, St Chad was built on Cheetham Hill in 1847 and St John Evangelist, on Chapel Street in Salford was completed between 1844 and 1848, replacing an earlier chapel. St John was an ambitious building in both scale and design being cruciform in plan and modelled on medieval minsters and abbeys in Decorative Gothic style, with a crossing tower and 73.2-metre steeple. It was elevated to the status of a cathedral in 1852, being one of the first Catholic cathedrals in England since the Reformation. Cathedral offices and a seminary school were added around a courtyard to the east of the church in 1872.

Nonconformist Chapels

Fig. 3.34 Unitarian Chapel and Sunday School, Upper Brook Street (Author, 2021).

Like the Catholic community, Nonconformism became more prominent in the built environment, and spread out from the city centre, as the congregations moved and expanded into the suburbs. Unitarianism had always been important to Manchester, with its central base remaining at Cross Street Chapel. But with the middle-class exodus from the centre, new chapels were constructed, such as Charles Barry's Unitarian Chapel on Brook Street, built between 1836 and 1839 (with a later attached Sunday School). It was located on the edge of the respectable residential suburb of Chorlton-on-Medlock, adjacent to the Dissenters' Rusholme Road Cemetery. What is interesting about Barry's design was the use of Gothic. Nonconformists had previously distinguished themselves architecturally from Anglicans by building in Neoclassical styles in marked contrast to the Gothic of Anglican churches. However, with the repeal of the 1828 Test and Corporation Act which had discriminated against non-Anglicans, Nonconformists could now participate more fully in the life of the British state. This led to a growing confidence amongst the community and a desire to be accepted and be treated on equal footing with Anglicanism. The shift to Gothic for Nonconformist chapels can be seen as an expression of this, as well as an assertion of the respectability of religious pluralism. This shared Gothic aesthetic may be seen as projecting a visual sense of equality between the different Christian denominations.

Fig. 3.35 Lancashire Independent College, Whalley Range (Author, 2022).

Congregationalists (Independents), together with Unitarians, Methodist and Quakers, were a strong Nonconformist influence on Manchester. During this phase Congregational chapels also became more ambitious in design, as illustrated by Edward Walters's striking Renaissance-style chapel with Veneto-Byzantine campanile in Castlefield, which was completed in 1858. Likewise, there was an expansion from the centre into the suburbs. Of particular note is the Congregationalist's educational college built in 1843 in the recently planned residential suburb of Samuel Brooks' Whalley Range estate (as Nonconformists had been excluded from studying at Oxford and Cambridge universities). It followed the founding of the Wesleyan Theological Institute (1842) on Wilmslow Road in Didsbury. But rather than a classical design, the Congregationalist distinguished themselves from the Methodist by building in Gothic. The impressive college building (Fig. 3.45) evokes the style of Nicholas Hawksmoor's Gothic All Souls College, Oxford, with its ashlar-faced facade with a cloister-like ground floor arcade of arches, and a fanciful central tower. Later in the nineteenth century, the Primitive Methodists also located their theological college in Whalley Range, building Hartley Hall on the neighbouring Alexandra Road South in 1878 using Gothic and Elizabethan styles.

Bourgeois Housing and the Age of the Suburban Villa

William Wyld's much reproduced painting, *Manchester from Kersal Moor*, is worth reflecting on as an introduction to a discussion of the middle-class flight to the countryside. It depicts a viewpoint of Manchester that the bourgeois residents of Broughton Park and The Cliff would have been familiar with. This watercolour painting was completed in 1852, two years before the publication of Charles Dickens's *Hard Times*. However, despite the many chimneys belching smoke, this is not a Dickensian image of 'Coketown'. The rustic, peasant couple in an Arcadian-looking foreground, surrounded by trees and foliage, with the sun in the background casting the city in soft light, makes this is a romanticised vision that naturalises industrial Manchester. It offers a positive image during a phase of transformation when the liberal elites were consciously reshaping and repackaging the city. Seen from without, the industrial city was more readily perceived as an object that could be tamed and managed. This, therefore, is a bourgeois view of Manchester looking in from the outside; a vision for the middle class who had escaped from the centre and now resided in suburban and rural villas.

Fig. 3.36 William Wyld, *Manchester from Kersal Moor*, 1852. Wikimedia Commons, public domain, https://commons.wikimedia.org/wiki/File:Wyld,_William_-_Manchester_from_Kersal_Moor,_with_rustic_figures_and_goats_-_Google_Art_Project.jpg

The middle-class exodus from the centre of Manchester that began in the previous phase resulted in the creation of an outer suburb. As Engels noted:

> Outside, beyond this girdle [of working-class housing], lives the upper and middle bourgeoisie, the middle bourgeoisie in regularly laid out streets in the vicinity of the working quarters, especially in Chorlton and the lower lying portions of Cheetham Hill; the upper bourgeoisie in remoter villas with gardens in Chorlton and Ardwick, or on the breezy heights of Cheetham Hill, Broughton and Pendleton, in free, wholesome country air, in fine comfortable homes, passed once every half or quarter hour by omnibuses going into the city. (2009, 86)

But the encroachment of railways and industries into middle-class suburbs such as Ardwick Green and The Crescent in Salford encouraged movement further afield into the residential parks and gated enclaves of Whalley Range, Broughton Park and Victoria Park. This in turn led to further speculative investments in suburbia. As with the 'Railway Mania' of the 1840s, investment in real estate was a way of absorbing surplus capital which could not find a profitable outlet in the primary economy of industrial production. In this sense, investing in suburbanisation (land and housing) was economically countercyclical.

Fielden Park in Didsbury, some distance south of the city centre, for instance, was laid out in 1863 in conjunction with the building of Palatine Road, and formed another compact area of large villas. This trend grew in popularity during the second half of the nineteenth century and was stimulated by the expansion of the local rail network which promoted commuter developments. Importantly, the separation of the public world of work and politics from the private life of the family, entailed by these investments, established the material underpinning for the rise of Victorian 'domestic ideology' with its assumption of two spheres (public and private) and separate gender roles for men and women. This led to the formative age of the suburban villa and the conspicuous consumption of private residences. As the historian F. M. L. Thompson argues:

> It was only in the setting of this kind of house, where the family could distance itself from the outside world in its own private fortress behind its own garden fence and privet hedge and yet could make a show of outward appearances that were sure to be noticed by the neighbours, that the suburban lifestyle of individual domesticity and group-monitored respectability could take hold. (1982, 175)

Although many houses were bespoke-designed by architects, the rise of middle-class suburbia led to the publication of pattern books, such as Samuel H. Brooks' *Rudimentary Treatise on the Erection of Dwelling-Houses* (1860) that provided a guide for the building of an ideal suburban villa, as well as the proliferation of household management books, after the incredible success of Mrs Beeton's famous manual.

Even though their number is steadily diminishing, Manchester still has a rich collection of residential urban villas. Middle-class houses tend to survive better than working-class ones and come in a diversity of forms and styles in marked contrast to the uniformity of redbrick by-law terraces. They were constructed by speculative builders who designed houses for different tastes. Mansions of various sizes—detached and semi-detached villas and middle-class residential terraces—were built in Neoclassical, Italianate, Gothic and Tudor/Elizabethan designs. And there are numerous, excellent examples still standing and worth visiting.

Fig. 3.37 Gaskell House, 84 Plymouth Grove (Author, 2025).

The Gaskell House on Plymouth Grove in Chorlton-on-Medlock is one of them. It dates to 1840 and is a good example of an early nineteenth-century Neoclassical (Greek Revival) villa that was possibly designed by Richard Lane. It is a relatively modest house, containing twenty rooms over two floors, with interesting classical motifs, as the capitals of the pilasters and portico columns of the front entrance echo those from the Tower of the Winds in Athens—these architectural details being emblematic of middle-class culture and aspiration. The Unitarian minister William Gaskell of Cross Street Chapel and his more famous novelist wife, Elizabeth Gaskell, moved into the house with their four children and five servants and lived in the property from 1850 until their deaths in 1884 and 1865 respectively.

Fig. 3.38 The Firs, Fallowfield. Photo by Richardhandscombe (2014), Wikimedia, CC BY-SA 2.5, https://commons.wikimedia.org/wiki/File:Chcc_blue_sky_2.jpg#/media/File:Chcc_blue_sky_2.jpg

The Firs (now Uttley House), in Fallowfield, however, was designed by Edward Walters for the Stockport-born engineering magnate Joseph Whitworth in 1850 as an Italianate mansion. Whitworth created the standard screw thread and inventor of the Whitworth rifle (amongst other things), which made him fabulously wealthy. His large, multi-room mansion was surrounded by a walled garden, as well as a fifty-two-acre estate (which is now part of Fallowfield Campus). Whitworth leased the house to C. P. Scott, the editor of the *Manchester Guardian*, in 1882.

Fig. 3.39 Addison Terrace, Victoria Park (Author, 2022).

A fine example of a stuccoed Tudor Gothic terrace can be found in Victoria Park on Daisy Bank Road. Addison Terrace, c.1850, consists of six pairs of houses for less wealthy middle-class residents. Number 102 was the home of Charles Halle, the Anglo-German conductor who founded Manchester's Halle Orchestra in 1858. It was later used by Ford Madox Brown, the Pre-Raphaelite, when he painted the murals in Manchester Town Hall.

Victoria Park has such a rich collection of villas that virtually every architectural style popular amongst middle-class Victorians is represented in the surviving assemblage of residential houses. Maryland, on Lower Park Road is illustrative of the Gothic. This was built in grey and yellow brick around 1870 in a typically Gothic asymmetrical design with a splendid entrance hall with a Gothic arcade. It was home of the pioneering chemist, Henry Roscoe, who was the Chair of Chemistry at Owens College (later Victoria University) and part of the set of middle-class intellectuals in south Manchester.

Fig. 3.40 Maryland, Victoria Park (Author, 2022).

During the second half of the nineteenth century, Manchester's leafy and spacious middle-class suburbs and residential parks became steadily in-filled with more modest villas, typically semi-detached houses following pattern book designs of the type popularised by Samuel H. Brooks. These tended to be all quite similar in design, often made to appear as one large, detached house, two storeys high, with attics with dormer windows and semi-lit basements, bay- or three-light Venetian style windows and prominent doorways reached by steps, set within walled grounds with front and back gardens. There are numerous such houses in Manchester, many still in residential use, although now frequently subdivided into apartments or converted into offices. Although their proliferation prompted the upper middle class to move further afield to mark their superior social status, these semi-detached villas embodied the social expansion of the middle class that now incorporated wider layers of managers, professionals and businessmen, as well as the spread of bourgeois culture.

Fig. 3.41 Semi-detached villa on 124-126 Palatine Road (Author, 2023).

The internal arrangement of these middle-class homes, with their multiple rooms, was therefore designed to accommodate bourgeois values on domesticity and household management. Internal space was subdivided into discrete rooms (dining room, drawing room, morning room etc.), halls and corridors which separated out different activities, as illustrated in the schematic floor plan of the ground floor of the Gaskell House. The compartmentalising of domestic space in this way enabled the physical division between family and servants, adult and child, male and female pursuits to be mediated through architecture. It helped codify behaviour and attitudes towards domesticity. Ironically, as these households were serviced through a largely female staff of servants, Victorian domestic ideology clearly only applied to the middle class, highlighting one of the many contradictions and hypocrisies of bourgeois liberalism.

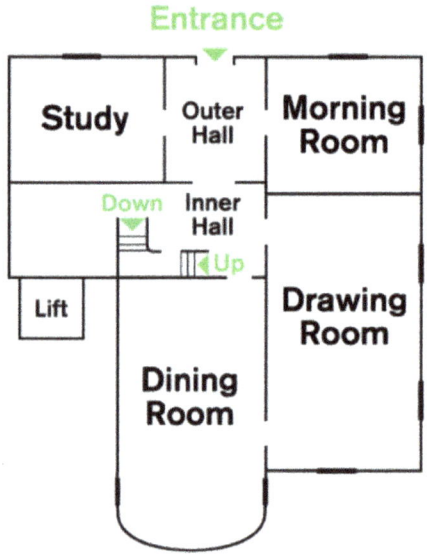

Fig. 3.42 Gaskell House floor plan (Elizabeth Gaskell's House, all rights reserved).

Walking along The Cliff in Higher Broughton, Salford, the lanes of Victoria Park or Didsbury, villas and mansions similar to the Gaskell House, The Firs, Addison Terrace, Maryland and pattern book semi-detached houses can be found. Although there are examples all around Manchester, the greatest concentration is to the south of the city, especially in the vicinity of the main arterial route of Oxford Road and Wilmslow Road, which passes Victoria Park and leads to Withington, Didsbury and Fielden Park. This became a bourgeois corridor through south Manchester, passing the working-class districts of Hulme and Chorlton-on-Medlock. It is surely Oxford Road/Wilmslow Road that Engels had in mind when he described how it was possibly for the bourgeoisie to travel from the suburbs into their businesses in the city centre 'without ever seeing that they are in the midst of the grimy misery that lurks to the right and to the left' (2009,

86). It is this concentration of villas that has earned south Manchester the reputation of being the 'posh' side of the city. These villas were originally situated in leafy and rural environs but were steadily swallowed up by the subsequent expansion of the city, forcing the more affluent and 'aspirational' middle class to retreat further into the countryside. The desire for a rural setting for one's home is reflected in the names given to Victorian suburban housing, like Rose Cottage, Oak House, Spring Bank, Woodstock etc., despite the reality of many of these properties being located in fairly built-up residential streets.

The use of horse-drawn omnibuses had permitted the further residential movement of Manchester's industrialist and businessmen away from the city centre and meant places like Withington and Didsbury became dormitory villages. The richest purchased or built mansions in more distant rural locations, such as the draper James Watts (owner of Watts Warehouse on Portland Street) who bought and developed the Tudor Gothic-style Abney Hall which lay just over the River Mersey in Cheadle, Cheshire. Watts hosted Prince Albert at Abney Hall when he visited Manchester to open the Arts Treasures Exhibition in 1857.

Fig. 3.43 Abney Hall, Cheadle (Author, 2023).

However, it was the arrival of the railway and the laying out of suburban lines that meant Manchester's middle-class commuter belt could now extend southward into the countryside of Cheshire (which was a more desirable location for villas and mansions than the more urbanised and industrialised landscapes to the north of Manchester). For instance, a station at Alderley Edge was opened in 1842 by the Manchester and Birmingham Railway. The company offered free season tickets to Manchester businessmen who built a substantial house within a mile of the station. By the 1850s, there were at least thirty 'handsome residences' concentrated on the slopes of Alderley Edge following Macclesfield Road and Woodbrook Road. These large Victorian villas and mansions, built in different architectural styles from Italianate, Tudor and Gothic along these roads, still represent some of the most expensive real estate in Britain, with Alderley Edge forming part of Cheshire's famous 'Golden Triangle'.

The opening of the suburban Manchester and South Junction and Altrincham Railway in 1849 created further opportunities for rail-based commuter investments. A residential village emerged at Bowden, near Hale Station, with many merchant villas aligned along Stamford Road and Green Walk. A subsequent development on the Manchester and South Junction and Altrincham took place at Sale in 1856, when the wealthy industrialist and banker, Samuel Brooks, the man responsible for laying out Whalley Range, bought another plot of land to invest in a new residential 'park', Brooklands. At the same time, the small market town of Altrincham grew essentially into a well-to-do, 'rural' suburb of Manchester due to the railway links into the city.

The three key patterns identified in this phase of development, namely the establishment of a railway infrastructure around Manchester, the zoning of the central business district and the construction of an inner suburban belt of working-class redbrick terraces followed by an outer one of middle-class villas and mansions, set the framework for future reconfigurations of this industrial city. Manchester expanded through absorbing a hinterland of emerging townships that emerged along the main thoroughfares to create a distinct inner and outer city. So, despite the formal boundaries of the borough being set, the city extended beyond these limits to form an informal 'greater' Manchester. The next phase of transformation, however, was defined by new types of interventions into the built environment, designed to instil a specific civic culture during the resurgence of mass politics following the expansion of the franchise with the reform Act of 1867. Amongst other things, this was expressed through an architecture of paternalism, articulated through the celebration of the Gothic. This symbolised, in architectural terms, a new conception of the relationship between social classes in the urban arena.

4. City of Civic Pride and Industrial Paternalism, c.1860–c.1890

Fig. 4.1 Manchester Town Hall and Albert Square. Photo by Mark Andrew (2012), Wikimedia Commons, CC BY 2.0, https://commons.wikimedia.org/wiki/File:Manchester_Town_Hall_from_Lloyd_St.jpg#/media/File:Manchester_Town_Hall_from_Lloyd_St.jpg

The realisation of Manchester Corporation's plan to construct a new town hall and public square in the heart of the central business district represented a decisive intervention into the built environment. Erected between 1868 and 1877, Manchester Town Hall together with Albert

Square created a new civic space, and was the defining feature of this phase of development. It reorientated the public focus of the centre, which had been Piccadilly Square and Esplanade, with a monumental building that towered above the surrounding district with its grand architecture enhanced by the open space of Albert Square. Together, Manchester's new town hall and square were a material expression of civic pride. They symbolised the wealth and power of the city's Corporation and the industrialists, merchants and bankers that underpinned it.

To examine this phase of development, this chapter is organised into five sections, starting with 'The Gothic Revival and the Architecture of Industrial Paternalism'. As well as the new Town Hall and Albert Square, this section will look at the other Gothic monumental buildings which come to dominate the cityscape and represent an architecture of bourgeois paternalism in an age of political reform. It is followed by another sub-phase, 'The Rational Reconfiguration of the Built Environment', in which the disciplinary and remedial institutions (workhouses, hospitals and prisons) are moved to the periphery, allowing the centre to become the focus of civic, cultural and commercial buildings. This is a time that a central 'shopping district' emerges with the first department stores and up-market shops, as well as a formative one in the rise of private gentlemen's clubs and societies. The third section, 'Later Nineteenth-Century Industrial Developments', then explores the geography of industry which expands along the rail and canal networks to form industrial corridors, especially to the east around the township of Gorton, where numerous engineering works were located. The movement to the urban fringes facilitated the construction of larger plants including whole industrial estates, as in William Houldsworth's 'industrial village' in Reddish. Section four, 'Working-Class Manchester and the Impact of Paternalism and Political Reform', takes a closer look as these industrial suburbs which become defined, not simply by by-law redbrick terraces, but also through the increasing presence of middle-class charitable institutions. Manchester Corporation gets directly involved in encouraging rational recreation and education by opening new parks and by establishing board schools. Other notable features in working-class districts during this sub-phase include the building of working men's Conservative clubs, the proliferation of ornate 'palace' pubs, and the more conspicuous presence of police stations. The final section, 'Suburbanisation, Places of Worship and Cosmopolitan Manchester', then explores manifestations of the 'golden age' of Victorian suburbanisation with the further growth of residential townships. This was a time when there was a degree of social mixing and blurring of the differences between suburban villas and by-law housing, as illustrated in terms of the 'middle-class terrace'. However, most of this sub-phase will be taken-up by a discussion of the rise of distinct, suburban communities, defined by different places of worship that gave expression to the existence of cosmopolitan Manchester. So, in addition to new Anglican churches, Nonconformist chapels and Catholic churches and institutions, the presence of a Greek Orthodox church and Armenian church will be analysed, together with the synagogues and Jewish institutions of Cheetham Hill, ending with a discussion of Manchester's new municipal cemeteries.

The Gothic Revival and the Architecture of Industrial Paternalism

Manchester Town Hall and Albert Square

The plan to erect a new town hall was conceived in 1863 as the Corporation sought to copy developments in other industrial cities and establish a town hall 'equal if not superior to any similar building in the country' (cited in Hartwell 2001, 71). Birmingham possessed a Neoclassical town hall in the design of a Roman temple, Liverpool completed the magnificent Greek Revivalist St George's Hall in 1854, while Leeds commissioned of an enormous French Renaissance town hall that was opened in 1858. Manchester, in contrast, chose a Gothic design, with Alfred Waterhouse winning the competition with his neo-Gothic-styled building that resembled a thirteenth-century Flemish cloth hall (a direct reference to the city's status as capital of the cotton industry). It occupied the triangular space of the old Town Yard, owned by the Corporation, and was fronted to the west by Albert Square, which had been created through the demolition and clearing of blocks of warehouses, workshops and back-to-back housing. The architecturally ornate western facade was three-hundred metres long, four storeys in height with a steeply pitched roof, and pavilions at the corners. But the central focus was the principal entrance and clock tower above, which rose to a height of eighty-seven metres and so came to dominate the city's skyline. Inside the main public room was the Great Hall with its hammer beam roof festooned with the coats of arms of the nations that Manchester traded with, and Ford Madox Brown's twelve paintings depicting the history of Manchester. The Great Hall was reached by a pair of grand staircases from the entrance foyer, with the whole interior richly decorated with painted ceilings and patterned polychrome floors of tiles and mosaics. In the words of Abel Heywood, the liberal major most associated with the completion of the building, it was a 'worthy monument of the industrial greatness of Manchester'.

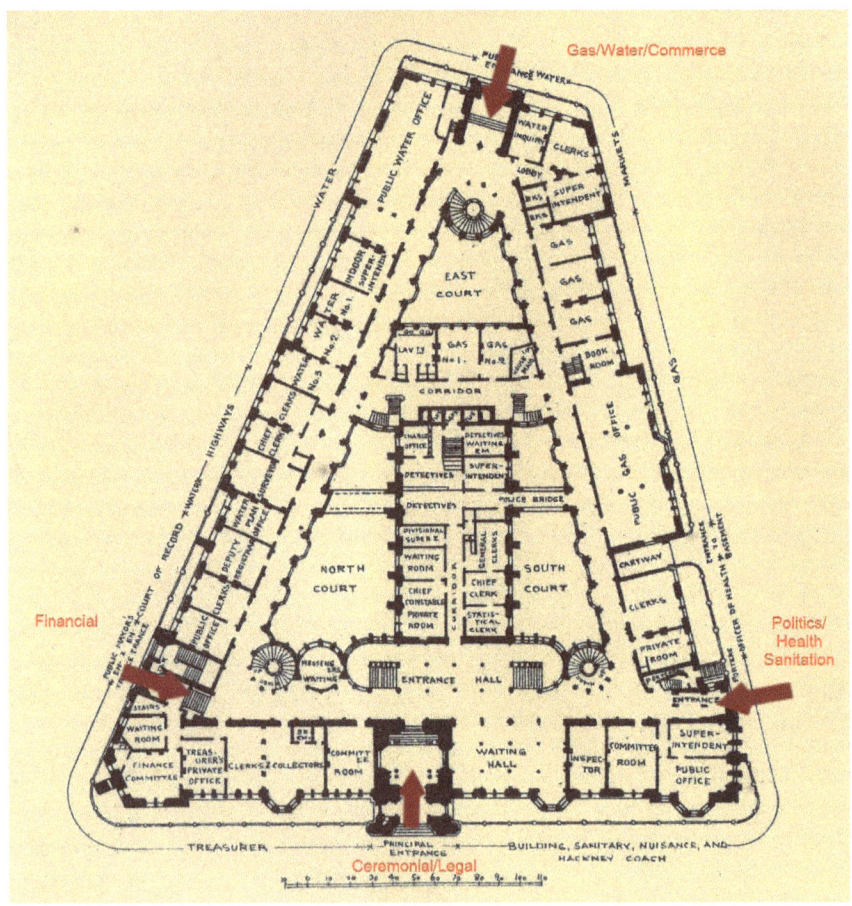

Fig. 4.2 Manchester Town Hall, ground floor plan, 1868 (after Crinson 2022, 106).

Mark Crinson has explored in an intriguing way how the Gothic architecture and plan of the new town hall 'embodied the disposition of Manchester's now dominant class' (2022, 107), and how the choice of

Gothic was integral to the transformation of the city's industrial culture. His study of the ground floor plans, for example, highlights how the new town hall played a multifunctional role in the life of the city. The four main public entrances had different functional and symbolic roles. The principal entrance facing Albert Square was largely ceremonial. It gave access to the grand stairways leading up into the Great Hall at the centre of the building. However, the other three doors provided structured ways into different parts of the building: the Lloyd Street entrance to rooms linked to municipal politics, health and sanitation; the Cooper Street entrance to commercial offices especially those related to the city's gas and water utilities, while the Princes Street entrance gave access to financial offices. As Crinson notes, it is striking that the space given over for political debate in the Manchester Town Hall was minimal when compared to the number of rooms related to the management of the Corporation's commercial monopoly of water and gas supplies.

Albert Square was named after the death of Prince Albert, with its centrepiece being Thomas Worthington's Gothic Albert Memorial (1877). Later other monuments were erected in the square including statues celebrating national and local liberal figures: William Gladstone (1878), Bishop James Fraser (1888), John Bright (1891) and banker Oliver Heywood (1894). This new civic space was a symbol of municipal power with the Gothic rather than the Italianate now becoming the favoured architectural style to express civic identity, ambition and association.

Fig. 4.3 South side of Albert Square (Author, 2022).

Accompanying Waterhouse's Gothic Town Hall were ranges of other Gothic buildings, lining Albert Square. Although the western side was demolished in the 1970s, the buildings along the southern range form an architectural essay on the Gothic. Echoing the style of the Town Hall was St Andrew's Chambers (1872) for the Scottish Widows Fund Life Assurance Society, on the corner of Mount Road. This is followed by Carlton House (1872), a club house, and example of free European Gothic style. Then comes Albert Chambers (1873) in Venetian Gothic and finally the splendid Memorial Hall (1863–1866) designed by Thomas Worthington in polychrome Venetian Gothic. This building was erected to commemorate the bicentenary of the creation of the Unitarian church in 1662. It was inspired by John Ruskin's influential *The Stones of Venice*, and an example of a Venetian palazzo reminiscent of a number of a famous buildings in Venice which Worthington had visited.

Gothic Monumental Buildings

Even though Italianate buildings continued to be built during the second half of the nineteenth century, the Gothic was the defining architectural style of this phase. It became fashionable and was the preferred design for all sorts of buildings, religious, domestic and commercial; but in particular, Gothic architecture was favoured for civic and public institutions. A. W. N. Pugin was the figure most directly associated for the Gothic Revival of the Victorian age. He had championed the moral qualities of the Gothic, arguing that it was the 'true' indigenous architectural heritage of Christian Britain (as opposed to the alien, pagan Classical tradition). The Gothic style, Pugin argued, epitomised the cultural and religious character of the nation and was a form of architecture that embodied a morality that could help mitigate the social problems generated by the strict commercial logic of industrial capitalism. It harked back to an imagined medieval past of communalism, paternalism and mutual cooperation and responsibilities that had been lost through rampant liberal individualism. These ideas became popular after Pugin's death in 1852 and were taken up by other architects, such as Alfred Waterhouse who started his career in Manchester (as well as Pugin's son, Edward who was active in the Manchester–Salford conurbation).

Fig. 4.4 University of Manchester, Oxford Road (Author, 2023).

It was Waterhouse who was responsible for the major civic buildings of this phase. Before he won the commission for the new Town Hall, Waterhouse had designed the Assize Courts (1859–1865) on Great Ducie Street in Flemish Gothic, a notable public building that was damaged beyond repair during the Manchester Blitz. However, his medieval-styled Strangeways Prison (1861–1869), that combines Romanesque and Gothic features survives, as does his magnificent Gothic Victoria University of Manchester (1869–1875) on Oxford Road with its tower, turrets, steep-pitched roof and Gothic arcades and windows. With these major monumental buildings, Waterhouse made his mark on the built environment of Manchester in a similar fashion to that of Richard Lane and Edward Walters had done in previous phases.

Fig. 4.5 Police and Sessions Court, Minshull Street (Author, 2023).

Other figures were also key to the spread of Manchester's Gothic architecture, especially Thomas Worthington, who has been previously mentioned. As well as Memorial Hall on Albert Square, Worthington was also responsible for the Police and Sessions Court, located on Minshull Street. This was built in Venetian Gothic and included an ornate clock tower, which was also a feature of another notable Worthington building that still survives, Nicholls Hospital in Ardwick.

The preference for Gothic style for governmental buildings continued in Manchester throughout the second half of the nineteenth century, and there are many noteworthy examples such as the Inland Revenue office on Mount Street, Lawrence Buildings (1874) and Queens Chambers (1876) on the corner of Deansgate and John Dalton Street. Both these Gothic buildings were constructed by the same firm and display statues of a young Queen Victoria in gabled niches on their facades. But perhaps the finest is one of the last monumental Gothic structures to be built in Manchester. The remarkable, cathedral-like John Rylands Library, constructed between 1890 and 1899 on Deansgate, was commissioned by Enriqueta Rylands in memory to her husband, one of the city's major cotton magnates and philanthropist. Its frontage resembles a medieval gatehouse with towers, corner turrets and battlements. Rylands Library is an excellent example of Victorian paternalism which became a trait of the second half of the nineteenth century when industrialists would charitably invest part of their wealth in the founding of cultural institutions for rational recreation for the working class.

Fig. 4.6 Rylands Library, Deansgate (Author, 2023).

The appeal of the Gothic for Manchester's elite lay as much in social and cultural reasons as in purely aesthetic ones. Following Pugin's polemics about the morality of the Gothic, it was a style of architecture that seemed most conducive for the politics of the period. After the triumph of liberalism during the so-called 'age of equipoise', economic and social problems resurfaced from the 1860s onwards. Manchester suffered acutely during the American Civil War (1861–1865) due to the impact of a 'cotton famine' which led to a severe depression in the cotton industry of Lancashire. This caused mass unemployment and impoverishment, which resulted in the return of open class politics, as evidenced in the Stalybridge Riots of 1863 that spread to other towns in Manchester's immediate hinterland.

The 1860s was also a time of renewed calls for parliamentary reform and the demand for the expansion of the franchise to incorporate sections of the working class. This culminated in the Reform Act of 1867 which gave birth to a new dynamic of mass electoral politics. Manchester gained another constituency in 1868, with Hugh Birley elected as MP marking the start of a Tory revival. After the 1884 Reform Act, the number of Manchester seats increased to six with local politics now dominated by conservatives rather than liberals. As well as widening the electorate, this new era of mass politics included the formal recognition of the organised working class. The Trades Union Congress was founded in 1868, holding its first meeting in Manchester at the Mechanics Institute on Princess Street, and the Trade Union Act of 1871 legalised trade unionism for the first time in Britain. In such a political climate, the architectural morality associated with the Gothic, with its emphasis on an ordered society of mutual cooperation, deference and responsibilities, became attractive. The Gothic provided the style of architecture for industrial paternalism. In contrast to the phase of liberal triumphalism, industrial paternalism was an ideology that acknowledged the existence of the working class but conceptualised its presence within a fixed social hierarchy dominated by the bourgeoisie that provided a nurturing and guiding hand. The Gothic, with its historical connotations harking back to an idealised, ordered community, served as an architectural vehicle to propagate this ideology. It is therefore significant that the opening of Manchester Town Hall on the 17th September 1877 was marked by a highly organised procession of around 50,000 working men from various trade societies in Manchester and Salford who marched in ordered groups behind trade banners. The town hall and public space of Albert Square created civic centre for regulating social mixing, with the Gothic architecture helping to project notions of shared interests and values that ideologically united the bourgeoisie and proletariat into an imagined paternalistic society and civic culture.

The Rational Reconfiguration of the Built Environment

The construction of the Gothic Town Hall alongside the opening up of a new public square was therefore an expression of civic pride and part of the long-term project to instil a civic culture through the use of architecture and the manipulation of the built environment. Consequently, it represented another phase in the rational reconfiguration of the city which started in the 1840s. As Simon Gunn highlights in his examination of the transformation of the industrial cities of Birmingham, Leeds and Manchester, Victorian urban reform involved the architectural, spatial and representational reorganisation of the centre.

> [T]he city centre became the locos of technical and aesthetic innovation, the place where new types of building, architectural styles, street lighting and shops were first open to public view. Increasingly the city was identified with its major monuments, squares and architectural landmarks, symbolically representing the new forms of urban modernity. (2000, 39)

In particular, two trends can be highlighted: 'the displacement of disciplinary and remedial institutions from the centre to the urban fringe', and the 'cleansing' of the city centre of inhabitants, rendering it open for commercial and cultural activities and social display.

Disciplinary and Remedial Institutions

The spatial shift of workhouses, hospitals and prisons from central areas to the periphery geographically separated poor wage labourers from those who would not or could not work, paupers, vagrants, the old and infirm and criminals. Although this marked a shift from the strategy pursued in the initial phase of industrialisation, the aim was the same—to consolidate the ethos of wage labour in working-class districts. This displacement of disciplinary and remedial institutions, however, was accompanied by a change in basic designs, as institutional architecture became influenced by liberal, utilitarian philosophy. These institutions no longer resembled Georgian country mansions, but applied new 'scientific' ideas about incarceration, surveillance, sanitation, order and control.

The New Poor Law, which was pushed through by the 'reforming' Liberal government in 1834, radically overhauled the old principles of poor relief. Although ostensibly to reduce costs, the primarily goal was to discipline the emerging working class into accepting the harsh logic of industrial capitalism. It was underpinned by utilitarian assumptions about human motivation and rested on the notion of 'less eligibility': that the conditions of poor relief should be worse than that of the poorest independent labourer. Outdoor relief was therefore ended and replaced with the workhouse system. To receive any help the poor had to be incarcerated in a workhouse and subjected to the rigours of family separation, forced labour and dire living conditions. The New Poor Law essentially criminalised pauperism. Disraeli may have been a Tory, but he was right to refer to this set up as 'Brutalitarianism'. It was undoubtedly one of the most pernicious government acts against the working class during the nineteenth century—an 'iron stick' used to instil social fear through the stigma of the workhouse. Hence the cruelty of the New Poor Law was intentional. The aim was to alter social consciousness and behaviour through stigmatising and shaming poverty and destitution, thus encouraging wage labour. Despite much opposition, the workhouse system was pushed through and in the process created a social division between the so-called 'respectable' and 'disrespectable' working class. As such, it represented a classic divide and rule strategy.

Fig. 4.7 Illustration of Barlow Moor Workhouse, 1856, unknown artist, public domain.

The passing of the Poor Law Amendment Act of 1834 forced parishes or townships to group together and form Poor Law Unions to administrate the system through electing boards of governors and setting up workhouses. In the Manchester conurbation, four poor law unions were established: Salford (1837), Chorlton-on-Medlock (1837), Prestwich (1837), and the Manchester Union (1841) which took over the running of the old Bridge Street Workhouse. However, with the imposition of the New Poor Law, new workhouse designs were commissioned. Many of these were influenced by the architectural ideas of Sampson Kempthorne, with his cruciform or hexagon-shaped plans that emphasised incarceration, segregation and observation. Workhouse architecture encompassed the principles of the New Poor Law, with the layout and organisation of the buildings designed to deter potential paupers and to discipline and reform inmates. The original Chorlton-on-Medlock Union Workhouse, built on Stretford New Road in Hulme, adopted such a 'Kempthorne' cruciform plan. However, from the mid-nineteenth century, workhouses were relocated to essentially rural locations on the edges of the conurbation. A new workhouse for the Manchester Union was built at Crumpsall on open high ground overlooking the Irk Valley in 1855, taking over the functions of the old Bridge Street Workhouse which was sold off to Victoria Station. It was a large complex site influenced by Kempthorne's designs and could accommodate 1,660 inmates. In the same year Chorlton Poor Law Union moved its workhouse at Hulme to a new, larger site at Withington, which could accommodate up to 1,500 paupers. This workhouse survives relatively intact and was clearly designed as a prestigious monumental building with the entrance symbolising power and authority, involving a high degree of architectural elaboration (as illustrated in the drawing and photograph of Barlow Moor Workhouse, Fig. 4.7).

Fig. 4.8 Barlow Moor Workhouse, main entrance and chapel (Author, 2023).

A similar pattern occurred at Salford where the old (1793), centrally placed workhouse on Greengate was closed and the institution moved to a new position on the periphery of the town at Eccles New Road in 1852. Prestwich Poor Law Union also moved its workhouse to Crumpsall in 1866, adjacent to the new Manchester Workhouse, and was built by the local architect, Thomas Worthington. Its administrative offices were housed in an attractive Italianate building (1862) with venetian windows, which is still standing on Cheetham Hill Road (as do the offices of Chorlton Poor Law Union, the Ormond Building at Grosvenor Square, Chorlton-on-Medlock).

Fig. 4.9 Prestwich Union Office (next to former Cheetham Town Hall), Cheetham Hill Road (Author, 2023).

In terms of penal reform, the ideas of John Howard, who had influenced the design of New Bailey Prison, with its emphasis on solitary confinement, were replaced with Jeremy Bentham's notions of surveillance. As a utilitarian philosopher and reformer, Bentham produced an innovative design for an ideal prison involving a 'panopticon' (an all-seeing eye) to reform prisoners. The basic idea was for prison cells to be arranged around a central observation point so that prisoners were always aware that they could be potentially observed by a warden, and so regulate their behaviour accordingly. This led to the development of radial prison designs in the mid-nineteenth century with wards of cells radiating out from an axial tower. At Manchester, Alfred Waterhouse was commissioned to design a prison and he adopted the new 'Benthamite' radial plan for penal institutions, with six wings radiating from a central hall. Strangeways Prison was located away from the centre on Bury New Road, but not so far that its physical presence was not felt in the city, with the tall minaret-like ventilation tower becoming a distinctive landmark in Manchester's skyline. The prison was completed and open for inmates in 1868, with the old, New Bailey Prison closing in 1871 and the buildings demolished.

Fig. 4.10 Strangeways Prison (and Assize Courts), 1930, unknown photographer. Image courtesy of Manchester Libraries.

Manchester Corporation had already built a second prison in 1848 at an out-of-town site on Hyde Road in Gorton—Belle Vue Prison. This also possessed a 'Benthamite' radial plan and could hold around five hundred prisoners, being in operation between 1848 and 1888, after which it was demolished. Famously, the police van carrying two Fenians to the Belle Vue gaol in 1867 was successfully ambushed on Hyde Road with the prisoners rescued by Irish republican supporters (although a police officer was accidentally shot dead in the process)—this incident was known at the time as the 'Manchester Outrage'.

The Royal Infirmary, at Piccadilly, remained central to Manchester's medical provisions throughout this period. But during the second half of the nineteenth century, new hospital installations were built on the periphery of the city and incorporated the new pavilion plan for medical institutions made famous by Florence Nightingale. These were barrack-type hospitals with wards housed in separate blocks linked to a central corridor in an attempt to overcome the problems of poor sanitation (which were still linked to traditional theories of miasmas). The focus of clinical architecture was segregation and ventilation. At Manchester, a number of new hospitals were built and added to the 'out of town' workhouses as state-funded Poor Law hospitals. Thomas Worthington built a pavilion-ward hospital attached to Barlow Moor Workhouse (1864–1866) with the design praised by Florence Nightingale, as well as Prestwich Union Workhouse (1866–1870). Other Poor Law hospitals were added to the Manchester Workhouse at Crumpsall in 1876 and the Salford Workhouse on Eccles New Road in 1882, with Prestwich Poor Law Union building an infirmary at Blackley in 1904. These institutions have in part survived by being integrated into the NHS system as Withington Hospital, North Manchester Hospital, Hope Hospital and Booth Hall Children's Hospital respectively. Another medical institution which was likewise relocated into the countryside at the edge of the Manchester conurbation was Pendlebury Children's Hospital. This voluntary hospital was moved from a central location to a much larger suburban site in Salford in 1873, where a pavilion-ward complex was built.

4. *City of Civic Pride and Industrial Paternalism, c.1860–c.1890* 165

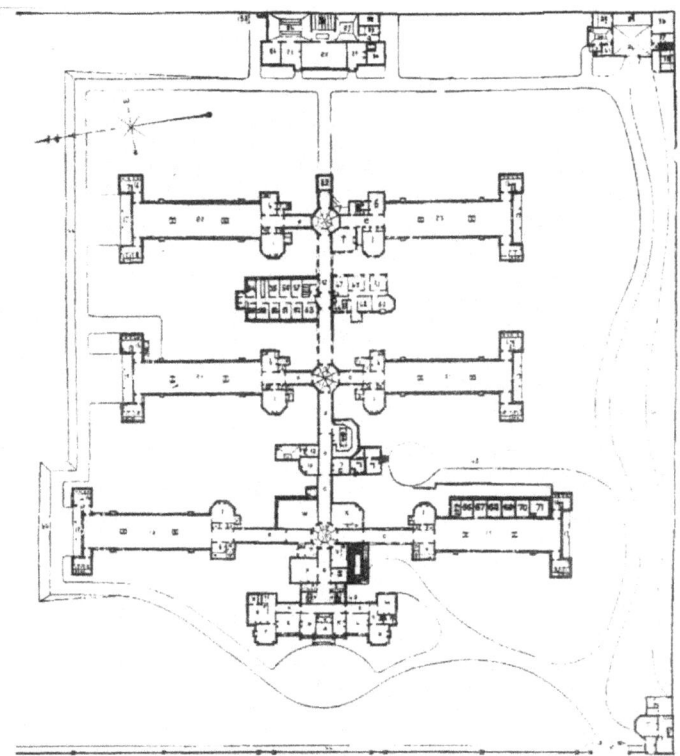

Fig. 4.11 Plan of Pendlebury Children's Hospital, Salford, 1873, public domain.

Other institutions were also moved from the centre to the periphery. The Victoria University of Manchester started as Owen's College founded in 1850 and first accommodated at Cobden House in Quay Street. It moved to Oxford Road after Waterhouse had constructed a purpose-built institution in Gothic style in 1873 arranged around a quadrangle, with Whitworth Hall and Manchester Museum aligning the street. This development influenced further reconfigurations with the city's key medical institutions being also relocated to Oxford Road. The Royal Eye Hospital was rebuilt there in 1886, and the Royal Infirmary, Saint Mary's maternity hospital, and the dental hospital were all moved to adjacent sites on Oxford Road in 1908 and 1909 respectively (as will be discussed in Chapter 5). Another, albeit later example of this trend was the movement of Manchester Grammar School in 1930 from its original site by the Cathedral and Cheetham school, to its current position in Rusholme.

Department Stores and Shops

The moving of these 'disciplinary and remedial institutions' to the suburbs allowed the city centre to become the locus of commerce and consumption. Alongside banking and warehousing distinct 'shopping districts' began to emerge, as Manchester responded to the retailing and commercial revolution of the high/late Victorian era. This growth of consumerism can be regarded as the flip side of the rise of middle-class suburbia (discussed in Chapter 3). Multi-room villas required furnishing: curtains, rugs and carpets, furniture of all types and an array of objects and commodities to decorate houses and facilitate the social and family rituals of Victorian domesticity. The bourgeois home was notoriously crammed full of 'things', reflecting the importance of conspicuous consumption for denoting status and class identity. This stimulated a new form of retail industry designed specifically to sell to the middle-class clientele. Shops were arranged together in rows to encourage window shopping with streets illuminated through the innovation of street lighting. Significantly, it was during the 1870s that the department store first appeared. As Gunn and Bell argue, 'The department store was the middle-class shop *par excellence* and it and the middle classes developed alongside each other in the Victorian and Edwardian period' (2003, 40). These stores fostered notions of luxury and exclusivity by offering a wide range of commercial goods within purpose-built retail palaces that were designed to seduce the consumer. Deansgate is a good illustration of these developments: in 1869, it was widened and straightened with gas street lighting introduced. It became home of one of Manchester most famous retail giants, Kendal, Milne and Faulkner (Kendals), which is purported to be Britain's first department store. Founded in 1836, the store was substantially rebuilt in 1873 with the original department building now a Waterstones bookshop (with the 1938 Art Deco store located opposite, although operating under the name of the House of Fraser). Other department stores followed in Kendal's footsteps such as the opening of Lewis's on Market Street in 1877, Affleck and Brown's on Oldham Street, and the now demolished Paulden's in Chorlton-on-Medlock. Of the original retailing structures that survive on Deansgate, the best is Barton Buildings with its a four-storey cast-iron and glass-roofed Barton Arcade. It could be entered from both Deansgate and St Ann's Square and contained numerous retailers displaying their goods from within individual glass-fronted shops.

As a consequence, Manchester's central shopping district expanded beyond Market Street and extended from the lower end of King Street and St Ann's Square into Deansgate, and from Piccadilly along Oldham Street. These streets have remained the focus of fashionable shopping, both upmarket and alternative, from the late nineteenth century onwards. Such continuity means that there are many great examples of Victorian shops. Some businesses, such as jewellers Arthur Kay on the corner of the Royal Exchange and music store Forsyth on Deansgate, still operate from their original nineteenth-century premises. However, to appreciate them generally requires looking up, as the original shopfronts tend to have been replaced. Still, there are some good survivors such as Hayward's Glass and China shop on Deansgate, which retains its street-level arcade and first-floor display windows all in Free Renaissance style. There is another interesting survivor at 19 King Street which has an example of a glass and iron shopfront. Further, it is King Street and Oldham Street that reveal the eclectic nature of Victorian retail architecture with virtually every shop built in a different style with variations on Classical, Italianate and Gothic designs.

Fig. 4.12 Barton Arcade, Deansgate (Author, 2022).

Fig. 4.13 Hayward's Building, Deansgate (Author, 2022).

Clubs and Societies

In addition to the burgeoning of retail facilities, and alongside the commercial and financial institutions of banks, warehouses and insurance companies, the central district became the favoured location of public and private gentlemen's clubs. These male fraternities and societies had always been an important feature of modern urban culture as they facilitated the social networking of the middle class and so helped forge collective identities. As Simon Gunn argues, private associations 'became a significant presence in urban life, forming a distinct social world known as 'clubland' (2000, 84). These clubs were crucial for the construction of bourgeois culture during the second half of the nineteenth century. Manchester had several, of which the Literary and Philosophical Society, established in 1781, was the most prestigious. However, it was during this phase of political reform that political clubs were established in the heart of the city in prominent, conspicuous buildings. This was clearly an expression of the rise of mass politics after the 1867 Reform Act, as

Liberals and Tories needed to engage with a widened franchise which now included sections of the male working class. Edward Salomans' Venetian Gothic Reform Club on King Street is illustrative of the way in which architecture was used for political display. It was built between 1870 and 1871 and is one of the largest surviving provincial clubhouses in the country. This Venetian palazzo is of three storeys with a *piano nobile* of polychrome arches and marble columns, and ornate oriel towers at the corners. In competition with the Liberals, the Conservatives built their central club house nearby at the corner of Cross Street and St Ann Street in 1876, Hanover House. This was a large, ornately decorated building in Italianate style in direct contrast to the Liberal's use of the Gothic.

Fig. 4.14 Reform Club, King Street (Author, 2025).

Other societies and institutions had their main premises in the central district of Manchester which were used as meeting rooms and club houses to consolidate members and to project a collective identity. Charlton House on Albert Square, which has already been mentioned, was the home of Manchester Arts Club, while in Kennedy Street, in what became the legal zone of the city, there was the Law Library. This was also built in 1885 in Venetian Gothic to provide a meeting place and reading room for the Manchester Law Society. It housed one of the oldest provincial law libraries. Another example can be found in the neighbouring Cooper Street, Waldorf House, which was the headquarters of Manchester's Freemasons, built in 1863 with numerous Masonic emblems in the architectural sculpture of the street facade.

Fig. 4.15 Law Library, Kennedy Street (Author, 2022).

Later Nineteenth-Century Industrial Developments

The major components of Manchester's industrial geography had been set during the initial phase of the factory take-off at the end of the eighteenth and beginning of the nineteenth century. Cotton mills had been established along the canal and river networks surrounding the centre with a particular focus on the Ancoats district to the north, which effectively became the world's first industrial estate. This pattern continued, although by the second half of the nineteenth century, industry had expanded out to form industrial suburbs in corridors along the lines of Rochdale, Ashton and Bolton canals and the tracks of the railway system.

4. City of Civic Pride and Industrial Paternalism, c.1860–c.1890   171

Fig. 4.16 Victoria Double Mill, Miles Platting (Author, 2021).

This linear expansion away from the more built-up inner-city districts allowed the construction of larger premises which then encourage further suburban industrial developments. Brunswick Mill, on the northern edge of Ancoats on Bradford Street and the Ashton Canal, represents a survivor from the start of this process. It was built around 1840 and at the time was one of the largest mills in the country. But in terms of developments in the second half of the nineteenth century, Victoria Mill at Miles Platting is the best example of this general trend. This was a six-storey double mill with shared engine house completed in two phases in 1869 and 1873. The tall central chimney, which forms a visual landmark in the area, has a stair tower wrapped round the lower part with Italianate architectural details. Victoria Mill was built alongside the Rochdale Canal for the cotton magnate William Holland who moved his business from Salford to a less built-up area to the north of Ancoats in order to construct a much bigger mill. Subsequently, Rochdale Canal became a popular location for industry with various textile mills, dye works, engineering plants and brick works aligning the canal stretching north-east into Newton Heath. Together with Gorton and Openshaw, Newton Heath became a major centre of engineering in the city, with the establishment of the carriage and wagon works for Lancashire and Yorkshire Railway in 1877 at Thorp Road, which grew into a huge complex of sidings and engine sheds. Newton Heath was also the home of the engineering company Mather and Platt since 1845 when the company moved to a large site, Park Works at Ten Acre Lane in 1900 (a factory visually immortalised in L. S. Lowry's 1943 painting *Going to Work*). Similar patterns of growth occurred along the Manchester, Bolton and Bury Canal and later railway lines creating the new working-class district of Charlestown in Salford, as well as along the route of the Liverpool railway line on Liverpool Street in Weaste where Ermen and Engels had their mill. However, the most concentrated area of industrial expansion occurred in east Manchester following the routes of the Ashton Canal and Sheffield railway line between Ashton New Road, Ashton Old Road and Hyde Road. This wide industrial corridor, comprising the townships of Beswick, Bradford, Clayton, Gorton and Openshaw, was dominated by engineering works and other major heavy industries such as mining, dye and chemical works and locomotive depots.

Engineering Works and East Manchester

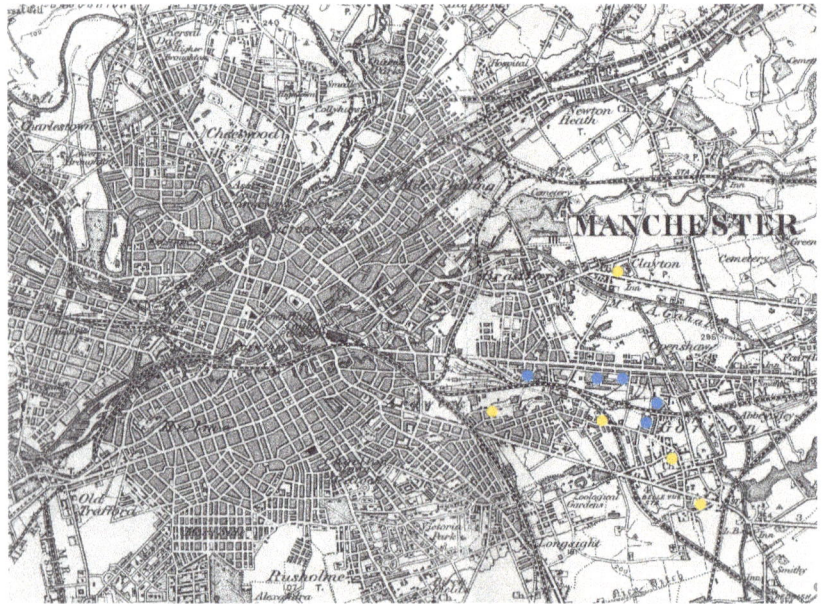

Fig. 4.17 Manchester and District Map, 1896, annotated by the author (showing location of major engineering works (blue dots) in East Manchester and new church foundations (yellow dots)), (section of Old Ordnance Survey Maps, England Sheet 85), Alan Godfrey Maps.

It may have been the centre of the cotton industry, but Manchester had always been more than a 'mill town'. In fact, textile production stimulated the engineering of tools and machinery, so from the start Manchester's leading industrialists included engineers such as the Scottish William Fairbairn and James Nasmyth, and the Stockport-born Joseph Whitworth (who developed the standard screw thread). By 1850, there were more than a hundred iron founders and engineering firms based in Manchester. However, it was with the coming of the railways that Manchester gained the national and international reputation as a centre for locomotive manufacturing.

Fig. 4.18 Gorton, 1933, showing Gorton Carriage Company, 'Gorton Tank' and Gorton Foundry (section of Ordnance Survey map, Lancashire Sheet 104.07), CC BY, National Library of Scotland.

Fig. 4.19 Gorton Foundry (Author, 2021).

East Manchester was the initial centre of railway engineering. As described in the previous phase of development, Ashbury Carriage and Iron Company moved to this area in 1847 and as a result other firms followed suit, exploiting the availability of cheap coal from the Manchester Coalfield. Bradford Colliery was the most important of these local mines and started sinking deep shafts from the 1840s onwards, utilising steam winding technology to lift the coal and ventilate the mine. Gorton Carriage Company was established in 1848 ('Gorton Tank') on the northern side of the Sheffield railway line and Gorton Foundry in 1854 immediately adjacent on the southern side of the track. These two companies became major employers and stimulated the growth of both Gorton and Openshaw, alongside Whitworth's factory and Crossley engineering, which were also based in this east Manchester industrial corridor. The scale and impact of these works on the built environment of Gorton can be seen in the section Ordnance Survey map of 1933 with the fantastical arrangement of rail tracks. The area of 'Gorton Tank' is now the site of Smithfield Market, but there are remains of Gorton Foundry at the corner of Gorton Lanes and Preston Street.

Fig. 4.20 Brookfield Unitarian Chapel, Gorton (showing the Peacock Mausoleum on the left) (Author, 2023).

The Beyer, Peacock and Company of Gorton Foundry manufactured famous locomotives that were exported around the world, especially to the British colonies. The two industrialists behind this enterprise, Charles Beyer and Richard Peacock, were both active in local politics and took a paternalistic interest in the development of the industrial suburb of Gorton. Peacock was a Liberal Unitarian, being the local MP between 1885 and his death in 1889. He commissioned Thomas Worthington to design Brookfield Unitarian Church in Gorton, which was built between 1869 and 1871, and is where Peacock is buried under an ornate Gothic mausoleum. Adjacent to the church was a Sunday School. Beyer, on the other hand, was a German industrialist of Jewish ancestry who moved to Manchester and converted to Christianity. In contrast to Peacock, Beyer was a Conservative and Anglican. He founded three churches in Gorton, all with associated Sunday Schools, including the rebuilding of the parish church which was renamed St James in 1871. As the founding member of Gorton Conservative Club, Beyer built the club house right next to St James. The spire of Beyer's St James visually relates and competes with the spire of Peacock's Brookfield Church in the low-lying, flat terrain of Gorton.

Fig. 4.21 St James, Gorton (Author, 2020).

Houldsworth's Industrial 'Village'

The major trend in this phase of moving industry to new sites in the immediate hinterland of Manchester found its purest expression in the creation of whole 'industrial villages' or 'model estates'. William Houldsworth's mill town at Reddish is an excellent example of this and the way that paternalistic politics dominated the thinking of industrialists. Houldsworth was an Ardwick-born cotton manufacturer. On taking over the family business he relocated the firm to Reddish near Stockport, taking advantage of the open land along the Stockport arm of the Ashton Canal (or 'Lanky' as it was called). In 1865 and 1872, Houldsworth built two large mills aligning the canal in association with streets of workers' housing arranged in a grid beside Houldsworth Mill (which is one of the largest mills ever built). As with other contemporary industrial villages, such as Saltaire in West Yorkshire, social division amongst the labour force were consciously reproduced in the differential size of the workers' terraces with larger foreman's and manager's houses with large front gardens, located fronting the mill on Houldsworth (which became locally known as 'Nob Row').

Fig. 4.22 Houldsworth Mill, Reddish (Author, 2020).

Fig. 4.23 Houldsworth Working Men's Club (Author, 2020).

Houldsworth, as an entrepreneur with political ambitions, was president of Manchester Conservative Association, he attempted to create a working-class base for Toryism through paternalistic endowments— 'clog Toryism' as it was called. At Reddish, Houldsworth commissioned a Working Men's Club, built in 1874, and employed Alfred Waterhouse to design a school (1876), St Elizabeth's church (named after his wife) and rectory (1883). Later a park with bowling greens was added to this model village. Houldsworth became a Conservative MP for Manchester North between 1883 and 1906 and was made a baronet in 1887.

Working-Class Manchester and the Impact of Paternalism and Political Reform

Industrial Suburbs and By-Law Housing

The physical expansion of Manchester's industrial base in the second half of the nineteenth century was accompanied by the simultaneous growth of suburban working-class districts to provide the labour for this phase of capital investment. The working-class industrial suburb of Gorton, for instance, was transformed from a minor village in open farmland to a major urban centre in its own right, physically joined to the wider Manchester conurbation. Gorton's population, for example, rose from 4,476 in 1851 to 55,417 in 1901. Far Lane still has a village feel to it, with several late eighteenth-century cottages aligning Gore Brook. Far Lane and the winding pre-industrial roads leading to St James (which had originated as a fifteenth-century chapel), Church Lane and Wellington Street, stand out in marked contrast to the ordered and gridded arrangement of redbrick by-law terraces, as depicted on the section of the 1905 Ordnance Survey map (see Fig. 4.24). Despite substantial slum clearances, the streets to the south of Hyde Road to the east of Wellington Road survive virtually intact. By-law houses built after Manchester's 1867 Act led to improved minimum standards, which means a substantial number of blocks of terraces have survived twentieth-century urban developments. As well as Gorton, examples of late Victorian and Edwardian by-law working-class houses can be found in the townships of Levenshulme, parts of Longsight, Rusholme and Moss Side. These come in the standard variety of forms of through terraces and 'tunnel backs', with backyards and ginnels (alley ways). Some would include small front yards and others embellished with a bay window to denote variations in wealth and status amongst working-class communities.

Fig. 4.24 Gorton, 1905 (section of Ordnance Survey map, Lancashire Sheet CIV.16), CC BY, National Library of Scotland.

4. City of Civic Pride and Industrial Paternalism, c.1860–c.1890

Fig. 4.25 Gorton by-law housing. Photograph by John Critchley, Dreamstimes.com.

Middle-Class Charitable Institutions

The middle class concern for working-class lives followed the pattern established earlier of promoting charitable institutions and recreational spaces to enhance health and morality through self-improvement. Manchester and Salford District Provident Society (DPS) had been set up in 1833 to reinforce the paternalistic ethics of charity so that it was directed towards the deserving poor. In the society's Annual Report of 1876–1877, its declared aims were 'the encouragement of industry and frugality; the suppression of mendacity and imposture; and the occasional relief of sickness and unavailable misfortune'. The widening of the franchise and the return of mass politics after the 1867 Reform Act intensified bourgeois anxieties about the urban poor. This in turn led to new waves of middle-class philanthropy and new interventions in the built environment of working-class districts. In 1876, the District Provident Society established the Manchester and Salford Provident Dispensaries Association to supervise the free medical help offered to the poor by dispensaries and to combat any abuse of the system. With the physical growth of the city, medical dispensaries were placed in various working-class districts such as Ardwick, Harpurhey, Hulme, Beswick and Salford. The one in Ancoats, the Ardwick and Ancoats Dispensary, made famous by Lowry's painting of the outpatient's clinic (*Ancoats Hospital Outpatients' Hall*, 1952), just about survives on Old Mill Street. It was built in 1874 in polychrome

Gothic with a central clock tower including elaborate tourelles, and managed by the Provident Dispensaries Association.

Fig. 4.26 Ardwick and Ancoats Dispensary, Mill Street. Photo by Pete Birkinshaw (2008), Wikimedia Commons, CC BY 2.0, https://commons.wikimedia.org/wiki/File:Ancoats_Hospital_(3192798312).jpg#/media/File:Ancoats_Hospital_(3192798312).jpg

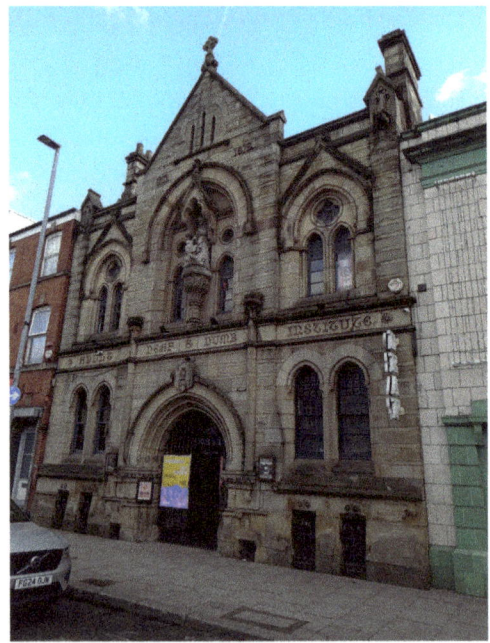

Fig. 4.27 Adult Deaf and Dumb Institute, Chorlton-on-Medlock (Author, 2025).

Other notable medical institutions established beyond the central district include the Adult Deaf and Dumb Institute on Grosvenor Street in Chorlton-on-Medlock. Like Ancoats Dispensary, this was an eye-catching building, constructed in Gothic in 1878 with elaborate architectural details such as the statute of Jesus healing a deaf man above the entrance. There is another survivor on Cheetham Hill, as the Clinical Hospital and Dispensary for Children moved from Stevensons Square to a new site at Park Place, where a hospital with twenty-five beds was opened in 1867. This later became the Northern Hospital for Women and Children.

Fig. 4.28 Northern Hospital for Women and Children, Park Place, Cheetham Hill (Author, 2023).

The reconfiguration of the central district of Manchester, therefore, led to the displacement and proliferation of many charitable institutions that were now more firmly embedded within working-class communities in working-class suburbs. As well as medical charities, orphanages and various public halls were built for paternalistic reasons. While charitable endowments of this kind only touched the surface of urban poverty and deprivation, they were highly visible monuments which were really designed to symbolise the munificence of their patrons.

Fig. 4.29 Nicholls Hospital, Ardwick (Author, 2021).

Nicholls Hospital, on Hyde Road in Ardwick, was built by the mill owner Benjamin Nicholls as a memorial to his son in 1879. It was designed by Thomas Worthington in Flemish Gothic with a massive central tower similar to the one he designed for the Police and Sessions Court on Minshull Street. Originally Nicholls Hospital ran as a boys' orphanage before becoming a secondary school (now part of Manchester City College). It still dominates the surrounding area and forms one Manchester's more obvious landmarks.

Another good example of this phenomenon is the Public Hall in Stretford. This was built by the multimillionaire industrialist John Rylands who lived nearby in his Italianate mansion at Longford Hall (which unfortunately has been demolished although the park in which it was located remains). Rylands, due to his vast accumulation of wealth, was one of Manchester's greatest philanthropists and contributed to many public works including orphanages, churches, libraries and public paths. Stretford Public Hall was just one of them, and perhaps the most prominent. It was built in 1878 and incorporated a library and lecturer theatres. The Gothic design with tall clock tower was clearly influenced by the other Manchester civic buildings of this phase, especially Waterhouse's new Town Hall. As such, it illustrates how the Gothic clock tower became the architectural signature of industrial paternalism.

Fig. 4.30 Stretford Public Hall, Chester Road (Author, 2022).

New Municipal Parks

Alongside the philanthropic activities of middle-class individuals, Manchester Corporation also played a direct role in encouraging rational recreation amongst the working class in the form of parks and sport facilities. The urban expansion of Manchester necessitated further developments, so in addition to the municipal-run Peel Park, Queens Park and Phillips Park, the Corporation bought land in Moss Side and commissioned a new public park which was opened as Alexandra Park in 1870. Its location, some distance from the centre and the earlier municipal parks, is indicative of the physical expansion of working-class districts to the south of Manchester. Despite the flat terrain of Moss Side, Alexandra Park remains the most elegant. It was designed by Alfred Derbyshire and included two lodges (one with a clock tower), a terrace walkway and circular paths, ovals and serpentine lake. There was also a gymnasium, bowling green and a sports and cricket ground with the aim of promoting healthier lifestyles for the working-class away from the 'evil' influence of the pub. The 'Band of Hope' temperance society placed a drinking fountain in the park to encourage just this. Parks were supposed to nurture sobriety and respectable social mixing. The late nineteenth century was a popular time for erecting public water fountains, especially in parks. Another fine example can be found in Philips Park which was installed in 1897 to celebrate the park's fiftieth anniversary. However, one of the unintended consequences of the rise of mass politics following the campaign for the widening of the franchise, was that the political policing of parks was challenged, most famously by the Hyde Park 'riot' in London in 1866 when sections of the railings were pulled down and the park occupied by the Reform League demonstrators. Despite much opposition, therefore, Alexandra Park, became an open venue for political rallies and mass meetings. Notably, Manchester's first May Day rally was held in the park in 1892 when Keir Hardie organised a May Day rally for the Independent Labour Party attended by a huge crowd of 60,000 people. This was the first celebration of International Workers' Day in Manchester. It is partially for this reason that Alexandra Park has become known as the 'people's park'. Across the Irwell, Salford Corporation followed Manchester's lead and built their second public park in Ordsall, which was opened in 1876.

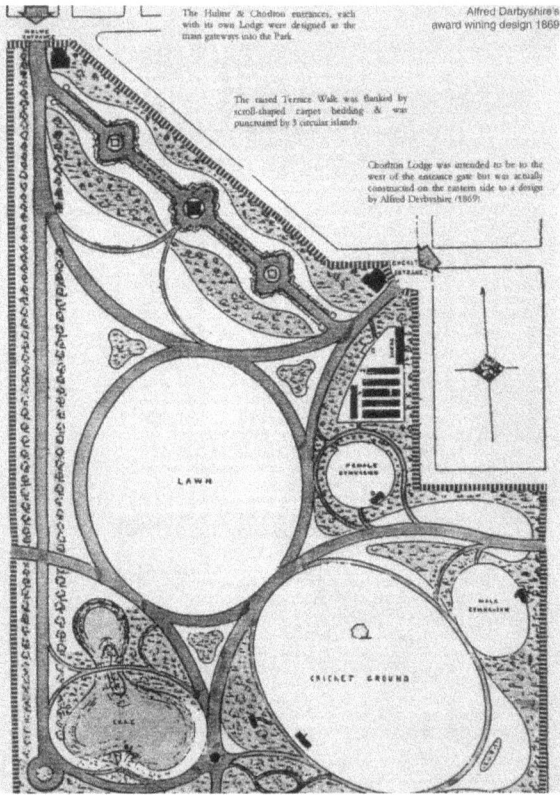

Fig. 4.31 Alexandra Park, Moss Side, plan by Alfred Darbyshire, 1869. Wikimedia Commons, public domain, https://commons.wikimedia.org/wiki/File:Plan_of_ Alexandra_Park,_Manchester.jpg#/media/File:Plan_of_Alexandra_Park,_Manchester.jpg

Board Schools

Political reform imposed a new electoral logic which required middle-class politicians to directly appeal to a working-class electorate. This was a novel development which necessitated the shaping and moulding of working-class political consciousness so that the status quo remained unchallenged, and society did not collapse into anarchy and revolution. In particular, the 1867 Reform Act promoted the idea that this new electorate needed to be educated to be worthy of the vote which led to educational reforms and the 1870 Education Act. This act allowed local authorities to establish board schools paid for by ratepayer's money. Between 1870 and 1902, Manchester Corporation built thirty-nine board schools, with the first being Vine Street School in Hulme, opening in 1874. These provided elementary education focused upon basic literacy and numeracy, as well as instilling 'good' behaviour. These board schools were all built within working-class suburbs in a common style of redbrick and terracotta Renaissance or Queen Anne influenced designs, such as the 1896 Varna Street School in Openshaw (which could accommodate over two thousand children). Eight board schools were erected in Hulme alone, seven in Ardwick and three in Ancoats; each had a memorial stone with a serial number. In contrast to the earlier church schools, board schools were all located within residential districts rather than placed in a public space next to a church. However, the 1870 Education Act did incentivise ecclesiastic bodies to build schools, so post-1870 there was a wave of new church schools all prominently positioned adjacent the founding institutions. Consequently, there was a proliferation of different types of schools as Anglicans, Catholics and Nonconformists were inspired to provide schools rather than see the education of their congregations pass to the school board office. In Ardwick, for instance, St Thomas's School was established by the church in 1872 and the Primitive Methodist next to their chapel at Higher Ardwick in 1874. Both competed with the seven board schools that had been located in the township.

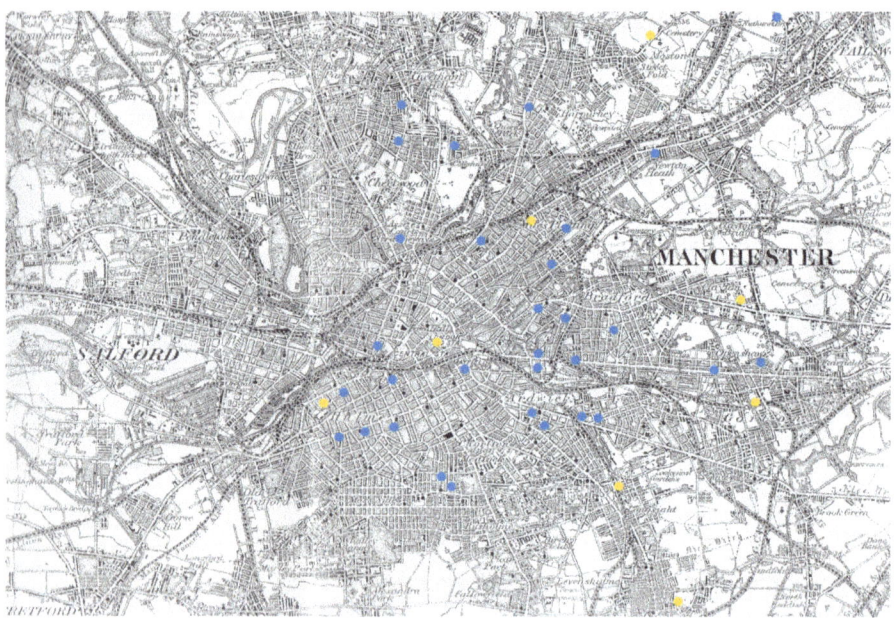

Fig. 4.32 Map of Manchester and Salford, 1913, showing location of Manchester Board Schools, annotated by the author (yellow dots = extant schools, blue dots = demolished schools).

The 1870 Education Act was also a far-reaching piece of reform in that it entitled middle-class women, who had been exclude from the political franchise, to vote and stand as board governors and so be able for the first time to officially participate in local politics. In Manchester, the suffragist Lydia Becker became the first woman to be elected to a school board and this enhanced her position as a leading campaigner to win votes for women. Manchester's School Board Office, which Becker would have visited to attend meetings, was built in 1878 on Deansgate as a Queen Anne style redbrick and terracotta building, known as Elliot House. Over the river, Salford Education Office, was located along the principal street of Chapel Street in a large French Renaissance-style building that was built in 1895.

Fig. 4.33 Varna Street School, Openshaw (Author, 2021).

Fig. 4.34 Elliot House, School Board Office, Deansgate (Author, 2022).

Working Men's Conservative Clubs

Another major consequence of the 1867 Reform Act was that it necessitated political parties to reach out to a new electorate and to create national party organisations that sought to mobilise voters. This resulted in the creation of political clubs at a local level. These were not just established in the centre of Manchester; they were also founded in all the surrounding working-class districts. Houldsworth's and

Beyer's moves to sponsor working men's Conservative associations at Reddish and Gorton were replicated elsewhere, at Ardwick, Blackley, Levenshulme, and Clayton for example, where the same pattern can be seen. What is striking is that it was the Tories who were far more proactive in 'wooing' the working class, in this respect, than the Liberals. Conservative club houses proliferate in Manchester's working-class districts, while Liberal or reform clubs are notable by their absence. Club building was therefore one of the means by which the Conservative Party gained a working-class base and this helps explain how the Tories came to dominate local politics at the end of the nineteenth century. Between 1885 and 1900 Conservative figures won twenty-one out of the thirty seats that were contested in Manchester, and this dominance is embodied in the built environment.

Fig. 4.35 Clayton Conservative Club (Author, 2021).

Pubs and Breweries

One of the ways that working men's clubs attracted clientele was through serving alcohol, sometimes at a discounted rate, and this is the main reason why some still manage to survive today. Manchester has always had a reputation for drinking. It was famous for the number of hostelers and could boast of possessing more pubs than any other equivalent town. But pubs were more than just places to consume the 'demon drink', as has already been discussed. They were also foci of working communities where people could talk business and politics, engage with trade union activity or participate in sporting clubs and societies. Despite the relentless efforts of the temperance movement to curb the culture of drinking and promote teetotalism, the public house remained popular throughout the nineteenth century. However, after the passing of the 1867 Reform Act there was a concern that licensing needed to be more tightly regulated. The Beer House Act of 1830 had liberalised the regulations governing the brewing and the sale of beer in the hope of weaning the working class off the consumption of the more dangerous gin. However, it resulted in the proliferation of beer houses across the city, as illustrated in the drink maps of Manchester produced by the temperance movement, as any rate payer could gain a license for a small fee. Through pressure of temperance societies and middle-class concerns that pubs fostered prostitution, gambling and criminality, the 1869 Wine and Beer House Act was passed. This brought the licensing of pubs under the control of local government which resulted in the raising of the license fee and the introduction of property qualifications for publicans. In turn this led to closing or the taking over of many beer houses by breweries and the construction of larger, multi-roomed beer houses. This was the start of the 'golden age' of pub building defined by the proliferation of grand ornate 'palace' pubs decorated in glazed tiles and stained glass with quirky architectural features and details to draw attention to the venue and attract customers.

Fig. 4.36 Derby Brewery Arms, Cheetham Hill (with the former Town Hall and Poor Law Union Office on the far right) (Author, 2020).

Manchester was served by several local breweries, such as the famous Boddingtons Strangeways Brewery, and there are still surviving examples. On Cheetham Hill can be found Joseph Holt's Derby Brewery on Empire Street, and on the edge of Moss Side is Hydes' Brewery, both dating to the 1860s, while on Monsall Road in Newton Heath is Wilson's brewery. These breweries consolidated their market position by opening large 'palace' pubs. For instance, along Cheetham Hill Road on the corner of Empire Street, Holt's positioned their Derby Brewery Arms, a five bay hotel and pub with central arched doorway with Ionic pilasters.

Derby Brewery Arms is still open to business, but many of these grand 'palace' pubs no longer function as hostelries, although their external structures still draw the eye. The Plymouth Grove (1873) in Chorlton-on-Medlock, and the White Lion (1880) in Withington are two excellent examples that illustrate the peculiarities of late Victorian and Edwardian pub designs. Both are large multiroomed and multifloored buildings which include grand entrances and unusual clock towers. Time underpinned the rhythms of recreation as well as work discipline, with the clock faces on these pubs echoing those on the facades of mills and civic buildings. Other public houses from this phase worth mentioning, as they can still be visited as pubs, include the Sawyers Arms (1873) on Deansgate, the Star and Garter (1877) on Fairfield Street, the Old Nags Head (1880) on Jackson Row.

Fig. 4.37 Plymouth Grove, Chorlton-on-Medlock (Author, 2022).

4. City of Civic Pride and Industrial Paternalism, c.1860–c.1890   191

Fig. 4.38 White Lion, Withington (Author, 2022).

Police Stations

While the middle class may have favoured indirect means to shape social behaviour so that the working class brought themselves to order, ultimately working-class discipline was imposed from above by local and central governmental authorities. The military barracks established in the first phase of industrialisation were still present, but the primary institution for maintaining control was the police. Manchester's 'New Police' had been formed in the 1840s. Although initially it struggled to gain legitimacy both amongst the working class and sections of the middle class, fear of public disorder and the spread of immorality meant that the police eventually became the main instrument for combating the 'criminal classes'. Respectable middle-class opinion viewed the police as the force to clamp down on drunkards, brawlers, vagrants and sex workers, and above all to protect private property. During the second half the nineteenth century, there were constant fears of crime waves, from the panics about garroters terrorising the streets in the mid-1860s, to concerns about the youth gangs of 'scuttlers' fighting during the 1870s and 1880s.

Fig. 4.39 Newton Street Police Station, central Manchester (Author, 2022).

Subsequently, the presence of the police became more conspicuous in the built environment. In the centre of Manchester is the Newton Street Police Station, now the Greater Manchester Police Museum. This was built in 1879 as the headquarters of Police Division A (when the force was split into five divisions). It still retains the original charge office, prison cells and a small morgue (a reflection of the nature of policing in the late nineteenth century). There is also a good example in the centre of Salford on Chapel Street, built in 1889, and placed in a visually prominent position on the corner of the approach road to Exchange Station. However, police stations were also erected throughout the suburbs especially within working districts, with several in Ancoats and Hulme, as well as Bradford, Chorlton-on-Medlock and Harpurhey. Old police stations can still be found at Goulden Street in Ancoats, Bridgewater Street in Castlefield and suburbs such as Levenshulme and Droylsden. The police faced great hostility from the working class and it was not uncommon for the 'peeler on the beat' to be physically attacked by organised gangs, as policing was directed at the poor and the places they frequented, public houses, brothels and gambling dens. Sieges of police stations to release prisoners by local communities were not uncommon.

Fig. 4.40 Chapel Street Police Station (with a police wagon shed painted blue on the right), Salford (Author, 2021).

An insight into respectable fear and fascination with crime can be found in memoirs of Manchester's so-called Sherlock Holmes, Jerome Caminada. He served as a police officer and detective between 1868 and 1899 and published his autobiography following his retirement. Amongst the case notes he published are accounts of a police raid on a queer and cross-dressing ball in a temperance hall in Hulme in 1880, the arrest of Irish republicans and the suppression of anarchist demonstrators in Ardwick Green in 1893. Caminada was reportedly responsible for the closure of four hundred public houses in his fight against vice and felony in Manchester.

Suburbanisation, Places of Worship and Cosmopolitan Manchester

The late nineteenth century marked the golden age of Victorian suburbanisation in Manchester and elsewhere. The residential townships that had emerged beyond the 1838 formal borders of the city, especially to the south, expanded and were consolidated as independent civic entities, first, by electing Local Boards of Health that helped regulate suburban growth, and then through the establishment of Urban District Councils. The town halls built for the UDCs of Withington (originally as a Local Board Office in 1881) and Levenshulme in 1898 are still standing and very much in use, the latter as an Antique Village. One of the distinctive features of suburbanisation during this phase was the way in which working-class housing began to penetrate previously middle-class residential areas. This is dramatically illustrated in Moss Side, which had been a picturesque village, described in the opening of Elizabeth Gaskell's 1848 published novel, *Mary Barton*. It possessed farms, such as the famous Pepperhill Farm, alongside fine houses and villas. A local board was formed in 1856 and Moss Side became an urban district council in 1894. Between these dates the whole area became laid out with a rigid north-south, east-west grid system of redbrick by-law terraces; an arrangement that stands out on district maps. Being built to higher specifications, these by-law houses were not demolished as slums, as occurred to the neighbouring Hulme in the post-war period, but were retained to form the residential heart of the area. Moss Side may have been unusual in that developments led to its wholesale transformation into a working-class district, in other suburbs (Rusholme, Longsight, Levenshulme, Fallowfield and Withington) there was more in the way of social mixing. This represented a significant change from the marked residential segregation of the mid-nineteenth-century city that had helped give rise to the popular contemporary notion of 'two-nation England'. The built environment of these suburbs, therefore, became characterised by a diversity of types of housing, particularly in terms of size and quality. Although this development should not be over-emphasised as class segregation was still the norm, there was a degree of architectural blurring on the fringes, with lower middle-class housing beginning to resemble more affluent working-class terraces. This blurring is best symbolised with the rise of the 'middle-class terrace'.

The 'Middle-Class Terrace'

As has already been noted, from the beginning of the second half of the nineteenth century, the leafy and spacious middle-class suburbs became infilled with more standardised villas, both detached and semi-detached. This trend accelerated with time. Obviously, grand houses were still constructed in a range of styles, but the trajectory was towards smaller and less architectural ambitious, semi-detached houses. These proliferated from the 1880s onwards, reflecting the growth of the lower middle class, and were increasingly arranged in tightly packed rows, which meant that these residential streets gave the appearance of being terraces (as can be seen in the photograph of Osbourne Road in Levenshulme). Alongside these semi-detached rows, actual terraces were built, usually consisting of short blocks of four houses, and again, tightly spaced. Middle-class streets, therefore, were no longer curved to evoke a rural setting, but were straight and gridded like other by-law terraces. At the same time, higher-end working-class houses gained small walled front gardens so that front doors did not open directly onto the street. Bay windows were added and entrances deeply recessed with more architecturally elaboration. In essence, they were modest versions of 'middle-class terraces' (as illustrated in the photograph of Forest Range, Levenshulme). Both types of late nineteenth-century housing were and remain ubiquitous. Being on the whole sought after property, they still form the core of Manchester's residential suburbs.

Fig. 4.41 A lower 'middle-class terrace' consisting of a tightly packed row of semi-detached houses, Osbourne Road, Levenshulme (Author, 2023).

Fig. 4.42 By-law terraces with front gardens and bay windows, Forest Range, Levenshulme (Author, 2023).

Fig. 4.43 Levenshulme, 1905, annotated by the author (the position of Anglican church shown as a red dot, the Methodist chapel a yellow dot and Congregationalis(section of Ordnance Survey map, Lancashire Sheet CIV.04), CC BY, National Library of Scotland.

The township of Levenshulme can serve as an example of this pattern. What had been a village on Stockport Road, the main south-east route out of Manchester, was slowly transformed into a small middle-class dormitory suburb with the arrival of the train station in 1842. In 1865 it was administered by a Local Board of Health and then by an Urban District Council from 1881. But by the late nineteenth century, Levenshulme was becoming a socially mixed district with the growth of a large working-class population. The 1905 Ordnance Survey Map reveals rows of detached villas and middle-class terraces to the east of the railway line especially on the northern side of Albert Road (labelled Coston Park and Rushford Park on the map), while the streets to the west of Stockport Road consist of a smaller, more tightly packed grid of working-class terraces.

The emergence of residential social mixing was a novel development and so must have had quite a disturbing impact on middle-class mentalities. It is therefore tempting to see the popularity of late Victorian paternalistic attitudes as being both a product of this new reality and a response to it. Paternalism provided the middle class with a mechanism for managing cross-class interactions in residential settings and for reimposing bourgeois social order in the era of mass politics following the widening of the franchise after 1867. Certainly, distinct suburban communities began to emerge during this phase which brought together different social groups. Religion played an essential role here, with various religious denominations providing the social glue, so to speak, for the forging of suburban communal identities.

Churches, chapels and other places of worship such as synagogues, as already noted, are an important category of monument when studying the built environment. As well as having a better survival rate in contrast to other types of buildings, they were institutions that straggled the strict class divide, being arenas for social mixing. Hence they can be viewed as monuments to the communities that they served. It is this angle of investigation that will be considered here. Places of worship and other religious-run institutions can be used, in particular, to map the fortunes of the various ethnic groups that were drawn into Manchester and set up home in the city. Industrial Manchester was a city of migrants that brought with them their religious affinities. The architecture and geography of these different denominations, therefore, was an expression and embodiment of cosmopolitan Manchester.

Anglican Churches

Anglican church foundations during this phase are a testament to both the expansion and consolidation of new suburban communities. At the same time, they indirectly reflect some of the tensions within Anglicanism during the mid-nineteenth century. The religious census of 1851, the first comprehensive statistical analysis of denominational affiliation, had shocked Victorian society, as it revealed the size of the dissenting community and the fact that church attendance was less than fifty percent. The dominant position of the Church of England seemed under threat from the rise of Nonconformity and what appeared to be the spread of secularism, especially amongst the working class. This worried the establishment. Catholicism was also expanding, with Catholic beliefs and practices directly influencing the Oxford Movement. One of the responses was to erect large and conspicuous ecclesiastical foundations designed by leading architects of the day. In Manchester a number of fine Anglican churches were built, especially within working-class districts that still visually dominate the surrounding topography. These include: William Butterfield's Church of St Cross in Clayton (1866); Joseph Crowther's St Benedict in West Gorton (1880), with its attached school and clergy house and distinctive Germanic-looking tower with corner tourelles, which forms an unmistakeable landmark when travelling in and out of Manchester by train; and the magnificent St Augustine at Pendlebury (1874), the 'Miners' Cathedral', which included a parsonage, gatehouse and school, all funded by the banker Edward Stanley Heywood for the local mining community. St Augustine is an imposing, tall structure, built so that it towered above the neighbouring mills. Its sheer physical presence is captured well in Lowry's 1920 painting of the church.

Nonconformist Chapels

In many places, these new Anglican foundations had to compete with those established by dissenting communities for their congregations. Churches and chapels were built adjacent to each other, and often visually referenced one another. A good example of this can be seen at Levenshulme. There had been a small Wesleyan Methodist chapel in Levenshulme since 1797, but with the growth of the township after the coming railways, there was a need for more ecclesiastical provisions. Charles Carrill-Worsley of Platt Hall, the major landowner in the area, provided the land and funds for the construction of the Anglican church of St Peter, together with a Sunday school, which was consecrated in 1860. St Peter was positioned in a far more prominent position than the earlier Methodist chapel and was more visually commanding, as it fronted the high street on Stockport Road and was built with a tower and spire, In response the Wesleyan Methodists relocated their chapel further along Stockport Road and built it on a larger scale with a tower and spire (which was taken down in the 1950s). It was between St Peter and the Wesleyan chapel on Stockport Road that the Congregationalist then placed their church in Gothic style in 1888, also with a prominent spire. As a consequence, these three ecclesiastical foundations form landmarks commanding the approaches to Levenshulme from either Stockport or Manchester, with the three spires referencing and challenging each other (see the above map, Fig. 4.43).

Fig. 4.44 Church of St Benedict, West Gorton (Author, 2023).

Catholic Churches and Institutions

Together with prestigious Anglican and Nonconformist churches and chapels, Roman Catholic institutions became more visible in the religious landscape of Manchester. This was a reflection of the increasing size of the Catholic population and a more tolerant attitude towards Catholicism. Despite the backlash against the Pope's attempt to restore the old Catholic hierarchy of bishoprics in England (known as the Papal Aggression of 1850), Catholic cathedrals were reintroduced. The Church of St John the Evangelist in Salford, completed in 1848, gained cathedral status in 1852, and the first Catholic Bishop of Salford, William Turner, was instrumental in promoting the building of another cathedral-like Church of the Holy Name of Jesus, in Chorlton-on-Medlock. Although a parish church, this is the largest ecclesiastical building in Manchester. It was not hidden away like the 'Hidden Gem' of St Mary in Mulberry Street, but constructed fronting Oxford Street, the main middle-class thoroughfare into the city from the south. The church was completed in 1871 in Gothic Decorative style, with the tower added in 1929.

Fig. 4.45 Church of the Holy Name of Jesus, Oxford Road (Author, 2023).

Fig. 4.46 Church and Friary of St Francis, Gorton (Author, 2023).

Another important Catholic foundation whose physical presence is still felt today is Edward Pugin's Franciscan friary in Gorton. Known locally as Gorton Monastery, this tall and imposing structure was completed between 1866 and 1872 as a showcase Gothic Revival building following Edward's father's architectural philosophy. Built in redbrick and stone dressing, the exterior is ornately decorated with the west front dominated by stepped buttresses that enhance the church's height. So, despite an absence of a tower, Gorton Monastery was a visual icon in east Manchester. Edward Pugin was also responsible for other important Catholic buildings, the earlier St Ann (1867) and his masterpiece, All Saints (1868), both built in Stretford for Sir Humphrey and Lady Annette de Trafford of Trafford Hall and Park.

St Bede's College, on Alexandra Road South, is another Catholic institution, built between 1877 and 1880 in an elegant building that made use of the failed Manchester Aquarium in Whalley Range. Its facade is decorated with portrait heads on the pediments of the ground floor windows and relief panels adorning its three-bay porch entrance. The college was established by the Bishop of Salford, Herbert Vaughan and became the Diocesan Junior Seminary in 1891.

These prestigious Catholic institutions reflected the growing size of the Catholic population in Manchester, which had expanded due to waves of Irish immigrants who migrated to find work especially as a consequence of the horrors of the Great Famine. But they also served other Catholic immigrant groups such as Italians and Poles. There was an influx of Italians into the city especially during the late nineteenth century, following the unification of Italy, that formed a community in an area of Ancoats which became known as 'Little Italy'. The Roman Catholic church on George Leigh Street, St Michael, survives with its attached school and clergy house, although they are now used as offices and a hostel. Polish refugees and immigrants also settled in Manchester during the nineteenth century and formed a small community in Angel Meadow.

The size of the Catholic population of Manchester resulted in the construction of a large garden cemetery in Moston, three miles north of the city centre on the east bank of the River Irk on an attractive sloping site. This was the first Roman Catholic cemetery of the city and opened in 1875 with an axial layout and a Camps Santo at its centre. Amongst the many Victorian and Edwardian memorials is the monument to the 'Manchester Martyrs', the three Irish nationalists who were hanged for their supposed part in the armed rescue of Fenian prisoners being transported to Belle Vue Prison in 1867. It takes the form of a Celtic Cross surrounded by Irish cultural symbols with the stones of the base quarried from the different counties of Ireland.

Fig. 4.47 St Bede's College, Whalley Range (Author, 2022).

Greek Orthodox Church

Other ecclesiastic foundations attest to the presence of other immigrant groups in Manchester that formed separate communities. For instance, Greek merchants were present in the city since the 1830s and they formed a small community in Upper Broughton. By 1860, this community was wealthy enough to build the Greek Church of the Annunciation on Bury New Road. Its classical form, with a Corinthian portico, stands out against the Gothic Revival styles of contemporary Anglican, Catholic and Nonconformist churches and chapels.

Fig. 4.48 Greek Orthodox Church, Bury New Road (Author, 2020).

Armenian Church

Manchester was also the home of the first Armenian community in Britain. During the nineteenth century, they settled as silk merchants, with around thirty Armenian businesses operating in the city by the 1860s. In 1870 on Upper Brook Street, this community built the first purpose-built Armenian church in the country.

Fig. 4.49 Armenian Church, Upper Brook Street (Author, 2022).

Synagogues and Jewish Institutions

Fig. 4.50 Spanish and Portuguese Synagogue, Cheetham Hill Road (Author, 2023).

In terms of cosmopolitan Manchester, however, perhaps the best example of an ethnic group using the built environment to help fashion a communal identity lies in the township of Cheetham Hill. It is in this district that Manchester's Jewish community became concentrated during the second half of the nineteenth century, and it is here that the landmarks of Manchester's Jewish heritage can be found, as illustrated by

Edward Salomons's fantastic 'Moresque' style synagogue for Sephardic Jews fronting Cheetham Hill Road. This was completed in 1874 and is now the home of the Manchester Jewish Museum.

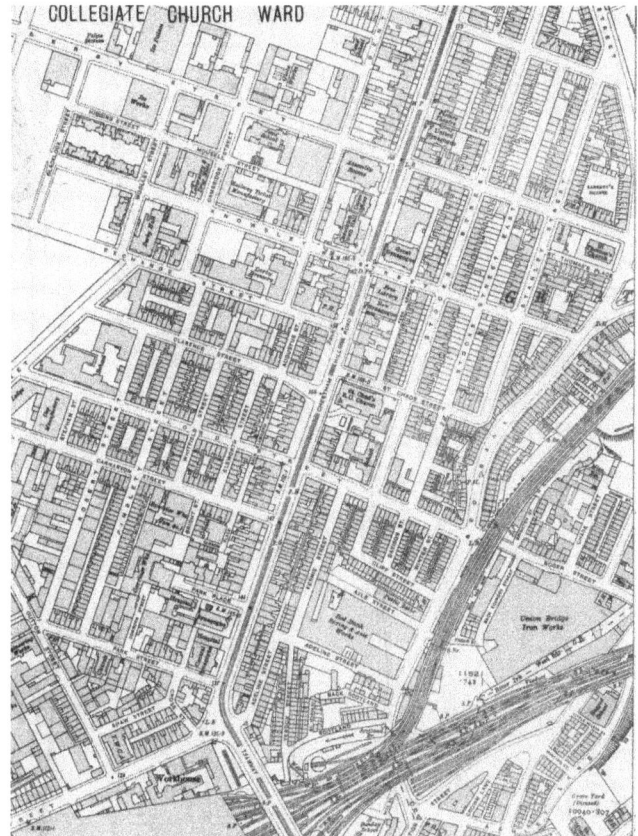

Fig. 4.51 Cheetham Hill Road, 1931 (section of Ordnance Survey map, Lancashire Sheet CXI.06), CC BY, National Library of Scotland.

The history of Jews in Manchester can be traced back to the eighteenth century, and by the mid-nineteenth century there was a well-established community. In 1858, the Great Synagogue opened on Cheetham Hill Road for Ashkenazi Jews and by the beginning of the twentieth century, the southern end of Cheetham had a considerable Jewish population with nine separate synagogues. Cheetham Hill Road (originally York Road) had initially been laid out in 1820 as part of a planned development for a middle-class suburb. The classical style town hall

(1856) and assembly rooms, and the Poor Law Union Office (1862), which still stand on the road, are a testament to this. However, with the encroachment of industry and especially following the building of Strangeways Prison, Cheetham Hill became a less fashionable residential district. Subsequently, during the second half of the nineteenth century, the area became a draw for poor Jewish immigrants, particularly refugees, fleeing antisemitic persecution in Eastern Europe during the 1880s, 1890s and 1900s. This created a dynamic and socially diverse community. The various synagogues reflected the religious schisms that divided the community between orthodox and reformed congregations, Ashkenazi and Sephardic traditions, for instance. Cheetham Hill was also a place where the relatively rich and absolutely poor lived side by side. It was the centre of Jewish business and trade, and the home of a growing Jewish working class. Red Bank, the road running down the bank of the Irk, in particular, became an infamous slum district of the Jewish poor and gained a reputation as being a breeding ground for working-class radicalism, sporting many Jewish trade unionists, socialists and revolutionaries.

Fig. 4.52 Manchester New Synagogue and Cheetham Branch, Manchester Free Library (left), Cheetham Hill Road (Author, 2023).

There are a number of existing buildings that relate to this late nineteenth-century Jewish community of Cheetham Hill. Even though Manchester's Great Synagogue was sadly demolished in 1986, the Spanish and Portuguese Synagogue and Manchester New Synagogue are still standing. The latter was built by William Ogden in 1889 in red brick and placed next to the Cheetham branch of Manchester Free Library (1876). Ogden also designed by the Talmud Torah School (1895) on Brent Street behind Cheetham Hill Road, which is decorated with Star of David tiles. And there are other notable surviving pieces of Jewish heritage in the township like the former Philanthropic Hall or Jewish Soup Kitchen (1906) on Southall Street, and the remains of Jewish owned factories and warehouses that still align Derby Street, such as the Anchor Cap Works.

The history of the Jewish community can be mapped through the geography of the city. During the twentieth century, rising affluence led middle-class sections of the community to move further up Cheetham Hill Road to the more leafy, middle-class suburbs of Crumpsall, Broughton, Prestwich and Whitefield (as well as to the south of the city and the dormitory villages of Fallowfield and Withington where there are two impressive early twentieth-century synagogues). This dispersal from Cheetham Hill, therefore, can be traced through new synagogue foundations.

Fig. 4.53 Jews' Burial Ground, Prestwich (Author, 2021).

As well as synagogues, the Manchester Jewish community also defined itself in terms of establishing separate cemeteries. The earliest one, Brindle Heath Jews' Burial Ground dates to 1794, as previously mentioned, but there are several others. The Prestwich Village Jews' Burial Ground was in use from 1841 to 1884 on Bury New Road (and can still be visited), and Manchester Reform Cemetery was opened at Whitefield in 1858. There are also Jewish cemeteries at Urmston (1878), Crumpsall (1884) and Blackley (1897), as well as Jewish sections in Manchester's municipal cemeteries.

Municipal Cemeteries

This brings us on to a consideration of a final significant intervention into the built environment that was shaped (in part) by religion, namely public cemeteries. For social history, cemeteries are excellent sources, providing insights into religious attitudes towards the treatment of the dead, as well as social divisions expressed in terms of the size and style of gravestone monuments. After the passing of the 1854 Burial Act, municipal authorities began to procure land and establish publicly owned burial grounds, as the old overflowing inner city graveyards were closed. These large municipal cemeteries were characteristically positioned around the periphery, on the outskirts of built-up areas.

Fig. 4.54 Map of Manchester and Salford, 1913, showing location of municipal cemeteries and large commercial cemeteries, annotated by the author (red dots = municipal cemeteries, yellow dots = large commercial cemeteries).

In the Manchester–Salford conurbation, it was the Salford city council that took a lead. Salford Borough Cemetery opened at Weaste in 1857 and was the first public cemetery after the 1850s Burial Acts. It was located in open ground by the bank of the Irwell, south of Pendleton, and is an example of the new 'garden cemetery' that became popular at the time. These cemeteries were designed like public parks to create a tranquil setting for mourning visitors. They were often landscaped to evoke Arcadia and Elysium Fields to aid reflective contemplation, and form great gardens of death. At Weaste, although the original four chapels and lodges have been demolished, the cemetery has a pleasant park feel about it, planned with trees and curving paths to facilitate perambulations. Weaste probably has the largest collection of Victorian monuments in the conurbation, including the Brotherton Memorial, to Salford's first MP Joseph Brotherton (1783–1857), who had campaigned for the cemetery, and Charles Halle, the founder of Manchester's Halle Orchestra. In 1902, Salford Borough Council open a second public cemetery at Agecroft, known as Salford Northern Cemetery, on the bank of the River Irwell. This was also a large cemetery, designed in sections of consecrated and unconsecrated areas, with an unusual central mortuary chapel with a clock tower still standing.

Fig. 4.55 Brotherton's funerary monument, Weaste Cemetery (Author, 2023).

Manchester Corporation was slower to respond to the Burial Acts, in part due to the fact that Manchester General Cemetery, established on 1837 by Rochdale Road in Harpurhey, provided a substantial out-of-town burial ground, despite it being a commercial cemetery. The first public cemetery in Manchester was Philips Park cemetery, designed by the landscape architect William Gay, and it opened in 1866. Like Weaste, it has an entrance lodge and mortuary chapels within the different sections of the cemetery to accommodate Anglican, Nonconformist and Catholic internments and circumvented via winding paths. There was also a Jewish section that was added. Infamously, Philips Park Cemetery suffered during the traumatic events of the Great Flood of 1872 when the Medlock burst its banks and washed numerous bodies downstream into the city centre, much to the horror of Mancunians.

Manchester's second public cemetery, Southern Cemetery, was opened in 1879 by Barlow Moor Road in Chorlton-cum-Hardy. It was placed on flat ground (unlike Philips Park) and was designed with a symmetrical geometric plan with chapels for the different sections. Like the other municipal cemeteries, Manchester's Southern Cemetery was not just open to different religious denominations. It was also a resting place for the rich as well as poor. The most notable burial in the cemetery is the monument to the millionaire industrialist John Rylands, who was buried in 1888 in the Dissenters section. It is also where the graves of police detective Jerome Caminada and the artist L. S. Lowry can be found.

Consequently, these four public cemeteries surrounding Salford and Manchester, reflect the growing religious toleration of the late nineteenth century and the way in which the treatment of the dead embodied middle-class paternalistic attitudes and notions of 'one nation'. Even though these cemeteries were open to all classes, religious and social differences were clearly expressed in terms of the location, size and prominence of the graves. Elaborate and prestigious monuments and mausoleums were placed in central areas, while the guinea graves and unmarked mass paupers' graves were relegated to the edge of the cemetery. In life and death, class divisions were maintained with the necropolis mirroring the metropolis.

At the same time that Salford and Manchester Corporations were establishing large municipal cemeteries, other local authorities in the townships around the centre were building smaller public cemeteries, such as at Peel Green, Eccles (1879), Stretford (1885), Urmston (1892) Droylsden (1894) and Gorton (1900).

By the end of this phase, Manchester had been transformed. It had reinvented itself, no longer the 'Coketown' or 'shock city' of industrialisation. Manchester had been consciously rebuilt as a city of civic pride, extolling the virtues of art, culture and politics, as well as trade and manufacture—a place of consumption alongside production. The reconfiguration of the built environment, which started in the 1840s, resulted in a city centre of commercial, cultural and civic institutions all housed in ornate monumental buildings with architectural pretension. This was a city of display and metropolitan grandeur, as epitomised by Waterhouse's Gothic Town Hall and Albert Square. Surrounding this centre, both industrial and residential suburbs emerged and took shape. Industry was concentrated along corridors radiating out following rivers, canals and train lines, especially to the east. Residential suburbs expanded and became formerly established around townships, resulting in the consolidation of both working-class and middle-class communities, with a degree of social mixing. Beyond this suburban sprawl, the rich set up more exclusive residential enclaves in the rural periphery of the conurbation. This general pattern of development that was firmly embedded by the end of the nineteenth century, remained relatively stable and so provided the basic urban framework for twentieth-century Manchester. But the underlying drive of capital accumulation, with the competitive class dynamics that this involved, meant that the city was forever in a state of becoming. The next phase was defined by the audacious project of making Manchester a major inland port through the digging of the 'The Big Ditch', Manchester Ship Canal, and the creation of the accompanying industrial estate of Trafford Park. Significantly, along with the impact of the so-called 'second Industrial Revolution' on Manchester's built environment, the next phase was defined by the rise of a popular urban leisure culture that challenged bourgeois notions of industrial paternalism. This coincided with a change in the dominant architectural fashion, a shift from the Gothic back to the Baroque.

5. City of Ambition and Popular Culture, c.1890–c.1920

Manchester Ship Canal, the Port of Manchester and Trafford Park

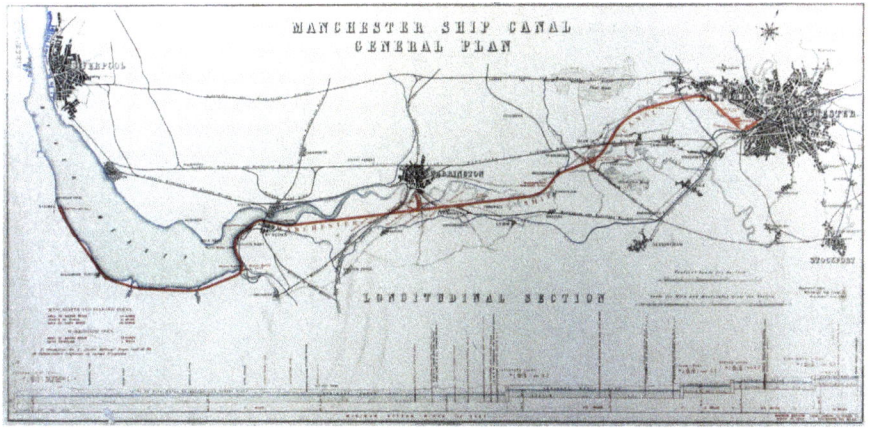

Fig. 5.1 Map of Manchester Ship Canal, 1890. Wikimedia Commons, public domain, https://commons.wikimedia.org/wiki/File:Plan_of_Manchester_Ship_Canal_1890.jpg#/media/File:Plan_of_Manchester_Ship_Canal_1890.jpg

The scale and ambition of the cutting of Manchester Ship Canal, the 'Big Ditch' as it became known, was truly impressive. Over thirty-six miles long, it took six years to build between 1887 and 1893 involving the labour of 17,000 navvies (with over 130 killed during its construction and many more permanently injured). Starting from Eastham on the south bank of the Mersey, six miles upstream from Liverpool, the canal ran through to the docks at Salford, which became the Port of Manchester. It allowed ocean-going merchant ships to sail directly into the city, making Manchester, at its height, the third largest port in the country. Although the project started as a private venture, championed by the engineer Daniel Adamson with the plan arranged at a famous meeting at 'The Towers' (his Gothic mansion in Didsbury) on 27th June 1882, it was completed by Manchester Corporation who bailed out the Ship Canal Company when faced with financial collapse. The canal was opened for traffic on 1st January 1894 with an official ceremony overseen by Queen Victoria on 21st May (the monarch's third and final royal visit to Manchester). The ship canal was a massive piece of civil engineering. It needed to be wide and deep enough to allow ships to pass each other and overcome a number of technical problems which required ingenious solutions. At Barton-upon-Irwell, a hydraulic swing aqueduct, the first and only one of its kind, was installed to carry the Bridgewater canal over the Ship Canal together with a swing bridge for the road, which could be opened to allow large ships to pass through.

Fig. 5.2 G. W. Bacon's Plan of Manchester and Salford, c. 1900. Image provided by The John Rylands Research Institute and Library, The University of Manchester.

The physical impact of the Ship Canal and, in particular, the docks on Manchester's topography was marked, as illustrated on Bacon's 1900 map. Not only did the canal's terminus cover a substantial area of land, but the Port of Manchester generated both industrial and urban developments in the southwestern side of the city. Working-class districts of densely blocked, terraced by-law housing rapidly covered wide areas of Ordsall and later Stretford. Most significantly the aristocrat, Humphrey de Trafford, who had opposed the whole Ship Canal project, admitted defeat and sold the family's 1,183-acre estate that sat immediately next to the canal in 1896. Trafford Park was substantially transformed into a planned industrial estate, financed by Ernest Terah Hooley and overseen by Marshall Stevens, who had been the General Manager of the Ship Canal Company. It took time to attract industrial investment, but it became the chief arm of the distributive trades of the Co-operative Wholesale Society (CWS) and the base of the British subsidiary of the American Westinghouse Electric Company, which manufactured turbines and electric generators. Other American firms set up business in Trafford Park including Ford Motors, who in 1911 established their first factory outside the USA making Model T Ford cars. These investments also incorporated the 'Village' designed on an American gridiron pattern with numbered avenues.

Fig. 5.3 Main entrance and the Dock Office, Port of Manchester, Ordsall (Author, 2013).

The Port of Manchester, together with the industrial estate at Trafford Park, proved a success and provided an economic boost for the city in the early twentieth century. It consolidated Manchester's status as a 'world city' with global connections and as a city of empire. This is reflected in many of the international names of the city centre streets, office buildings and warehouses constructed at the time such as India House (1906), Asia House (1909), Canada House (1909), Orient House (1914) etc. The construction of the Ship Canal House on King Street in 1924 can also be viewed as an expression of the prestige and economic impact of the project. Harry S. Fairhurst's Neoclassical design was one of the tallest office buildings in the country, located on the most prominent streets in the central business district of Manchester. Fairhurst was also the architect behind the Art Deco main entrance and Dock Office built in 1925, one of the few original structures of Salford Quays still standing. The wider economic impact of the Ship Canal is that it shifted the industrial focus of Manchester to the south-west fringes, where it is still based today. The sheer scale of these related projects meant that the canal, docks and industrial estate became a source of great civic and individual pride. For instance, on his death at his home in Devonport, Devon, in 1936 Marshall Stevens' body was brought back to Manchester and buried under a large monolith in the graveyard of the church of St Catherine on the bank of Manchester Ship Canal at Burton-upon-Irwell.

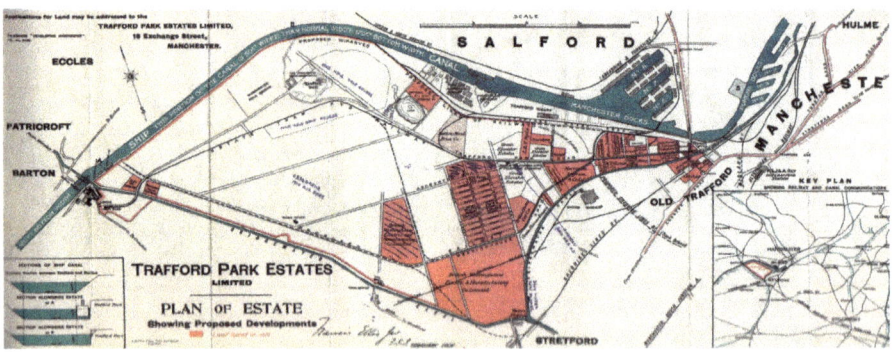

Fig. 5.4 Map of Trafford Park Estate, 1902. Image courtesy of Manchester Libraries.

The immediate rationale behind the Ship Canal was the need to reduce the price of transport into Manchester by bypassing Liverpool, as Mersey Docks charged high rates. But the scheme was devised in a context of a widespread fear amongst the elites that Britain was facing a period of economic decline. The final decades of the nineteenth century are sometimes referred to as the 'Great Depression'. It was not so much that the economy was declining (as it was still expanding), but rather that prices and profits were depressed in part due to competition from Germany and the USA. Britain was being undercut by its nearest industrial rivals who were catching up and, in some sectors, overtaking. This sense of decline preoccupied contemporaries who sought solutions in utilising the British Empire as a form of economic protection, and stimulating entrepreneurship through investing in the new capital-intensive industries of the 'second Industrial Revolution'—chemicals, motor cars and electrical engineering. Manchester Ship Canal and Port, together with Trafford Park Estate, therefore, can be seen as a localised response to these national concerns. The canal opened up opportunities for more direct trade with the colonies, and beyond, while Trafford Park became a hub for advanced engineering and new methods of production, such as 'Fordism'.

While perceptions of economic decline plagued the minds of the capitalist class, for workers the period was defined by the relative rise in living standards. Wages were increasing and imports of cheap food from the New World caused a fall in prices. Alongside economic prosperity, the growing strength of trade unions led to the reduction of working hours, and by the early 1890s, many workers were enjoying two-day weekends and bank holidays. With more free time and disposable income, these changing patterns of work led to the emergence of a working-class culture, distinct from dominant middle-class values, which expressed itself in the rise of a flourishing popular culture.

It must be noted that the final phase in this study of the making and transformation of industrial Manchester was the most intensive in terms of building growth. This was a phase that witnessed the formal expansion of the city boundaries to incorporate the surrounding satellite townships and ambitious building programmes within both inner and outer Manchester, so much so that the majority of the extant pre-World War II architecture dates from this phase. This is not simply a reflection of survival patterns. In the late nineteenth and early twentieth century, there was a marked boom in the building trade characterised by considerable capital investments in fixed real estate. As David Harvey (1973) has perceptively observed, in times of overaccumulation and resulting falling rates of profit, economic surpluses tend to be invested in the urban built environment. Consequently, the explosion of building work during this phase might be viewed as another Mancunium response to the uncertainties of the era of the 'Great Depression'.

This means that there is a vast amount of potential material to analyse, far more than any other phase in this study. To capture these developments in the late nineteenth and early twentieth century, this final phase will be broken down in terms of five subsections highlighting major interventions in the built environment that correspond to wider socio-economic patterns in the history of Manchester. Firstly, following the opening discussion on the Ship Canal, the Port of Manchester and Trafford Park, further transport innovations will be examined in 'Transport Innovations and the Creation of "Greater Manchester"'. The late nineteenth century saw the growth of the city's railways, with a new central station, and the establishment of a municipal tram network which had a profound spatial impact. Electric tramways helped integrate the suburban townships with the centre and so laid the infrastructure for the growth of 'Greater Manchester'. Secondly, 'The Baroque Revival and the Architecture of Decadence' will explore the shift in the dominant architectural style with the embrace of Baroque Revivalism through a look at the Midland Hotel and some of the other major examples of Baroque civic buildings: London Road Police and Fire Station, insurance buildings, banks and the Royal Exchange, as well as medical institutions on Oxford Road. The fashion for the Baroque and the use of terracotta, faience and glazed tiles in elaborately decorated monumental buildings may be seen as an expression of the superficial opulence and decadence of the time. The next subsection, 'Municipal Interventions and the Incorporation of "Greater Manchester"' will then turn attention to important municipal interventions with the expansion of the powers of Manchester Corporation. This may have been the phase when the surrounding suburban townships were formally incorporated into the city, but this was made possible by the extension of the municipal run utilities of water, gas and electricity. The city council was the driving force behind a distinctive civic culture that emerged at this time through creating and administrating new educational institutions, a branch library system, municipal swimming pools, housing, parks and recreation grounds throughout the newly expanded conurbation. Fourthly, 'Conspicuous Leisure and Popular Culture' will examine the rise of urban leisure and popular culture in Manchester at the turn of the century in terms of the geography of theatres, cinemas, pubs, sporting venues and pleasure gardens, which become a notable feature of the city and an intrinsic element of its urban identity. This discussion of the architecture of popular culture will then lead on to the final subsection which analyses the way in which the working class presence became a more visible component of Manchester, 'The Working Class and the Built Environment'. The late nineteenth century saw the resurgence of class politics and the emergence of a socialist and labour movement. This corresponded with a general decline in liberal values of class deference and acquiescence, especially during the period known as the Labour Unrest, 1910–1914. Although there are very few buildings of the labour movement still standing, the working-class presence in the city can be traced in the new charitable institutions established to alleviate poverty, the co-operative movement that was based in Manchester, and the places and spaces of working-class politics and protests.

This chapter concludes with a discussion of the end of the phase, characterised by a new era of urban development. This is defined by the establishment of garden suburbs and semi-rural council estates, and the corresponding end to the redbrick terraced working-class districts which had been such an iconic feature of the Victorian and Edwardian city.

Transport Innovations and the Creation of 'Greater Manchester'

The French impressionist painter, Pierre Adolphe Valette, who lived and worked in Manchester from 1905 until 1928, produced some of the most evocative paintings of the Edwardian city. In a series of large-scale canvases, Adolphe Valette captured the atmosphere of Manchester's streets and waterways cloaked in fog, mist and rain, from the street scenes of Albert Square and All Saints (Chorlton-on-Medlock) to the river scenes of the Irwell and the Medlock. These blurred and watery scenes, in which the solid city becomes almost liquid-like, convey aspects of the urban dynamics and transformations at the turn of the century, as Manchester embraced rising modernity.

Fig. 5.5 Adolphe Valette, *Oxford Road, Manchester*, 1910. Image courtesy of Manchester Art Galleries.

Adolphe Valette's 1910 composition titled *Oxford Road, Manchester* stands out in this respect as a study of modes of transports, old and new. It depicts the main thoroughfare leading into the city from the south at the point where the viaduct of Manchester South Junction and Altrincham Railway crosses the road. While the presence of a rail locomotive is indicated by the steam rising from behind the building on the right, pedestrians are shown strolling purposely along the pavements, with horse-drawn carriages, an electric tram, and even a motorcar moving in and out of the city. The overhead cables powering the new tram network are clearly visible, with the looming presence of Alfred Waterhouse's Refuge Assurance Building seen under construction in the background.

New Railways and Train Stations

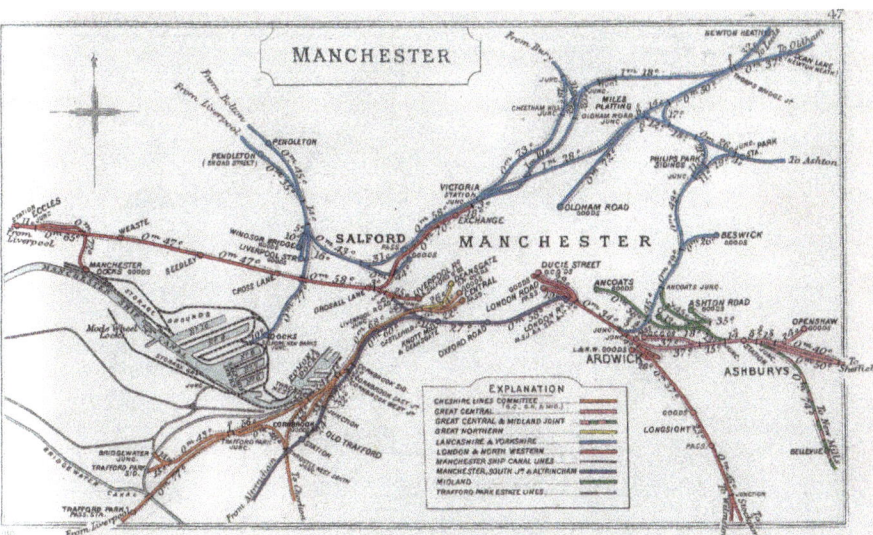

Fig. 5.6 Map of Manchester and Salford railways, 1910. Wikimedia Commons, public domain, https://commons.wikimedia.org/wiki/File:Manchester_RJD_47. JPG#/media/File:Manchester_RJD_47.JPG

This phase of development was characterised by significant new improvements in Manchester's transport infrastructure. This was not just defined by the transformation of the city into a port with the completion of the Manchester Ship Canal, but also by innovations in the rail and tram networks which became integrated together. The 1910 map of Manchester and Salford railways (Fig. 5.6) depicts the network at its height, tightly integrated with the train lines and sidings of Trafford Park and the Port of Manchester. It was in 1880 that Manchester gained a new, fourth railway terminus with Central Station opening on the southern edge of the business district by the Cheshire Lines Committee. It served the Midland Railway which ran an express service to London St Pancras, as well as the Great Northern and Manchester Sheffield and Lincolnshire Railway. Although closed in 1969 due to the post-Beecham 'rationalisation' of the network, the huge wrought-iron and glass train shed survives, now used as a conference centre (G-Mex). On the western side of the station is the enormous five-storey Great Northern Goods Warehouse, opened in 1898, and the Great Northern Railway

Offices, which form a single integrated range stretching along the entire southern limit of Deansgate from Peter Street. The warehouse was directly connected to the Port of Manchester and Trafford Park, together with the canal network, as it was built over the line of the Manchester and Salford Junction Canal with a specialised hydraulic system to move goods direct to and from barges.

Fig. 5.7 Great Northern Railway Offices, Deansgate (Author, 2023).

Fig. 5.8 Victoria Station (Author, 2025).

5. *City of Ambition and Popular Culture, c.1890–c.1920* 223

It was also during the 1880s that the terminus at Piccadilly (London Road Station) was enlarged when the present glass train-shed roof was installed, supported by wrought iron trusses and columns, elaborately decorated with foliated 'Corinthian' capitals. Victoria Station (Fig. 5.8) also underwent several expansions during the later nineteenth century, and by 1909 it had reached its peak, with seventeen platforms and a new station building. This was an impressive four-storey structure with thirty-one bays, constructed with a neo-Baroque facade at right angles to the original Hunts Bank Station for the Lancashire and Yorkshire Railway. Victoria Station has the best surviving station facilities, with an Edwardian wood-panelled booking hall complete with a magnificent glazed tiled map of the Lancashire and Yorkshire Railway network, a café with a glass dome and the original first-class restaurant and adjacent bookstall, all with coloured, Art Nouveau mosaic lettering. Immediately adjacent to Victoria Station, over the River Irwell in Salford, was Exchange Station, established in 1884 for the London and North Western Railway. The station was subsequently demolished with only the approach roads from Deansgate and Blackfriars and the retaining walls indicating its former presence.

Fig. 5.9 Castlefield's railway viaducts (Author, 2011).

The colour coding and table of the 1910 map of the Manchester and Salford railways (see Fig. 5.6) indicates that the network was built and maintained by private companies that competed with each other. It is this that led to the proliferation of lines—a distinctive feature of Britain's railway infrastructure, in contrast to the state-initiated continental developments. The combined brilliance and total irrationality of such a privatised system is superbly illustrated in Manchester at Castlefield, where four separate viaducts converge as they span the Bridgewater Canal Basin. These were all built in different materials and architectural styles, from the plain brick-built viaducts of Manchester and South Junction and Altrincham Railways of 1846 and 1849, to the crenelated brick and wrought iron viaduct of the Midland Railway of 1877, and the castellated tubular steel columns of the Great Northern Railway of 1898, both of which ran out of Central Station.

Trams

Adolphe Valette's painting of Oxford Road, as noted earlier, contains the silhouette of an electric tram. What is interesting about the composition is that it records the privileged status of trams in terms of traffic management. The central part of the road is clearly left open to allow the free movement and passing of trams up and down Oxford Road, while horse and carriages, as well as the motor car, are confined to the sides of the road. Certainly, the establishment of Manchester Corporation Tramways in 1901 represented an important and successful achievement. The municipal authorities took over and electrified the tram services in Manchester and expanded public transport for the working class, which consolidated the integration of suburban townships with the city centre. Horse-drawn omnibuses were first introduced in Manchester by John Greenwood in 1824 to serve middle-class commuters who lived in affluent suburbs. This network was expanded in 1865 when the Manchester Carriage Company was formed to run services throughout the city and then grew again with the emergence of the Manchester Carriage and Tramways Company in 1880, as the 1870 Tramways Act granted municipal authority powers to lay tramways (although it also prevented them from directly operating tram services). But when the Corporation took full control in 1901, a more integrated and modernised electric tram system was established, with Manchester possessing the second largest network in the country, outside London.

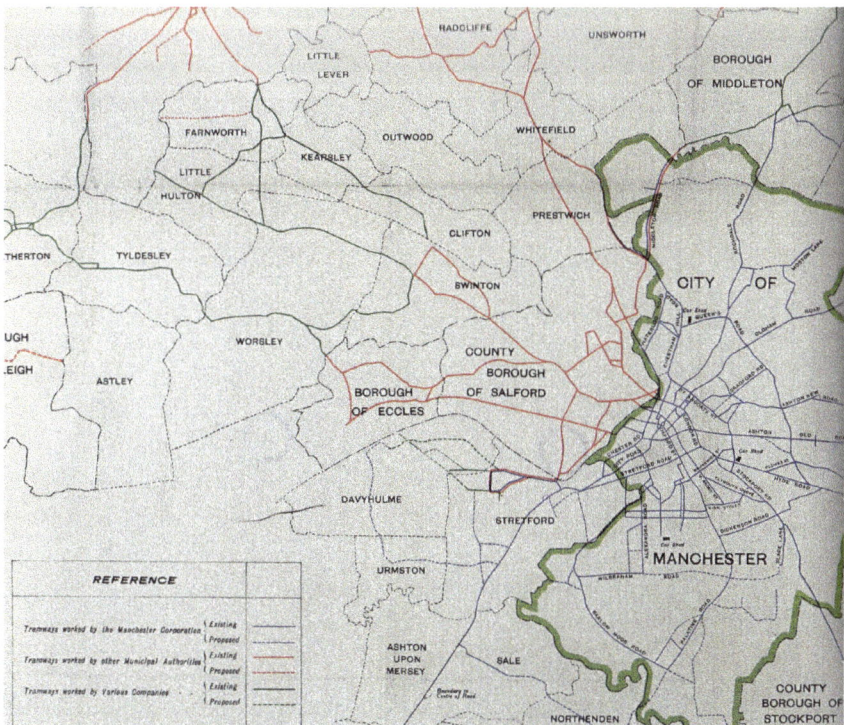

Fig. 5.10 Manchester Corporation, existing and proposed tramways in Manchester and neighbouring boroughs and districts, 1916. Image courtesy of Manchester Libraries.

The introduction of the cheap, one-penny fares in 1888 allowed skilled and semi-skilled workers to move out from the inner suburbs, and was a key factor in the geographical expansion of the city with the proletarianisation of previous middle-class suburbs, such as Rusholme, Fallowfield and Levenshulme. Trams were 'gondolas of the people', to use Richard Hoggart's phrase, that allowed suburban living to be enjoyed by sections of the working class. By the end of the nineteenth century and start of the twentieth century, new blocks of by-law terraced houses extended beyond the inner working-class districts in all directions around the city, as housing building followed new tram routes.

The transformative nature of tramways in helping forge a 'Greater Manchester' is reflected in the time zone map produced by Manchester City Council in 1916 (Fig. 5.11). This depicts how trams running along the main arterial roads created a star-shaped urban pattern, as suburbs of up to five miles from the centre could be reached in under half an hour. As a result, passenger numbers rapidly increased in early twentieth-century Manchester, as trams encouraged the spread and growth of suburbs. Penny fares also altered leisure activities of the urban population, facilitating shopping trips and travel to sporting events which now became feasible on a regular basis.

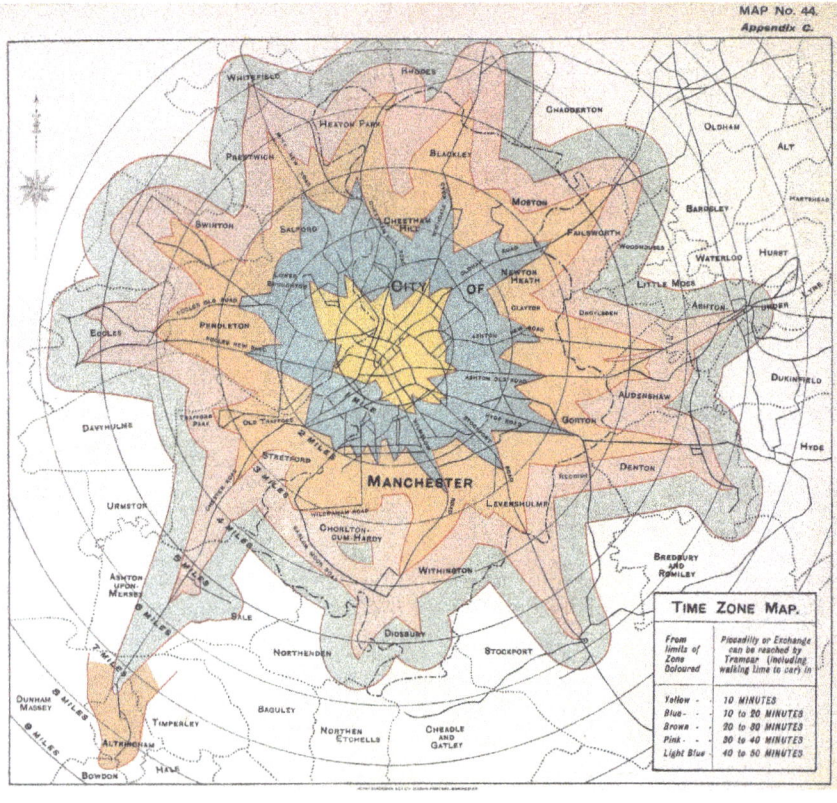

Fig. 5.11 Time-zone map of tramways in Manchester and surrounding districts, 1916. Image courtesy of Manchester Libraries.

Despite the geographical and social impact of electric trams, by the end of the 1930s they had become obsolete with the car and bus becoming the more favoured form of transport. The last electric tram ran in 1949. However, although this Edwardian municipal tram network has long gone, two of the three car sheds, or tram depots, survive; one on Cheetham Hill, at Queens Road, and the other at Ardwick on Hyde Road, both of which are currently used as depots for Stagecoach buses. The civic pride embodied in these municipal investments is expressed in the use of the Corporation's coat of arms to adorn the front of the car sheds at the Cheetham Hill depot.

Fig. 5.12 Queens Road Tram Depot, Cheetham Hill (Author, 2021).

Returning to Valette's 1910 painting of Oxford Road, it is significant that different modes of transport are depicted juxtaposed. Alongside a tram and motorcar are horse-drawn carriages. This illustrates that, despite the new innovations, traditional forms of transport still dominated Manchester's streets as the city remained dependent on the horse—a feature attested by the presence of horse troughs. Although most have long since been removed, there are occasional reminders of what have been a ubiquitous feature of street furniture. A late nineteenth-century example can be found in Withington, on Copson Street which originally stood at the junction of Wilmslow Road and Palatine Road. Another, in its original location, can be found on the junction of Manchester Road and Audenshaw Road, erected in 1879 with the inscription 'A righteous man regardeth of the life of his beast'. Others can be found in Greater Manchester, some in association with drinking fountains.

The Baroque Revival and the Architecture of Decadence

Midland Hotel

Midland Railway built the Midland Hotel next to the Central Station terminus as a northern counterpoint to Midland Grand Hotel at St Pancras Station. Although perhaps not as impressive as George Gilbert Scott's London hotel, Charles Trubshaw's Manchester's Midland Hotel is widely regarded as one of the region's finest. It was built between 1898 and 1903 on a two-acre site facing onto St Peter's Square, and included a Palm Court (winter garden), consort hall-cum-theatre, Turkish baths, among other recreational and retail facilities, alongside four-hundred bedrooms. It may not have been attached to the station like the hotel at St Pancras, but a covered walkway joined the hotel to the train station to protect travellers from Manchester's inclement weather. The Midlands was a grand, up-market hotel, visited by many famous guests. It is claimed that the car manufacturers Charles Rolls and Henry Royce met at the hotel on 4th May 1904 and decided to go into business together, an event commemorated on a plaque in the entrance foyer. The size, design and architecture of the building reflected its status as the city's premier hotel. It was opulently decorated on all four facades in glazed terracotta and faience tiles from Burmantofts in Leeds, with impressive architectural sculpture such as the sequence of panels on the building's western façade, depicting the arts: literature, sculpture, architecture and painting (emblems of bourgeois culture).

Fig. 5.13 Midland Hotel (Author, 2022).

The Midland Hotel is a fine example of Baroque Revivalism, an architectural style that became fashionable at the turn of the century so much so that it began to define the Edwardian era. By the late nineteenth century, the city centre was endowed with many grand public buildings in many different architectural styles, with Classical, Italian Renaissance and Gothic structures juxtaposed together. Such architectural historicism and eclecticism were prominent features of the cityscape, a pattern that continued into the twentieth century. The proliferation of different architectural styles reflected the increasing commercialisation and commodification of the built environment. Yet at the same time, it is notable that richly ornamented Baroque designs grew more popular during this phase of development, overtaking interest in the Gothic, to become the most prominent style of the age. Many conspicuous commercial and public buildings constructed at the time were influenced by Baroque Revival designs, as well as related Jacobean and Queen Anne styles that focused upon surface decoration and ornamentation, exploiting the potential of terracotta and faience ceramic wares in blocks and slabs, as well as bricks and tiles, glazed or unglazed.

The London Road Police and Fire Station, along with Midland Hotel, is a standout example of Manchester's Baroque Revival. It was completed in 1906 as the headquarters of the fire brigade, and incorporated a police station, ambulance station and coroner's court (amongst other things). The building was clearly designed as a monument to municipal power and order on the southern approach into the city by Piccadilly railway terminus, combining Hawksmoorish turrets, terracotta sculpture and architectural modelling with allegorical representations of Courage, Vigilance, Justice, Truth, etc. It was from this site that working-class demonstrators were hosed down to stop them from marching into the city centre during a 1931 unemployment protest.

Fig. 5.14 London Road Police and Fire Station (Author, 2023).

Insurance Buildings, Banks and the Royal Exchange

The Baroque was also a popular style for insurance offices and banks. The Refuge Assurance Building on Oxford Road, which was built in three stages between 1891 and 1932 and designed principally by Alfred and Paul Waterhouse, is another great example of the use of the Baroque on a commercial structure. Valette's 1910 *Oxford Street, Manchester* shows it under construction. It was clad in pressed brick and terracotta and includes a sixteenth-century Italian-style clock tower which forms a distinctive feature on Manchester's skyline. The vast open business hall on the ground floor is sumptuously decorated in Burmantofts faience and glazed brick in butterscotch shades. The size and grandeur of the structure is an architectural statement of the prominence of Manchester as a major centre of insurance.

There are many other examples of Baroque Revival insurance and commercial offices, particularly on the main thoroughfares of the central business district, such as on Oxford Street (Tootal Building, 1898 and St James' Building, 1912), Whitworth Street (Harry Smith Fairhurst's India House, 1906 and Lancaster House, 1910) and Cross Street, which has the most attractive collection of Edwardian office blocks. Here can be found several examples of the work of the Manchester-based architect Charles Heathcote, who specialised in Edwardian Baroque, including his insurance building, Eagle Star House (1911), and Lloyds Bank (1915) which was built out of Portland stone.

Fig. 5.15 Refuge Assurance Building, Oxford Road (Author, 2023).

Fig. 5.16 Eagle Star House, Cross Street (Author, 2022).

Heathcote (along with Fairhurst) was an architect who made an enduring mark on Manchester during this phase. Buildings of his design, for instance, dominate the view looking up King Street to Spring Gardens, which include the former Parrs Bank (1902) on the corner of York Street, another superb example of Heathcote's use of bold Edwardian Baroque, this time in red sandstone. He even helped plan Trafford Park industrial estate, being employed by both British Westinghouse and Ford Motor Company.

Fig. 5.17 Parrs Bank, Spring Gardens (Author, 2023).

Another commercial building worth noting here alongside this discussion of insurance buildings and banks, is the Royal Exchange. This institution, like the Royal Infirmary, was a constant throughout the five phases of this study. It was first established in 1729 and substantially rebuilt and enlarged four times during its history. The structure that stands today was the result of a remodelling of the Mills and Murgatroyd Exchange of 1867, by Bradshaw, Gass and Hope between 1914 and 1921. The exterior was extensively rebuilt, with the pedimented entrance portico on Cross Street removed to allow for the widening of the street, and the whole structure heightened and enlarged so that it filled an entire city block. The final exchange was therefore a mega-structure that could accommodate all eleven thousand members and represented the largest trading building in the world. It had an Italianate Neoclassical designed facade with numerous Baroque architectural details: Corinthian columns and pilasters; balustraded parapets and an elaborate colonnaded corner tower with turret.

Fig. 5.18 The Royal Exchange (from the corner of Cross Street and Market Street) (Author, 2022).

Medical Institutions and Oxford Road

Baroque architecture was also embraced by Manchester's medical institutions that were relocated from the city centre and grouped together on Oxford Road by the Victoria University during the late nineteenth and early twentieth century (thus consolidating Oxford Road's status as the preeminent route into the city). This group included: the Royal Eye Hospital (1886); the Royal Infirmary (1908); Dental Hospital (1909); and St Mary's Maternity Hospital (1909). Of these, both the Dental Hospital and Royal Infirmary were constructed in a striking Greenwich Baroque style, utilising redbrick and Portland stone. The grand entrance to the Royal Infirmary had a central domed tower with a relief showing the Good Samaritan, with the pavilions either side with colonnaded corner towers (although only one of the pavilions survives due to war damage). The Royal Eye Hospital and St

Mary's in contrast were built in redbrick and terracotta with Baroque details. Opposite, and forming part of this Edwardian group of civic institutions on Oxford Road, is the Whitworth Institute, now Art Gallery. This Jacobean-style building was founded through a bequest from the famous industrialist Joseph Whitworth, and was set within a park and constructed in stages between 1894 to 1908 in redbrick and terracotta.

Fig. 5.19 The Royal Infirmary, Oxford Road (Author, 2023).

The wholesale embracing of the Baroque style (as well as Jacobean and Queen Anne styles) was a national fashion and certainly architects such as Heathcote and Fairhurst were following the latest trends. Terracotta and faience had the added advantage of durability—resistant to the effects of smoke and soot—and therefore ideal materials for buildings in cities like Manchester, with its infamous wet weather. However, the Baroque Revival also gave architectural expression to the wider ambitions and anxieties of the time. Richly decorated buildings conveyed the wealth and exuberance of the Edwardian era, and so were appropriate for a time of growing conspicuous consumption and display. But it is hard to detect the social or moral message these Baroque buildings were attempting to project, in contrast to the earlier phases of Classical,

Italianate and Gothic designs. The detailed ornamentation was just surface deep and therefore the Baroque Revival represented quite a superficial splendour. It might be seen as a form of architectural decadence that masked the growing concerns about Britain's place in the world of industrial competitors. It is therefore ironic that, in this final phase of the expansion of industrial Manchester, the dominant architectural style returns to that favoured during the initial phase of development. It is as if the tradition of architectural historicism that had started in the eighteenth century had run out of road and lost direction.

Municipal Interventions and the Incorporation of 'Greater Manchester'

The late nineteenth and early twentieth century was characterised by the expansion of municipal power in Manchester, which saw the formal incorporation of suburban townships into the city, as well as a more interventionist approach on behalf of the city council in terms of managing and regulating the built environment. In particular, it was the improvements in the transport infrastructure, especially the establishment of an integrated tram network, alongside the local rail lines and stations, that laid the basis for the extension of the municipal boundaries. Between 1885 and 1931, Manchester successively subsumed the surrounding townships. In 1885, Harpurhey, Bradford and Rusholme were added to the original borough, followed by Crumpsall, Blackley and Moston, Newtown Heath, Clayton, Openshaw and West Gorton in 1890. Heaton Park was incorporated in 1903, Moss Side, Chorlton-cum-Hardy , Withington, Burnage and Didsbury in 1904, while Levenshulme and the rest of Gorton were added in 1909. The city of Manchester then reached its geographic and demographic extent with the acquisition of Wythenshawe in 1931. As one writer in the 1930s complained:

> Manchester, like a mouth gaping enormously, swallowed up village after village. After Fallowfield went Withington, then Didsbury. Soon the great jaws were mumbling at the edge of Cheshire. The engulfed villages lay only half digested in the monster's stomach. Each of them still preserved

some resemblance to what it had been once, though some were more decayed than others. (cited in Kidd and Wyke 2016, 311)

Fig. 5.20 Manchester's civic boundaries, 1931 (Kidd 2002, 202, all rights reserved).

This expansion of the city's boundaries coincided with the extension of the municipal powers as rising rates made the city council more prosperous. Although liberal political philosophy still permeated elite thinking, Manchester did embrace what became known as 'municipal socialism' (or more accurately 'municipal capitalism') after the success of places like Birmingham when Joseph Chamberlain was mayor and pioneered the philosophy of the 'civic gospel'. This led to significant interventions at the turn of the century, involving large-scale capital investments with a focus on improving public utilities. In part, this was a reflection of the changing political climate due to the impact of the rise of new socialist politics and the social democracy of labourism which triggered a move towards New Liberalism and a more social approach to the problems of urbanism. Major municipal projects undertaken in Manchester included the construction of Thirlmere Aqueduct, which was completed by 1894, the opening of the Ship Canal and the Port of Manchester in the same year, and the electrification of the tram system in 1901. The city councils in both Manchester and Salford saw their responsibility as providing fresh water, gas and electricity supplies, an efficient public transport network, as well as an effective sewage disposal system. These public utilities became directly controlled by the municipal authorities and became a new source of civic pride.

Gas, Water and Electricity Installations

In Salford, the Corporation Gas Board office still stands in Bloom Street. This Worthington-like, Gothic building with a central tower with corner tourelles, was built in 1880 and acted as the public front of the Bloom Street Gas Works. Although both Manchester and Salford possessed a number of gas works by the end of the nineteenth century, with the distinctive steel gas holders forming iconic landmarks well into the twentieth century, these have all now been removed, apart from two at Bradford Road Gas Works which have been left as a reminder of what used to be a common urban sight in working-class districts (as this is where gas works were typically positioned).

Fig. 5.21 Gas Board Offices, Bloom Street, Salford (Author, 2023).

Fig. 5.22 Gas holder at Bradford Road Gas Works (Author, 2023).

If the Manchester Ship Canal was evidence of the scale of ambition and geographical reach of the Corporation, so was the opening of the Thirlmere Aqueduct which was built in phases between 1890 and 1925 by Manchester Corporation Water Works. From 1894, the Thirlmere Aqueduct brought millions of gallons of water daily from the Lake District along a ninety-six-mile pipeline directly into the city, solving Manchester's supply problems.

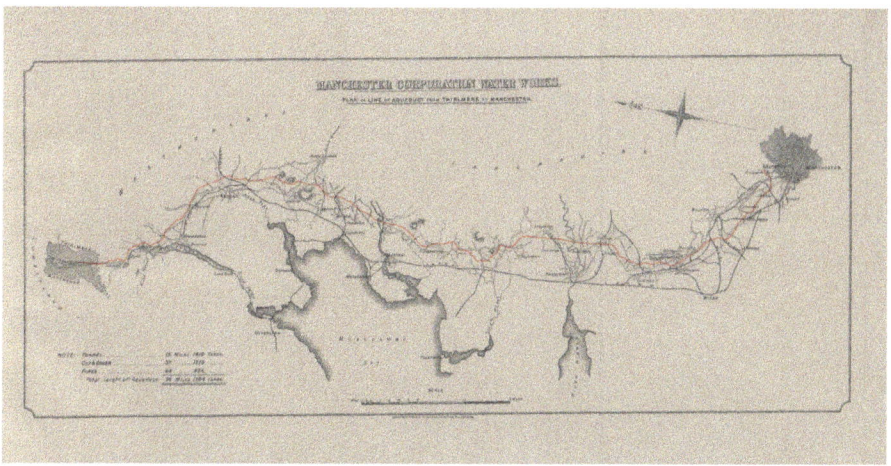

Fig. 5.23 Manchester Corporation Water Works – Plan of line of Aqueduct from Thirlmere to Manchester, 1894, Wikipedia Commons, https://commons.wikimedia.org/wiki/File:Blacklock_%26_Co.(1894)_p73_-_Manchester_Corporation_Water_Works_-_Plan_of_Line_of_Aqueduct_from_Thirlmere_to_Manchester.jpg

In addition to securing an adequate supply of water for an expanding city, Manchester Corporation was responsible for constructing a high-pressure hydraulic system to power lifts, cranes and cotton baling presses in textile warehouses within the city centre. There were originally three power stations driving this hydraulic system in Whitworth Street, Pitt Street and Water Street. Only the one in Water Street survives, integrated now into the People's History Museum. This was completed in 1909 and designed by Henry Price, the Corporation's architect (whose other works will be discussed in more detail below).

Fig. 5.24 Hydraulic Pumping Station, Water Street (Author, 2023).

Fig. 5.25 Wilburn Street Basin, Salford (Author, 2023).

The supply of fresh water was linked to the issue of sanitation, which both Manchester and Salford corporations increasingly took direct responsibility for. In 1890, for instance, the Manchester authorities constructed a series of intercepting sewers that carried waste away to a treatment plant at Davyhulme where a sewage works was constructed in 1894, which is still in operation today. It was during this decade that further local by-laws were passed to make sure all new residential housing was equipped with indoor plumbing and to force landlords to refit existing housing. Similar developments took place in Salford, where a surviving waste management basin can be found at Wilburn Street, opening onto the River Irwell. This site was developed by Salford Corporation in the 1880s to collect 'night-soil' to transport it to the market gardens on Chat Moss. The basin contains purpose-built chutes to deposit the human waste into waiting river barges.

Fig. 5.26 Manchester Corporation Electricity Works sub-station, Heaton Moor (Author, 2023).

In contrast to gas and water, the supply of electricity was something specifically new to this phase, and the local authorities were directly involved from the start. Manchester Corporation built its first coal-fired electrical power station in Dickinson Street in 1893 (off Portland Street). Although this building is no longer standing, there is a lot that still survives, as much of the infrastructure of power stations and sub-stations is still in use today. It is significant that both Salford and Manchester Corporation Electricity Works were high-quality designs, reflecting pride in the local government's role in providing this new form of power. The electricity stations at Fredrick Road, Salford, and Winser Street by the Rochdale Canal in Manchester, for instance, were housed in monumental structures that remain prominent buildings in today's cityscape. As municipal installations, these electricity works characteristically display the city's coat of arms. The 1902 sub-station at Heaton Moor, for instance, built as a Baroque-styled redbrick and terracotta structure has the initials M. C. E. W (Manchester Corporation Electricity Works) proudly inscribed above the entrance and below the segmental pediment bearing Manchester Corporation's coat of arms. It is interesting that the middle-class suburb of Heaton Moor was not and did not become part of the City of Manchester. The extension of municipal facilities beyond the boundaries of the city therefore reveals the expansionist aspirations of the council. Other, smaller sub-stations from this phase can be found dotted throughout Greater Manchester, such as the one integrated in a street of by-law terraced housing at the end of Brailsford Street in Fallowfield (which also prominently displays the city's coat of arms on the side of the structure).

Fig. 5.27 Electricity substations, Brailsford Road, Fallowfield (with a plague displaying the city's coat of arms) (Author, 2023).

Educational Institutions

By the early twentieth century, the civic amenities that local government were directly involved in had broadened and now involved the provision of technical and further education, the building of municipal housing, alongside the creation and supervision of public parks, baths and wash houses as well as district libraries. It was the broadening and extension of these municipal interventions into the suburban townships that helped integrate the expanding city. Municipal schools, libraries, swimming baths and parks were the means for both forging local communities and constructing a collective Mancunian identity.

Anxieties about Britain's perceived economic decline in face of competition from its industrial revivals prompted concerns that the country was suffering from entrepreneurial and technological shortcomings. It was feared that weaknesses in education meant that Britain was being outpaced in technology and so needed to emulate the Technische Hochschulen (technical universities) of its greatest rival, Germany. In Manchester, the Corporation responded by setting up the Municipal Technical School in 1892 which was housed in a prestigious new building on Sackville Street, opened by the Prime Minister of the time, Arthur Balfour, in 1902. This grand five-storey building in Loire style was lavishly decorated with Burmantofts terracotta panels with Renaissance motifs, as well as the city's coat of arms. The school soon became one of the country's leading centres for technical and scientific education and became integrated into the Victoria University of Manchester in 1905 as the Faculty of Technology. It was extended in 1927 with a large block facing Whitworth Street (although this was not fully completed until 1957).

Fig. 5.28 Manchester Municipal Technical School, Sackville Street (Author, 2023).

Fig. 5.29 Royal Salford Technical Institute, Chapel Street (Author, 2023).

A similar development occurred in Salford with the establishment of the Royal Salford Technical Institute in 1896 which later became part of the University of Salford. This formed a long, three-storey, Renaissance-style structure in redbrick with fine terracotta panels, with reliefs representing the Arts and Sciences.

It was also in 1892 that Manchester's School of Art that had been housed in 1880 Gothic building on Cavendish Street in Grosvenor Square in Chorlton-on-Medlock became the Municipal School of Art. The building was extended in 1897 in redbrick and orange terracotta. Between 1893 and 1899, the famous Arts and Craft artist and socialist, Walter Crane, was Director of Design at the Municipal School of Art, and the artist Adolphe Valette taught there between 1906 and 1920, influencing the work of L. S. Lowry, who was one of his pupils.

5. City of Ambition and Popular Culture, c.1890–c.1920

Fig. 5.30 Manchester Central School, Whitworth Street (Author, 2022).

The 1870 Education Act had allowed local authorities to open Board Schools, but this was replaced by the 1902 Education Act, known as the Balfour Act. This established local educational authorities (LEA) which would directly administer a system of primary, secondary and technical schools. Manchester's thirty-nine Board Schools were brought into LEA control and new schools established throughout the expanded borough. Manchester Central School on Whitworth Street, now Shena Simon College, was opened in 1900 as the city's 34th Board School (and was taken over by the LEA to become the Central High School in 1920). It was built in redbrick and orange terracotta with a polygonal corner turret, and became the hub of secondary education in Manchester, associated with five other high schools in the city.

District Libraries

Fig. 5.31 Crumpsall and Cheetham District Library (Author, 2022).

Fig. 5.32 Didsbury District Library (Author, 2023).

Together with these educational provisions, Manchester Corporation had responsibility for setting up district libraries throughout the borough in order to encourage rational recreation and further learning amongst the population. The free library movement had been embraced by the city authorities after the passing of the 1850 Public Libraries Act (as has been discussed in Chapter 3). Liberals regarded the free library as central to the creation of a civic public sphere, focused on individual rational recreation and self-help. But it was also perceived as an institution that could help shape new urban communities. The open plan design of the interior of most libraries provided space for social interaction (albeit under the discipline of silence) and cultural display. Alongside the books, libraries were often decorated with busts, paintings and mosaics depicting the 'great and the good' in terms of national and local figures of importance. So, a distinctive feature of Manchester's library developments was the coexistence of a central library together with branch libraries in residential districts. By 1895, the city had eleven branches and many more were to follow as the city boundaries expanded.

Such municipal building projects led to the creation of the City Architect's Department in 1902. The first person to hold the office of City Architecture was Henry Price. During his tenure between 1902 and his retirement in 1934, Price was responsible for many of the city's landmark municipal buildings, including several libraries. Crumpsall and Cheetham District Library, completed in 1911, was one of them (Fig. 5.31). It is an Edwardian Baroque structure with two symmetrical gables and semi-domed porch, with the facade decorations including four cartouche panels with the names of Scott, Milton, Shakespeare and Dickens. Unfortunately, the library has moved to a new location making the future of the building uncertain. Other examples of Price's libraries are still very much in use. Price designed three of Manchester's Carnegie libraries (named after the Scottish-American industrialist and major philanthropist who endowed many public libraries in the United States, Britain and the British Empire) at Chorlton, Didsbury and Withington. Chorlton District Library was opened in 1914 also in Edwardian Baroque, while at Didsbury he adopted a Gothic design for his 1915 library (Fig. 5.32), and a Neoclassical one for his library at Withington (1927). Each of these libraries was positioned in a prominent public location and the use of different architectural styles gave a distinct identity to each township. At Levenshulme there is a small, Carnegie-funded library built in 1904 by James Jepson in Jacobean style, placed adjacent to the Chapel Street Board School, the municipal park and directly opposite Levenshulme's wash house and what was to become the public baths. This library therefore formed the nucleus of a new township centre known as Back

Levenshulme, that served an undifferentiated working-class community living in the blocks of Edwardian by-law housing that were rapidly being built at the time on the eastern side of Stockport Road. Consequently, this township became geographically and socially split between the earlier middle-class suburb that grew up around Levenshulme station on the western side of Stockport Road, which became more socially mixed, and this solid, working-class district on the eastern side.

Slightly later in date, the erection of Central Library at St Peter's Square at the heart of the city, represents the culmination of this phase of municipal library building. This was the headquarters of Manchester's free public library network and by far the largest reference collection in the city. It was designed by E. Vincent Harris, and built between 1930 and 1934 as an enormous circular structure in Portland stone in a design inspired by the Pantheon in Rome, with its rotunda dome and an interior reading room resembling the one at the British Museum. This was clearly a monument of civic pride and symbol of British imperialism (as well as the Pantheon, the exterior gives a nod towards the facade of the Colosseum). It was opened by King George V with a commemorative plaque by the entrance directly celebrating empire and Britain's colonies: 'George V, by the grace of God of Great Britain, Ireland and the British Dominions beyond the seas King, Defender of the Faith, Emperor of India, opened this library'. At the time, it was the world's largest municipal library and regarded as the 'British Museum of the North'.

Fig. 5.33 Manchester Central Library (Author, 2025).

Public Swimming Baths

Fig. 5.34 Victoria Baths, Chorlton-on-Medlock (Author, 2022).

As City Architect, Henry Price was responsible for designing municipal swimming baths as well as public libraries. Like libraries, baths became iconic landmarks in the townships of Manchester and emblems of local civic pride. By 1838, the Corporation could boast of possessing thirty-five swimming baths, the largest and most prestigious of these being Victoria Baths on Hathersage Road in Chorlton-on-Medlock. This grand Baroque Revival structure, with steep gables and a clock cupola, was ornately decorated with polychrome brickwork and terracotta with separate entrances for Males First Class, Males Second Class and Females (an expression of Britain's entrenched class and gendered hierarchies). On its opening, the Lord Mayor of Manchester described the building as a 'water palace'. The interior is generously tiled, especially in the first-class entrance foyer and staircase. It housed three swimming pools, as well as Turkish and Russian baths, together with a laundry and wash house. There was even a flat for Manchester's Superintendent of Baths and Wash Houses. Although used for most of the twentieth century, Victoria Bath was closed like many of the other municipal swimming baths in Manchester. It has been recently restored, but very few of the city's other Edwardian swimming baths survive today. Most have been closed and demolished.

Fig. 5.35 Harpurhey Baths, Rochdale Road (Author, 2022).

Harpurhey Baths, dated to 1909, is an example of a Henry Price's designed district swimming pool and wash house. It is symmetrical and built in redbrick and orange terracotta with the typical separate entrances for men and women. It was closed in 2001 but survived by being put to new purposes. The only Edwardian baths still used for its original intention is Withington Baths. Completed in 1913, this is another example of the work of Henry Price.

Municipal Housing

In terms of housing, the Corporation had been indirectly involved by setting minimum standards in the form of by-law regulations. These were steadily tightened during the second half of the nineteenth century, improving the general housing stock. The 1867 Manchester Improvement Act was the most important, and only by-law housing built after this date has survived post-war slum clearances and redevelopments. However, it was during the turn of the century that a more direct, hands-on interventionist approach was adopted by both Manchester and Salford local authorities to deal with the problem of poor, substandard working-class housing. Ancoats in Manchester had been a notorious slum with many courts and back-to-backs. The clearance of these properties along Oldham Road allowed the Corporation to erect its first municipal housing, which was completed in 1894. This consisted of a five-storey, redbrick block, arranged around a courtyard with balconies, and ground-floor shops with Queen Anne detailing of terracotta oriel windows and gables. It proudly displays the Corporation's coat-of-arms in a large panel above the entrance on Oldham Road. The block could accommodate 237 double tenements and 48 single tenements, and represented a massive improvement in Ancoats' housing stock. Still, high rents meant that these Victoria Square apartments were not fully occupied in its early years, and so they were not an immediate success in alleviating poverty living. A similar municipal residential block was built on Pollard Street on the other side of Ancoats, which has subsequently been demolished. This lack of success limited the Corporation's ambitions in municipal housing, although there was an experiment in relocating working-class families to the countryside of the outer suburbs with the building of Blackley Cottages in 1903–1904. This anticipated a marked shift in housing policy which was to define the end of this phase of development.

Fig. 5.36 Victoria Square apartments, Oldham Road, Ancoats (Author, 2023).

Other early municipal housing schemes included Salford Corporation's New Barrack Estate on Regents Road in Salford. This was built between 1900 and 1904 for dock workers at Salford Quays on the site of the early nineteenth-century Infantry Barracks in Ordsall, and comprised 353 houses and thirty-two shops in a formal layout focused around Regent Square. It was designed by the architect Henry Lord in a Queen Anne style and included community provisions of a church, St Ignatius, and the now legendry Salford Lads Club (after the famous photograph of The Smiths album *The Queen is Dead*).

Fig. 5.37 Salford Lads Club, New Barrack Estate, Ordsall (and Ragnhild Steinshamn) (Author, 2021).

Suburban Parks and Recreational Spaces

Further, municipal parks became a major element in Manchester's urban geography with the Corporation's Parks and Cemeteries Committee responsible for establishing and maintaining parks and recreation spaces throughout the expanded borough. Manchester already had four large municipal parks, with Philips, Peel and Queens parks opening in 1846 and Alexandra Park in 1870. However, it was during the Edwardian period that there was a significant proliferation of local parks, both large and small, with every suburban township possessing at least one. To a certain extent there was a democratisation of parks as public spaces in the sense that parks became equipped with a diverse range of amenities which encouraged social mixing of different groups and classes of people. The presence of bandstands, boating lakes, water fountains and various sporting facilities such as bowling greens, tennis courts and football and cricket pitches led to social gatherings and crowds in parks which were no longer just places for promenading and individual perambulations. However, despite a degree of democratisation, parks were contested public spaces. Radical political gatherings were not welcomed and there were ongoing conflicts in Manchester around the right to hold political rallies and marches in its municipal parks.

Fig. 5.38 Manchester and District, 1896, showing major municipal parks in Manchester, annotated by the author (red dots = Phase 3; blue dots = Phase 4; yellow dots = Phase 5), (section of Old Ordnance Survey Maps, England Sheet 85), Alan Godfrey Maps.

It was Manchester's relentless growth that encroached on the aristocratic estates surrounding the city which opened up opportunities for the Corporation to acquire land, as the proprietors were incentivised to sell up and move on. In north Manchester, the 190-acre Boggart Hole Clough (which had been the property of the Carrill-Worsley Estate) was purchased and transformed into a country park with promenades, boating lakes, bowling green and tennis courts. Even though the Corporation attempted to police activities by banning political meetings, this was popularly resisted. Boggart Hole Clough was the focus of a campaign for free speech during 1896, with mass open-air meetings held regularly on a Sunday, with speakers including leading political figures such as by Keir Hardie, the founder of the Labour Party, and the suffragette champion, Emmeline Pankhurst. Also, on the northern edge of Manchester was Heaton Park, which was sold to Manchester City Council in 1902 by the Earl of Wilton, along with the eighteenth-century Heaton Hall. This 600-acre estate was transformed into a public park complete with a bandstand, boating lake and municipal golf course, which was opened to the public in 1912 in the former deer park. The classical facade of the Old Manchester Town Hall was moved to Heaton Park to form a monument to Manchester's civic history, which symbolically asserted municipal and public control over a former aristocratic, privately owned space. At the time, Heaton Park was the largest municipal park in Europe and served as a model for future park developments in the city. Nearer the city centre in Fallowfield, is Platt Fields Hall and park, home of the Worsley family, who put up their estate up for sale in 1907 as it was becoming surrounded by urban housing. It was bought by Manchester Corporation in 1908 and then landscaped into a municipal park with recreational facilities, including the usual boating lake, tennis courts, football and cricket pitches and bowling greens. In Salford a similar development took place when the city council bought Buile Hill mansion and the 86-acre estate in Pendelton in 1903 to convert it into a municipal park and museum.

As well as these new large municipal parks, there were numerous smaller ones in every locality in Edwardian Manchester. Some of these were totally new developments, such as Levenshulme Park (1902), Sunny Brow Park in Gorton (1905) and Crumpsall Park (1908), while others transformed the houses and grounds of urban villas, such as Birchfield Park (1888) and Crowcroft Park (1900) in Longsight, and Brookdale Park (1909) in Newtown Heath. These smaller, local parks were also contested public spaces as illustrated in the way that Ardwick Green became the scene of a major political incident around free speech in 1893. The Manchester Anarchist Communist Group used Ardwick Green as a venue to hold regular public speeches on a Sunday, which the local vicar of St Thomas objected to. The police responded, triggering a series of arrests and counter-demonstrations on each Sunday between September and December, recorded in some detail in police detective Jerome Caminada's casebook. This politicising of the public space of the park was also reflected in the citing of monuments commemorating the First World War. Ardwick Green has a fine one, a cenotaph in Portland stone to the Eighth Ardwick Battalion (embossed with the city's coat of arms), as does Boggart Hole Clough which consists of a bronze statue of Winged Victory standing on a globe on top of tall ashlar pedestal. It is perhaps no coincidence that both parks were sites of well publicised political protests. The placing of war memorials was one way that the municipal authority could reassert control of these public spaces.

Conspicuous Leisure and Popular Culture

In 1899 the Norwegian-American economist and sociologist Thorstein Veblen published his influential book *The Theory of the Leisure Class*, in which he introduced the concepts of conspicuous consumption and conspicuous leisure. Although heavily influenced by developments in the so-called 'Gilded Age' of the USA, these concepts can be usefully applied more generally. They certainly can be used to analyse the commercial and cultural developments in Manchester at the end of the nineteenth century, which witnessed the rise of elite shopping, with the growth of department stores such as Kendal's and Lewis's, as well as the expansion of prestigious cultural institutions, especially the proliferation of theatre and concert venues. Buying luxury goods and engaging in elite leisure pursuits became a fashionable way to demonstrate wealth and display rising social status. What was significant in the late nineteenth century was that these new patterns of consumption and leisure were embraced by a widening section of the population, a consequence of rising living standards and the shortening of working hours. This distinctive feature of this phase, therefore, was not so much the consuming habits of the bourgeoisie, but the spread of an urban leisure culture reflected in the music hall, cinema and organised sport venues, especially football. This was a formative time in the making of modern popular culture.

Theatres

Fig. 5.39 New Theatre (Opera House), Quay Street (Author, 2025).

Manchester had possessed a theatre since the end of the eighteenth century and Theatre Royal, built on Peter Street in 1844, represents the earliest surviving one. It was during the late nineteenth century that Peter Street, together with the adjoining Oxford Street and Quay Street, became the main focus of elite and popular entertainment venues in the city. The local theatrical architect Alfred Darbyshire built Manchester's Comedy Theatre in 1884 on Peter Street. This became the Gaiety Theatre when bought by Annie Horniman in 1908 and the unofficial home of what was known as the Manchester school of dramatists. It was demolished in 1959, but another theatre designed by Darbyshire still stands, the Palace Theatre of Varieties. This was completed in 1891 on Oxford Street on the corner of Whitworth Street. The ornate interior and domed auditorium survive, even though the exterior was subsequently clad in ugly beige tiles. At the other end of the Oxford Street–Peter

Street–Quay Street entertainment zone is the Opera House, formerly the New Theatre. This was established in 1912 and built in Neoclassical style with a facade of fluted Iconic columns and tympanum containing a relief, 'The Dawn of the Heroic Age', with the words 'The play mirrors life' below. The Halle Orchestra also had its home in this axis of streets, being first based in the Free Trade Hall on Peter Street from its inception in 1858.

Cinemas

Yet Manchester's premier entertainment zone encompassed popular, as well as elite culture. The city was quick to embrace the new popular entertainment of the moving picture at the turn of the century, and the first purpose-built cinemas were opened after the Cinematograph Act of 1909. One of the most prominent of these was the Picture House built in 1911 on Oxford Street in orange terracotta and redbrick. It is now a McDonalds. The readily affordable price for a seat meant that picture-going became a popular entertainment open to most Mancunians. Cinema buildings consequently multiplied. Other examples of Edwardian cinemas still stand, though none are used for their original purpose (apart from the 1923 Baroque-style Savoy, in Heaton Moor).

Fig. 5.40 Picture House, Oxford Street (Author, 2023).

Fig. 5.41 Grosvenor Picture Palace, Oxford Road (Author, 2025).

Grosvenor Picture Palace was opened on the corner of Grosvenor Street and Oxford Road in 1915, and at the time it was the largest cinema outside London, with a capacity to seat a thousand people. It was built in green and cream faience and terracotta tiles in what was described then as 'Roman-Corinthian of later Renaissance influence'. It is now a pub. There is also an early cinema still standing in Salford on Chapel Street. This is another ornate, showcase building with an orange terracotta exterior, decorated with Baroque swags and garlands, with a corner dome. It was opened in 1912 and is now a church.

Along with the picture house, the music hall figured prominently in Manchester's popular culture. The development of the music hall can be traced back to the mid-nineteenth century and emerged out of the tradition of pub music and concerts. The number of music halls proliferated at the turn of the century, entertaining audiences of predominantly working- and lower middle-class punters. Manchester had an array of music halls of different sizes, including two new huge halls opened in 1904, the Hippodrome on Oxford Street and the Ardwick Empire at Ardwick Green, both sadly gone. There are virtually no purpose-built Edwardian music halls and theatres left, apart from the sad remains of Hulme Hippodrome, and Victoria Theatre on Great Clowes Street in Salford, both of which are currently in a very poor state of repair, despite being listed buildings.

5. City of Ambition and Popular Culture, c.1890–c.1920   259

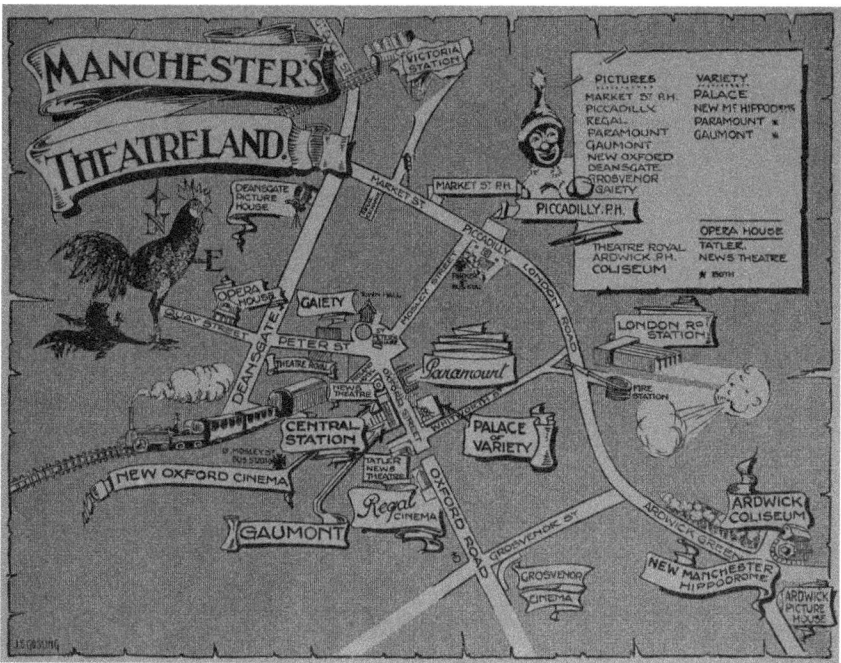

Fig. 5.42 J. Gosling's map of Manchester's Theatreland, 1937. Image courtesy of Chetham Library.

This 1937 map of Manchester's theatreland, or more accurately the central entertainment venues, highlights the zoning of theatres, cinemas and variety halls along Quay Street, Peter Street, Oxford Street and Road axis, and a concentration at the top of Ardwick Green. This pattern enhanced the status of Oxford Road as the principal thoroughfare into the city, with major buildings aligned along its route.

The 'Palace' Public House

The Edwardian era was also the heyday for the large and ornate 'palace' public house, representing continuity in the traditional pastime of beer drinking, which has remained a highly popular leisure activity in Manchester. 'The quickest way out of Manchester', as the old saying has it, 'is through the doors of a pub'! And Manchester had numerous public houses and several local breweries. Unfortunately, many of these large Edwardian hostelries have now gone and Manchester does not have the grand public houses common to other cities, such as Liverpool. However, it still retains some good smaller examples, such as the marvellous Mr Thomas's Chop House on Cross Street. This narrow Jacobean-styled structure was originally designed with a shop at the front and a chop house behind. It dates to 1901 and has an attractive interior of Art Nouveau pale terracotta tiles. The pub was one of the regular haunts of the artist L. S. Lowry. Other late Victorian and Edwardian pubs with tiled and ceramic interiors survive, such as: the Marble Arch Inn on Rochdale Road with its floor mosaics, glazed bricks and tiles and wall frieze listing alcoholic drinks and cordials; and Peveril of the Peak, with its late Victorian green ceramic faced exterior and interior rooms lined with a dado of green and cream tiles.

Fig. 5.43 Mr Thomas's Chop House, Cross Street (Author, 2021).

Sports Arenas

Organised leisure, in particular sporting activities, became an important element that defined the rise of popular culture. Clubs, associations and societies were established to support a range of leisure activities, and purpose-built venues constructed to house them. This development was not simply an extension of bourgeois 'rational recreation'. Although organised sports, especially football, were a way to channel the 'natural' rowdiness of working-class youth and teach them discipline, these activities were enthusiastically taken up by working people and refashioned to suit their own habits and tastes. Manchester was at the centre of these developments in popular culture, being the city in which the Football League was founded in 1888 and the Professional Footballers' Association established in 1907. Manchester United, formed in 1902, had originated as Newton Heath Football club, set up by the workers of the Lancashire and Yorkshire Railway Company in 1878, while Manchester City started off as the church football team of St Mark in West Gorton in 1880 as a way of drawing youth away from the allure of street gangs and 'scuttling', becoming Manchester City in 1894.

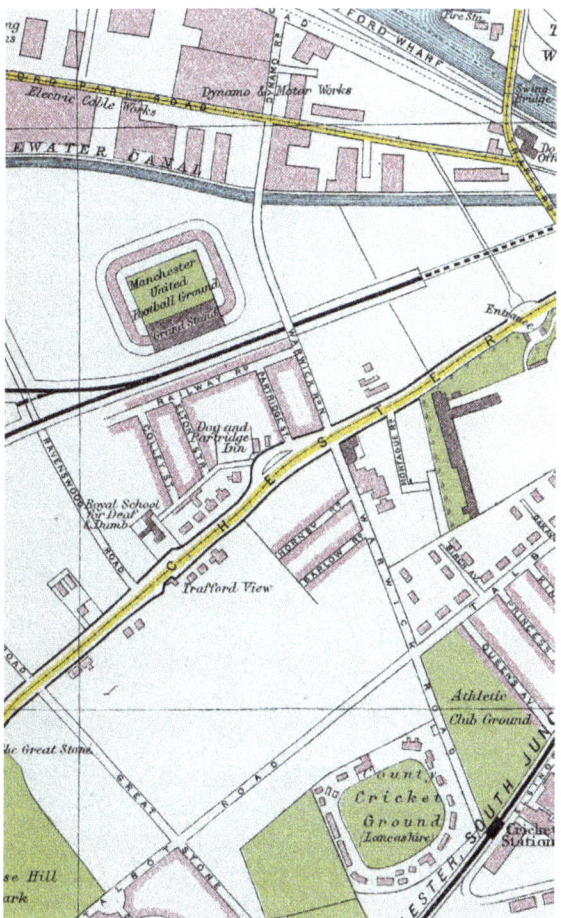

Fig. 5.44 The location of the football and cricket grounds at Old Trafford, c.1922, public domain.

Organised football required organised venues as it was a spectator sport, so football pitches and grounds became a conspicuous component of Manchester's physical fabric. United initially moved between several grounds, but success in the 1900s meant that the team relocated to a new ground at Old Trafford in 1910. It was a purpose-built stadium designed by Scottish industrial engineer Archibald Leitch, who subsequently became a prolific designer of football stadiums. Old Trafford could accommodate 80,000 spectators with the ground located near the new working-class districts around Manchester Docks and serviced by rail. City moved to a new purpose-built stadium in 1922, being relocated from Hyde Road to Maine Road in Moss Side, with a similar capacity to that of Old Trafford. Both stadiums became an integral part of the social identity of their working-class supporters.

Fig. 5.45 The Pavilion, Old Trafford Cricket Ground. Photo by Anthony O'Neil (2013), Wikimedia Commons, CC BY-SA 2.0, https://commons.wikimedia.org/wiki/File:Enlarged_pavilion_at_Old_Trafford_geograph-3720447-by-Anthony-ONeil.jpg#/media/File:Enlarged_pavilion_at_Old_Trafford_geograph-3720447-by-Anthony-ONeil.jpg

The 1922 map (Fig. 5.44) illustrates how the football ground at Old Trafford was placed close to the cricket ground that had been founded by Manchester Cricket Club in 1857. This became home of the Lancashire County Cricket Club in 1864. The late Victorian pavilion, built in 1895, still stands, although it has been disappointingly swallowed up by twenty-first-century redevelopments.

Spectator sports located in designated places and housed in purpose-built venues, therefore, were characteristic of the rise of popular culture. This was a highly commercialised culture and the basis of the leisure industry that flourished at the time. Other mass sporting events that attracted large crowds included the annual Manchester and Salford Regatta and horse racing meetings. Kersal Moor had been the traditional site of the popular Manchester races, but the racecourse moved between several venues during the nineteenth century and in the early twentieth century, with Manchester Racecourse Company shifting from grounds in Weaste back to Castle Irwell. A new course, stand and stables were built at Castle Irwell, and race meetings were regularly held there between 1901 and 1963. Now the only reminder that there was a popular racecourse at Castle Irwell is the boarded up Art Deco Racecourse Hotel, on Littleton Road. The 1923 map (Fig. 5.46) shows the racecourse and illustrates the size of this sporting venue located so close to the built-up centre of the Manchester and Salford conurbation. What is also striking about the map is how it depicts the prominence of sporting venues. Alongside the racecourse are football and cricket grounds, as well as a greyhound racecourse, recreational parks, playing fields and a golf course.

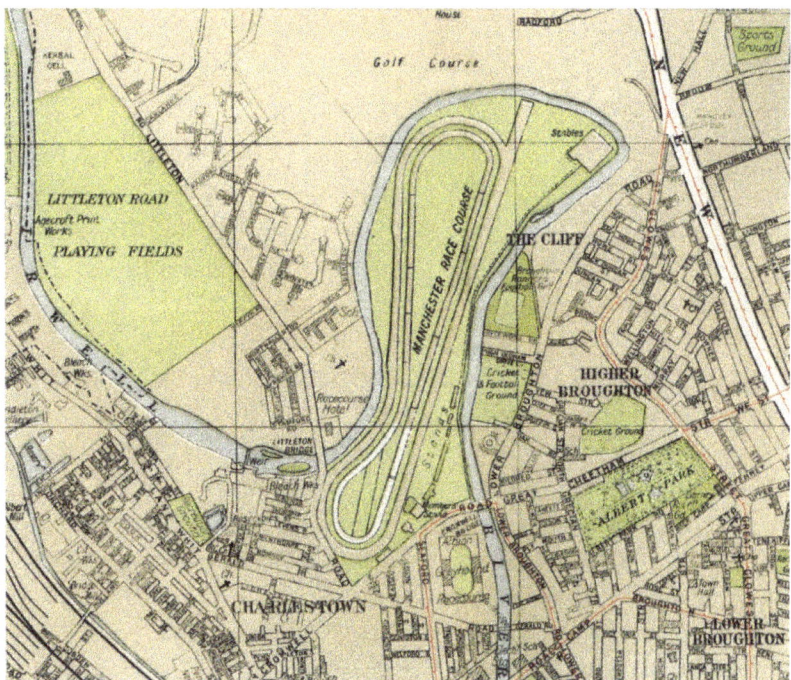

Fig. 5.46 The Castle Irwell racecourse, c.1923, public domain.

Fig. 5.47 Manchester and Salford Tennis and Racquet Club, Blackfriars Road, Salford (Author, 2025).

Although spectator sports facilitated social mixing, organised leisure was very much shaped by social class. While football was predominantly a working-class sport, golf and tennis were middle-class pursuits. It was during the later nineteenth century that the modern game of tennis took shape. The Manchester and Salford Tennis and Racquet Club was founded in 1874 and since 1880 was based on Blackfriars Road in Salford. Remarkably, the building survives and contains an indoor tennis court, as well as a squash court that was added as an upper floor in 1925.

Pleasure Gardens and Leisure Venues

Other major spaces associated with this new mass urban leisure culture included pleasure gardens, especially those at Belle Vue in Gorton, which combined a zoological garden and amusement park with sporting facilities. Established in 1836 by John Jennison, by the turn of the century it had expanded to cover 165 acres, serviced by two train stations and trams running up and down Hyde Road and Stockport Road. The scale and range of spectacles, entertainments and amusements at Bell Vue was truly impressive, and this 'palace garden' attracted over two million visitors a year in its heyday. Sporting events became a permanent feature of Belle Vue's attractions after an athletic stadium was added in 1887.

Greyhound racing was introduced in 1926 with the construction of the UK's first purpose-built greyhound stadium, and a speedway track built in 1928. Only the greyhound track remained in use after the gardens were closed in 1980.

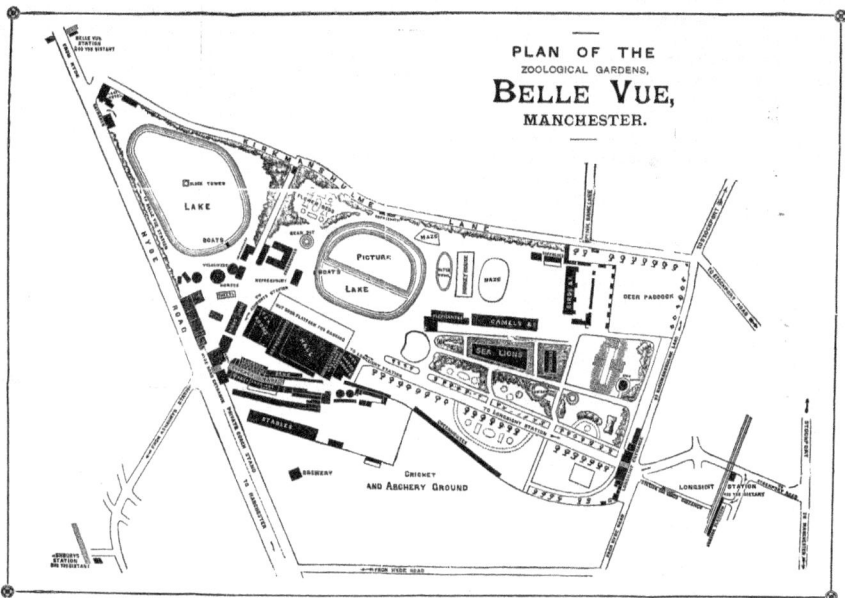

Fig. 5.48 Official guide to the Belle Vue Zoological Gardens, c.1892, Wikimedia Commons, public domain, https://commons.wikimedia.org/wiki/File:Belle_ vue_zoological_gardens_plan_1892.jpg

Competing with Belle Vue, on the other side of the city at Stretford, was White City Amusement Park, which was opened in 1907 on what had been the former site of Manchester Botanical Gardens that had hosted the Art and Treasure Exhibition of 1857. Unlike Belle Vue, White City success was short lived, as it was closed in 1928 when a stadium was built for greyhound and speedway racing. Only the gateway for the original Botanical Gardens remains standing as a physical reminder of the previous existence of White City (now a retail park).

This mass urban leisure culture, which was one of the defining components of popular culture at the turn of the twentieth century, was not simply confined to the large and central venues of Manchester; its presence was felt throughout the city's inner and outer suburbs. Each township possessed its own mix of entertainment venues, small local cinemas, theatres, and a variety of pubs and clubs together with the municipal-run recreational grounds, tennis courts, bowling greens and swimming baths. These survived well into the twentieth century but are now rapidly disappearing. Those venues that remain generally do so by changing function. The 1907-built Temperance Billiard Hall in Chorlton-cum-Hardy in a good example of this. The cue sports of billiards and snooker became popular pastimes from the late nineteenth century onwards, and many billiards and snooker halls were built throughout the city. Very few of the original Edwardian halls survive. The one in the southern suburb of Chorlton still stands by being converted into a pub, which is quite ironic given that it was built by the Temperance Billiard Hall Company in an attempt to lure working people away from the dangers of heavy drinking. It was located on a prominent position on the high street, Manchester Road, adjacent to the district library. The ornate Baroque facade in redbrick and terracotta, with a Venetian and domed entrance pavilion, was consciously designed to attract customers. The company built several other Temperance Billiard Halls in Manchester's suburban townships (Cheetham, Gorton, Harpurhey, Moss Side and Rusholme) all to a similar design with their distinctive semi-cylindrical, barrel roofs, but the hall in Chorlton is the best preserved.

Fig. 5.49 Temperance Billiard Hall, Manchester Road, Chorlton-cum-Hardy (with Chorlton District Library to the right) (Author, 2024).

Another notable survivor from the formative age of popular culture lies in the other side of the city in Cheetham Hill. On Derby Street is the former Manchester Ice Palace built in 1910. At the time, this was the largest indoor ice rink in Britain, and it quickly became one of Manchester's most fashionable venues in the city used for ice skating and ice hockey. It was closed in the 1960s and is now used as a warehouse for clothing shops. The grand Baroque frontage with its pedimented entrance and signage in yellow terracotta dressings is imposing, even without the white marble gladding that originally covered the redbrick facade.

The Working Class and the Built Environment

The rise of popular culture meant the working class became more visible in the built environment of Manchester. In part this can be explained by rising standards of living in the late nineteenth century and an increasing amount of free time—the latter, in particular, a consequence of the reforming pressure exerted by trade unions and political campaigns. This was the time of 'New Unionism' and increased working-class militancy and political consciousness. The London match girls' strike of 1888 and London Dock Strike of 1889 triggered a national movement amongst the unskilled and semi-skilled which made the working class more combative and confrontational in contrast to the conciliatory approach of the earlier craft unions. This growth of industrial unions coincided with the rise of socialist politics and political organisations, returning the country to open class polarisations last seen in the era of Chartism. The high point of this movement was the period of industrial militancy between 1910 and 1914 often referred to as the Labour Unrest (or more appropriately the Labour Revolt) which continued after the First World War right up to the General Strike of May 1926, and saw the British state once again employ the military to police and constrain an insurgent working class. In Manchester and Salford, branches of the Social Democratic Federation (SDF), the first British Marxist political party, were established in 1885 and 1884 respectively, with the Salford members meeting in the Black Horse pub on The Crescent, as well as Hyndman Hall on Liverpool Road (named after the founder of the organisation), both of which have since been demolished. The Independent Labour Party, formed in Bradford in 1892 under the influence of Keir Hardie, soon had a presence in Manchester with the first Independent Labour councillor, Jesse Butler, elected in Openshaw in 1894. There were also more local initiatives such as Charles Rowley's Ancoats Brotherhood, inspired by the work of William Morris, that attempted to bring art and literature to the working class. Manchester–Salford was one of the centres of the Labour Unrest with a virtual general strike in the conurbation during the summer of 1911 when transport workers (seaman, sailors and dock workers of Manchester Ship Canal and Salford Quays) joined with railway workers and carters, with solidarity action from striking miners at Agecroft and Pendlebury, which brought the city to a standstill. Despite soldiers being deployed to help the police restore order, the strike gained enormous concessions.

Although not in a direct way, these general developments did have an impact of Manchester built environment by encouraging the working class to be more assertive in establishing their own places and spaces in terms of creating new clubs, associations and societies to improve the situation for ordinary people. These could be explicitly political, like Manchester's Clarion Club, or more religious and social in nature such as the Salvation Army, friendly societies and the co-operative movement.

The increased presence of the working class may have occurred within a context of rising living standards, but it was also shaped by the gross inequality that defined this era in which fantastic wealth coexisted with abject poverty. General improvements in standards of living did not hide the fact that pauperism and destitution was a continual feature of the industrial city. The reconfigurations of Manchester in the nineteenth century transformed the centre into a prestigious commercial and cultural district shorn of residence, but the poor were not removed entirely. Pushed to the margins and the peripheral parts of the city centre, such as the area behind Deansgate or Angel Meadow, the inner-city poor were a reminder of the squalor that industrial capitalism inherently generated. However, during the late Victorian and Edwardian period new attitudes and approaches to the poor began to emerge, born out of fear and anxiety of growing class antagonism. In Manchester, it is notable that a number of institutions directed at the working class, including what had been regarded as the 'undeserving poor' were established at this time.

Charitable Institutions

The Wood Street Mission, a charity founded by the Methodist Alfred Alsop to help those excluded from the official Poor Law relief, 'street arabs, neglected children, outcasts and poor people of our slums' (cited in Kidd 1985, 58), had their headquarters in Wood Street behind Deansgate since 1873. Between 1896 and 1907, the site was substantially rebuilt and refurbished. The offices of Wood Street Mission extended to Bridge Street and were decorated with green and cream faience, with two panels each containing a smiling child. The mission included a Ragged School, a Sunday School, Hall for the Poor, home of destitute and neglected boys, as well as a Temperance and Band of Hope department. A Working Men's Church was extended in 1905 and located immediately beside the mission. This is the only surviving church connected with the Labour Church movement that was founded by John Trevor in Manchester in 1891.

Fig. 5.50 Manchester and Salford Street Children Mission, Bridge Street (Author, 2022).

In the notorious slum district of Angel Meadow, a home for working girls was added to the 1866 Ragged School in 1891. This provided accommodation for servants who would have otherwise had to use lodging houses. On Great Ancoats Street, the Methodists opened a Women's Night Shelter in 1899 for similar reasons. This Arts and Crafts building had a coffee tavern on the ground floor and in the rest of the building 'a night shelter, a home for women needing "further care and discipline" and a home for domestic servants, who were being offered an alternative to the moral perils of the lodging house' (Hartwell 2001, 286). There was a Methodist Men's hostel on Hood Street in Ancoats.

Fig. 5.51 Working Men's Church, Wood Street (Author, 2022).

The prominence of these charitable institutions within the physical fabric of Manchester was indicative of a shift of thinking away from the cruel logic of utilitarian liberal philosophy that had underpinned the horrors of the New Poor Law and the workhouse. Pauperism could no longer be understood and treated simply in terms of individual character flaws. However, new approaches to the alleviation of poverty were not principally driven by government at either a national or local level, but through the actions of charities, individuals and wider social movements. In particular, the emergence of working-class, self-help organisations to improve the welfare of ordinary people was a characteristic trend associated with the rise of popular culture. These organisations adopted different methods and philosophies, from trade unionism and socialist politics, through to the temperance movement, the Salvation army, friendly societies and the co-operative organisation.

Fig. 5.52 Charter Street Ragged School and Working Girls Home (Author, 2012).

Fig. 5.53 Onwards Building, Deansgate (Author, 2025).

The campaign for temperance from alcohol was a nineteenth-century social movement in Britain, with links to Nonconformism and to a certain extent the labour movement. In response to the prevalence of drink in the city, Manchester became one of the key centres. Temperance halls had been attached to a number of mechanic institutes during the 1850s, such as the ones in Salford and Chorlton-on-Medlock. But the movement gathered force towards the end of the century with several temperance clubs and institutions established in purpose-built halls (such as the temperance billiard halls discussed above). However, the most prominent temperance building in Manchester is the Onwards Building in Deansgate. This was erected by a federation of temperance societies for the Band of Hope in 1903–1904, and designed by one of the leading architects of the day, Charles Heathcote, with distinctive porthole-like windows. 'Onward' was the title of the Band of Hope's newspaper and the name of the group is displayed on an elaborate keystone in the building's entrance. The interior of the main hall on the third floor is richly decorated in green tiles which carry the names of the societies and individuals that supported the construction of the building.

Supportive of the temperance movement was the Salvation Army, founded in 1865 by a Methodist preacher, William Booth, from Nottingham. By the Edwardian era, it had grown into a national organisation with branches in every major city and town, including Manchester. Although few original buildings (headquarters, halls, hospitals and lodging houses) survive, there is a small Edwardian Salvation Army Hall on Toxteth Street in Openshaw.

Friendly societies, set up for the mutual benefit of its members, have a long history; they thrived in the nineteenth century especially, after the passing of the Friendly Society Act of 1875. In Manchester, the main society was the Manchester Unity of Oddfellows, a non-profit mutual organisation founded in 1810. During the nineteenth century, this expanded into seventy-four lodges involving thousands of paying members. The impressive Baroque-styled fraternity office, dated to 1915, still stands on Grosvenor Street in Chorlton-on-Medlock. But in terms of Manchester's working-class associational culture, it is the shops, offices and businesses of the co-operative movement that are the most conspicuous and prevalent.

Fig. 5.54 Oddfellows Hall, Grosvenor Street (Author, 2023).

Co-Operative Buildings

The origin of the co-operative movement is often traced back to the Rochdale Pioneers who founded a consumers' co-operative, Rochdale Society of Equitable Pioneers, in 1844 and opened a grocery shop with members rewarded a dividend from any profits. This set-up proved successful, and it was adopted by similar co-operative societies throughout the country with the aim of providing 'cradle to grave' goods and services to working-class communities in industrial areas. In Manchester, the North of England Co-operative Wholesale Industrial and Provident Society was established in 1863, later renamed the Co-operative Wholesale Society (CWS). The CWS grew rapidly, and by 1890 had established branch networks across northern and midland towns. Manchester remained the headquarters of the organisation with a central office established on Corporation Street, opposite Victoria Station. This was an imposing Baroque structure (despite losing its corner domes) built between 1905–1909. Further CWS offices were subsequently added, with this part of Manchester becoming and remaining the 'co-operative quarter' of the city. The expansion of the business was remarkable, with the CWS building its own canal-side flour mill at Trafford Park. Across the Greater Manchester conurbation there were several co-operative societies, each with their own network of stores, warehouses and factories all serving specific working-class suburbs. These were not simply utilitarian, functional structures. They were showcase buildings that stood out against the blocks of redbrick terraced by-law housing within which they were situated.

The scale and architectural elaboration of the headquarters of the Pendleton branch is illustrative of the ambitions of CWS. The principal building was built between 1887 and 1903 in redbrick and terracotta, and contained offices, warehouses, committee rooms and assembly rooms. The exterior decoration is very ornate with a tall octagonal turret and many Dutch gables. Co-op shops linked to this Pendleton headquarters can be found at Wellington Street, Higher Broughton and Gerald Road in Charlestown. Both of these are elaborate structures decorated with Edwardian Baroque details in yellow and green terracotta.

Fig. 5.55 Co-operative Wholesale Society headquarters, Corporation Street (Author, 2020).

Fig. 5.56 Pendleton Co-operative Industrial Society, Broughton Road (Author, 2021).

Similar buildings can be found throughout the working-class districts of Greater Manchester, such as the assembly hall and shops of the Beswick Co-operative Society in Longsight. This fine Edwardian Baroque structure dated to 1913 was carefully positioned to visually dominate a new development of redbrick by-law terraced housing. The rich material heritage of the co-operative movement (that largely goes unnoticed) includes banks, insurance offices, bakeries and factories such as Co-operative Sundries Manufactory in Droylsden. This factory is decorated in the society's beehive badge, echoing the city of Manchester's symbol of worker bees.

Fig. 5.57 Beswick Co-operative Society Assembly Hall, Northmoor Road, Longsight (Author, 2021).

Fig. 5.58 Co-operative Sundries Manufactory, Greenside Lane, Droylsden (Author, 2023).

Places and Spaces of the Labour Movement

In terms of buildings of the labour movement in Manchester, there are very few. Trade union activity was fundamentally linked to the workplace. Union meetings occurred either inside factories or outside by the gates. For instance, at the turn of the nineteenth century on Trafford Road, near the main entrance to Manchester Docks, there were many public debates amongst the dock workers involving some of the greatest socialist speakers of the time, such as William Morris, James Connolly and Tom Mann. Few purpose-built trade union or socialist structures were constructed in Manchester. This is not to say there were not any. The Amalgamated Association of Operative Cotton Spinners, formed in 1870, had its headquarters at 115 Newton Street in a building that still stands. The Manchester Mechanics Institute on Princess Street (as well as others in the city) was also used by trade unionists, being the site of the first meeting of the Trades Union Congress in 1868. However, by the turn of the twentieth century, mechanic institutes were in decline and the Princess Street offices had been taken over by Manchester Corporation and used for teacher training purposes. But with the rise of an organised socialist movement, a number of socialist halls and clubs were established. Openshaw, the township in east Manchester that voted for the first Independent Labour Party councillor in 1894, possessed a socialist hall for the Openshaw Socialist Society. This was a simple redbrick structure on Margaret Street, paid for and built by members of the society in 1908–1909. Its second-floor hall could seat four hundred people and was decorated with a mural painted by William Crane. The first secretary of the club was the Droylsden-born Harry Pollitt, who was one of the founding members of the Communist Party of Great Britain and its future long-standing General Secretary. Sadly, the building was demolished in the 1970s. This is also true of the socialist Clarion Club with its Clarion Café-cum-meeting room on Market Street, were Marks and Spencer's store stands now. This club opened in 1903 and was handsomely furnished and decorated with stain glass windows and a socialist-themed frieze. The Clarion Club and movement was linked the radical newspaper *The Clarion* published by Robert Blatchford in Manchester since 1891. The Clarion Club was a national organisation and, amongst other things, promoted healthy outdoor activities combined with socialist propaganda. There was a Clarion cyclist club as well as clubs for ramblers, footballers, swimmers etc. The movement declined after the First World War, and the

Clarion Café closed in 1936 and was subsequently demolished (although the City Buildings where *The Clarion* newspaper was printed still stand, by Victoria station).

Buildings directly linked to the early socialist movement may be few and far between in central Manchester, but there are existing examples in the North West, such as the Bolton Socialist Club at 16 Wood Street, in Bolton in Greater Manchester. This socialist society was founded in 1888 and moved into Wood Street in 1905. There is also the Socialist Institute on Vernon Street in Nelson, built in 1907. The institute became associated with Victor Grayson, who was elected as an MP for Colne Valley when standing as an Independent Labour Party candidate in 1907.

The ownership and accumulation of property was not the priority of the labour and socialist movement; political agitation and organisation was. Offices and halls were hired as and when they were required or could be afforded. The central halls of Manchester Nonconformist denominations were often used, such as Wesleyan Albert Memorial Hall on Peter Street, in which the Labour Party hosted a conference in 1917 to vote to join Lloyd George's wartime coalition. Purpose-built socialist or trade union buildings were rare and those that did exist were not generally viewed as worthy of preservation. The places and spaces of the labour movement were fluid. However, the struggle over public spaces and the rights of workers to collectively use them for mass protests and political meetings was an important dimension of the labour and socialist movement in the late nineteenth century, and something that can be linked back to plebeian politics of Peterloo and Chartism. Although restricted by the infilling or building over of previous open spaces, the earlier radical tradition of 'platform politics' was never eradicated. In 1874, for instance, during the agricultural worker's lockout, Pomona Gardens was used for a solidarity demonstration in support of the National Agricultural Workers Union, involving a crowd of 50,000 trade unionists. But it was the creation of new parks and gardens during the second half of the nineteenth century that offered renewed opportunities. As has already been noted, Manchester's municipal parks became key sites of protest and conflict. Alexandra Park had been the rally point of Manchester's first International Worker's Day, or May Day, march in 1892 against much opposition from the municipal authorities, and there were sustained free speech campaigns at Ardwick Green in 1893 and Boggart Hole Clough in 1896. Further, public squares had always been used for political demonstration and this trend intensified at the turn of the century. In particular, Stevenson Square in the

Northern Quarter was a notorious site for street orators, demonstrations and public gatherings from Chartists to Suffragettes and Communists. In 1905, thousands gathered in the square to celebrate Annie Kenney's release from prison, while in 1911 during the strike wave in Manchester linked to the 'Great Unrest', rallies were held in the square with speakers including the young Harry Pollitt. There was even a demonstration of over 5,000 in 1920 to protest against the government's involvement in military attacks against Bolshevik Russia. During the General Strike of 1926, which was solidly supported in Manchester, there were constant parades, processions and mass meetings of striking workers from across the different industries throughout the nine days of action, which made use of public spaces such as the large rally in support of the strike that took place in Platt Fields Park on Sunday 9th May.

Fig. 5.59 Tramway workers meeting during the 1926 General Strike in Albert Square, photographer unknown. Image courtesy of Manchester Libraries.

Beyond the urban arena, there were some famous campaigns around the rights of access to the surrounding moors instigated by local socialists and trade unionists. On Sunday 6th September 1896, 10,000 people marched from the centre of Bolton up to Winter Hill to successfully enforce a public right of way to the moors that had been closed by the owner of Smithills Hall estate. This was a forerunner of the more well-known events at Kinder Scout on Sunday 24th April in 1932, when members of the Youth Communist League from Manchester, including Benny Rothman, organised and led a mass trespass to secure public access to the Pennines. The 'ramblers' included the young singer song-writer Ewan MacColl (then James Miller), who wrote 'The Manchester Rambler' (1932) as a tribute. The chorus goes:

> I'm a rambler, I'm a rambler from Manchester way
> I get all me pleasure the hard moorland way
> I may be a wage-slave on Monday
> But I am a free man on Sunday.

The End of Late Victorian and Edwardian Manchester

At the end of the Edwardian era, the transformation of industrial Manchester was complete and it was no-longer the 'shock city' of capitalism, the epicentre of the country's cotton industry. Textile manufacturing, warehousing and marketing may still have been central, but Manchester was now a fully-fledged modern city, overseen by a confident and ambitious Corporation. Its economic foundation rested on more than just cotton, and encompassed engineering, banking and insurance, as well as burgeoning retail and leisure sectors. Manchester had moved on from its image of a Dickensian 'coke-town' of brutal functionality, to become a rich and diverse bourgeois city of some grandeur that also accommodated a dynamic urban popular culture. It was a city of pleasure as well as work, a global metropolis with a cosmopolitan population to match; Britain's second city of empire. Such developments manifested themselves in the patterning of the urban environment. Manchester possessed a well-organised central business district with zones for commerce and leisure. Beyond, an integrated suburban network of townships was established along the main arterial roads out of the centre, creating a concentric arrangement of industrial and working-class townships followed by a ring of more affluent suburbs. Binding these elements together was a shared infrastructure of urban utilities, especially the electric tram system, and a common architectural language of ornate Edwardian Baroque and Jacobean styles intermixed with standard, redbrick by-law terraces. The prosperity and confidence of late Victorian and Edwardian Manchester is reflected in the fact that the majority of the pre-Second World War buildings still standing today, both in the centre and many of the surrounding townships, date from this time.

Thomas Marr's 1904 map of Manchester and Salford (Fig. 5.60), which colour codes the district in terms of types of business property and dwelling-house, dramatically highlights the urban zoning at the turn of the twentieth century. There is a large commercial core of offices, followed by a zone of industry along the lines of the river courses and railway infrastructure, with an inner ring of slums, back-to-back housing and an outer ring of by-law terraces. Further out, more suburban areas of middle-class housing with gardens can just be seen. However, this 1904 map is also evidence that the distinctive pattern of urban development that can be traced back to the 1840s was coming to an end. Marr's map was drawn up to assist urban improvements through slum clearances. All the property coloured black and dark brown on the map would become earmarked for demolition.

Fig. 5.60 Map used as frontispiece in T. Marr, *Housing Conditions in Manchester & Salford* (Manchester: Sherratt and Hughes, 1904), https://archive.org/details/housingcondition00marr/page/n5/mode/1up, public domain.

The early twentieth century, therefore, both defined a high point in terms of the transformation of the industrial city, and also the start of a very different pattern of urban development in Manchester. Although the boundaries between urban phases and periods are inherently blurred due to the dynamic nature of urbanism, which is always in a state of flux and becoming, there were distinct changes in the built environment at this time. In particular, the passing of the Housing and Town Planning Act of 1919, or the Addison Act, led to a clear break in Manchester's Victorian and Edwardian cityscape, as it resulted in the end of the construction of gridded rows of redbrick by-law terraces and the move towards council estates and garden suburbs of semi-detached houses arranged in closes or cul-de-sacs.

The 1919 act gave local authorities powers and funds to build houses. It incorporated the recommendations made by the Paymaster-General of Lloyd-George's government, Tudor Walters, in his report on housing policy at the end of the First World War. Tudor Walters was inspired by the utopian urban planning ideas of Ebenezer Howard and the garden-city movement, and called for the construction of semi-detached housing in spacious estates beyond the heavily built-up central areas of the industrial city.

Wythenshawe Garden City

In Manchester, Ebenezer Howard's ideas had initially inspired the construction of Chorltonville Garden Village, in Chorlton-cum-Hardy to the south of the city. This was an estate of semi-detached houses designed around a village green between 1908 and 1911. Howard's ideas also lay behind the local architect Edgar Wood's Fairfield Garden Village in Droylsden, comprising neo-Georgian houses planned and built between 1913 and 1922. But it was when these urban planning ideas were taken up Manchester Corporation after the 1919 housing act that fundamental changes occurred with the building of council houses and council estates in greenfield, 'out-of-town' locations. Although the Corporation had previously played with the idea of garden suburbs when it constructed Blakely Cottages in 1904, and built Temple Square as a 'home for heroes' on Cheetham Hill for men returning from active service in 1919, these projects were on a relatively minor scale. It was when large-scale working-class council estates were planned that a qualitative urban transformation occurred. During the 1920s, the Corporation built the Anson Estate in Longsight and Burnage Garden Village. They also purchased land in Cheshire, over ten miles from Manchester centre, for the planned development of Wythenshawe Garden City. This was an ambitious project of social engineering, with Wythenshawe becoming the largest council housing estate in Europe. The idea, pursued by the Manchester politicians Ernest and Shena Simon, was to take the Mancunian working class out of the inner-city slums of Hulme and Ancoats, transplanting them to the leafy countryside. Ernest and Shena Simon bought Wythenshawe Hall and the surrounding land and donated it to the Corporation. In 1931, the whole estate was incorporated into the city.

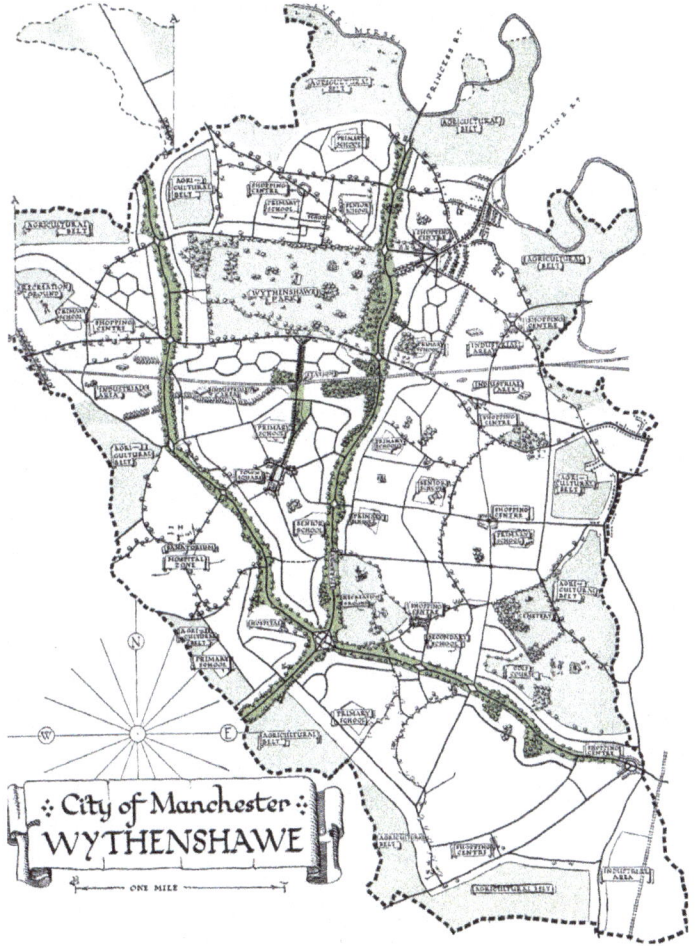

Fig. 5.61 Barry Parker's plan for Wythenshawe Garden City, 1928, public domain.

Fig. 5.62 Ordnance Survey Map of Wythenshawe Estate, 1951, public domain.

Only a few of the Arts and Crafts styled council houses in Wythenshawe were built before the Second World War, but the 1951 Ordnance Survey map captures the new urban geography of cul-de-sacs and winding, serpentine avenues, surrounded by open countryside. This represented a strikingly contrasting urban morphology to the one that had previously dominated Manchester's built environment, and so can be used to define the end of the Victorian and Edwardian urban phase of the city's development. However, rather than representing a new phase in the expansion of industrial Manchester, these urban changes mark the start of the city's industrial decline.

Conclusion

Fig. C.1 L. S. Lowry, *The Lake*, 1937 (© The Lowry Collection, Salford).

Lowry painted *The Lake* in 1937, just three years before T. S. Eliot composed *East Coker*. It presents a bleak urban scene without any sense of the hope that can be found within Eliot's poem. Supposedly a view of the River Irwell after a flooding at The Crescent in Salford, it is in fact a composite painting that projects Lowry's inner state of mind onto an imagined industrial scene with such desolation and despair. It is a piece of psychogeography. The tiny figurers by the river edge seem trapped and forlorn amongst the detritus of industrial decay. Although not necessarily his conscious intention, Lowry's paintings of this period capture a sense of crisis and decline the followed in the wake of the Wall Street Crash and the world economic slump of the 1930s. This is a Manchester shorn of its confidence, ambition and industrial swagger—in short, an urban dystopia.

Manchester, that had been the key centre of the Industrial Revolution, was in steady decline during the middle decades of the twentieth century. Despite the Ship Canal and Trafford Park helping offset the worst effects of the 'Great Depression' in the 1930s, the city never returned to the peaks of the late Victorian and Edwardian era. From a population high of 766,311 in the 1931 Census it would drop to a low of 392,819 by 2001, almost halving in size! The cotton industry that had driven Manchester's urban explosion was in catastrophic decline after the Second World War and 'Cottonopolis' ceased to exist, with the Royal Exchange closing for trading in 1968. Manchester's engineering sector and carriage works likewise rapidly contracted from the late sixties onwards, with the subsequent loss of thousands of manufacturing jobs. As Alan Kidd records '(b)etween 1966 and 1972 one in three manual jobs in manufacturing were lost and one quarter of all factories and workshops closed' (2002, 192). And by 1980, even shipping to the Port of Manchester had all but disappeared, with the docks left abandoned.

This dramatic reversal in the city's economic and industrial fortunes from its high point at the turn of the century was reflected in the physical fabric of the city. After the completion of the Central Library (1934) and Town Hall Extension (1937), there were no new civic monuments designed on such a grand scale. The regression in public building schemes is symbolised by the fact that the closure and demolition of the Royal Infirmary at Piccadilly, which had served as the focus of one of Manchester's key public spaces since the mid-eighteenth century, did not lead to the construction of a new civic building (despite discussions to erect a new art gallery on the site). The plot was left empty before being turned into a sunken garden in the 1930s—Piccadilly Gardens, with the only physical trace of the lost hospital being a stretch of the base for the railings that once surrounded the complex.

Fig. C.2 Royal Infirmary railings, Piccadilly (Author, 2023).

With the dramatic decline of the cotton industry, the prestigious commercial buildings in the city centre, cotton warehouses, banks and insurance offices steadily closed their doors to business and were left empty. Beyond the central district around the inner industrial belt, factories, workshops, canals and railway depots were shut and abandoned during the post-war period. The associated working-class townships were depopulated and many of the redbrick terraced houses boarded up or demolished. Whole districts, such as Hulme and Chorlton-on-Medlock, were systematically levelled, a process evocatively captured in Shirley Barker's extraordinary street photographs from the 1960s and 1970s.

This sharp decline of industrial Manchester has not been reversed, but a new post-industrial city began to emerge during the 1980s in response to another general shift in the dynamics of capitalism. It now rested on an economy based upon services not manufacturing. Manchester had retained its importance as a commercial and transport centre, and this was utilised to restructure the urban economy towards education, health, sport and leisure, alongside other public and commercial services. The hollowed-out centre of the city that had become depopulated and full of empty buildings and offices was subsequently slowly reserviced and redeveloped. Importantly, it was with the rise of post-industrial Manchester that a new concern for the built environment began to emerge, as the city's industrial heritage was viewed as a tourist attraction, and so a potential revenue source. Castlefield was designated a conservation area in 1980 and became the first urban heritage park, which led to the repair and restoration of the canal basin and associated warehouses. This Castlefield redevelopment set the model for further industrial heritage projects, such as Salford Quays, with the current regeneration of Ancoats and New Islington being one of the latest phases in the revamping of the inner city.

Fig. C.3 Manchester University 1968, Shirley Baker (© 2025, Nan Levy for the Estate of Shirley Baker. All rights reserved).

However, Manchester's makeover has been fuelled by a particular business model. As explored in Jamie Peck and Kevin Ward's *City of Revolution: Restructuring Manchester* and Issac Rose's more recently published *The Rentier City: Manchester and the Making of the Neoliberal Metropolis*, an entrepreneurial approach has been adopted, driven by commercial and developer interests, rather than local communities and democracy—the so-called 'Manchester Model'. This has led to a rather sterile built environment in which 'heritage' has been cleaned and sanitised and made fit for the city's vibrant cultural economy. The past has been commodified and therefore stripped of its complexity. Manchester's post-industrial redevelopment may have led to a new interest in the city's 'heritage', but at an expense of decontextualising it, so it can be accommodated within a highly commercial urban infrastructure. Renovated old canals, warehouses and railway arches have now become the setting and backdrop for pubs, clubs and fashionable eateries. Mills have been converted into lucrative student accommodation and luxury apartments.

In my view, Manchester's industrial past deserves much better than this. It is richly layered and complex, being open to multiple readings and interpretations. In this sense, Manchester's built environment forms a palimpsest with traces and marks of the past inscribed in the physical fabric of the present. Appreciating this requires a contextual approach. One of the main aims of this study is to illustrate the value of an archaeological 'gaze' when moving through the city. Examining the built environment contextually in terms of material, spatial and temporal patterns of development is an important way of making sense of Manchester. The urban palimpsest forms part of the city's 'living archaeology'. Bringing this to attention helps render visible the overlooked and ignored in the built environment, and so opens up possibilities for historical imagination. It allows us to construct narratives that simultaneously situate ourselves within the material, spatial and temporal matrix of both past and present. In the preface to his *The Making of the English Working Class*, E. P. Thompson famously declared that he was 'seeking to rescue the poor stockinger, the Luddite cropper, the "obsolete" hand-loom weaver, the "utopian" artisan and even the deluded follower of Joanna Southcott, from the enormous condescension of posterity' (1968, 13). While the built environment may not 'speak' so directly, or in the same way as written texts, the physical fabric of the city does provide tangible links into the past. After all, it is all around us and as such, readily accessible and experienced on a daily basis. Contemplating a blocked Georgian pedimented doorway in a back alley at the centre of Manchester can be both interesting and rewarding. It is this 'living archaeology' of the remains of old streets, canals, train lines, houses, churches, parks and industrial remnants, that allows us to connect with the lives and communities of the people that made and transformed Manchester: the hand-loom weavers, mill hands, navigators, engineers etc. So, it is through engaging with this 'living archaeology' that we can begin to construct narratives that link the past with the present.

The narrative I have been reading through analysing and interpreting Manchester's material remains relates to the city's industrial past—the making of the 'shock city' of industrial capitalism and its transformation into a Victorian, bourgeois city. It was a process that unfolded over two hundred years, from the early eighteenth to the early twentieth century, driven by the dual dynamics of competitive capital accumulation and class polarisation. Manchester was the city of capital and labour. The sequence of five phases of development, from the Georgian boom town to the city of ambition and popular culture during the Edwardian era, is defined by this dynamic that resulted in new industrial and commercial enterprises, transport innovations, residential and housing developments, as well as a diverse range of religious, cultural and civic institutions. The built environment was shaped by socio-economic forces of capitalism. It was the arena where communal and class identities were constituted, and a means by which dominant ideas and values were projected into the world. The places and spaces and buildings of Manchester are consequently steeped in this social history. Making this explicit by analytically breaking down Manchester's palimpsest in this way not only enhances our appreciation of the built environment, allowing us to situate ourselves in terms of the past, it also helps us to critically reflect on the transformation of Manchester in the present and whose interests it serves, along with the possibilities of building an alternative city.

Fig. C.4 Statue of Friedrich Engels, Tony Wilson Place, Manchester (looking out towards 'The Engels' penthouse in 'Manc-Hatten' (Author, 2025).

At the moment, the entrepreneurial model of urban regeneration may seem omnipotent, with the ongoing drive for private developers to construct high-end residential tower blocks and skyscrapers; a process that leads to Manchester's past being steadily commodified, stripped of meaning and value. A striking example of this was noted by *The Guardian* newspaper in June 2024, in an article that drew attention to the fact that one of the new developments in the city's emerging 'Manchatten' skyline is a tower block at the end of Deansgate that includes a multimillion-pound penthouse named 'The Engels'. The irony of repurposing Manchester's radical history for profit would be hilarious if it was not so obscene, given the current crisis of affordable housing and the state of homelessness in the city centre. However, as well as the naming of a luxury apartment, the figure of Friedrich Engels has been more viscerally referenced in the contemporary urban fabric in the form of a 3.7-metre concrete statue of the man standing in Tony Wilson Place (on the site of an old Gaythorn gas works). This was erected in 2017 as part of the artist Phil Collins' installation for the Manchester International Festival, and represents one of the very few public monuments to Engels' historical presence in the city. The statue has an intriguing biography. Constructed in the 1970s during the Soviet era and installed in a village in eastern Ukraine, it was broken in half and discarded after the banning of symbols of the former communist era in 2015, before it was acquired by Collins and transported to Manchester. Significantly, it still bears traces of the Ukrainian national colours of blue and yellow that were painted on its legs during the Orange Revolution of 2004–2005. Engels may be wrongly associated with the Stalinist Soviet empire, but he was a revolutionary. This is often downplayed or ignored in both popular and academic accounts of his life, but Engels, like Marx, wanted to smash the capitalist order and usher forth communism. It was his experience of living in Manchester during the 1840s that was instrumental in the shaping of Marxism into a theory of proletarian revolution, as he himself acknowledged in later writings. Tramping the streets, visiting the 'rookeries' and cellar dwellings of working-class Manchester gave him insights into the dynamics and contradictions of capitalism, as well as the social forces that could lead to its demise. Engels' subsequent study of industrial urbanism during the era of Chartism following the General Strike of 1842 was therefore critical for the development of both his and Marx's thinking. Above all, *The Condition of the Working Class in England* helped them, philosophically and politically, identify the working class as the agency of revolutionary change, with socialism and communism the result of proletarian self-emancipation. So, perhaps it is only appropriate that Engels should have the last words in this analysis of the built environment of Manchester, the birth place of industrial capitalism and the labour movement. In his pamphlet, *The Housing Question,* published in 1872, Engels returned to the issue of the capitalist metropolis and the perpetual housing crisis brought by the free-market system. Engels concluded his study by echoing the words with which he ended *The Condition of the Working Class in England* some thirty years earlier.

> Only the proletariat created by modern large-scale industry, liberated from all fetters including those which chained it to the land, and herded together in big cities, is in a position to accomplish the great social transformation which will put an end to all class exploitation and all class rule. (2021, 29)

Bibliography

Alexander Park Heritage Group (2017) *Alexander Park Manchester, A Park for the People Since 1870*, Alexander Park Heritage Group, Manchester.

Al-Othman, H. (2024) 'Luxury Penthouse in Manchester Named after Friedrich Engels', *The Guardian*, 9/06/2024, https://www.theguardian.com/business/article/2024/jun/09/luxury-penthouse-in-manchester-named-after-friedrich-engels

Archer, J. H. G. (ed.) (1985) *Art and Architecture in Victorian Manchester*, Manchester University Press, Manchester.

Baker, S (2018) *Without a Trace: Manchester and Salford in the 1960s*, The History Press, Cheltenham.

Barnes, S. F. (2009) *Manchester Board Schools 1870–1902*, Victorian Society, London.

Bradshaw, L. D. (1987) *Visitors to Manchester: A Selection of British and Foreign Visitors' Descriptions of Manchester from c1538 to 1865*, Neil Richardson, Radcliffe.

Briggs, A. (1963) *Victorian Cities*, Penguin Books, London.

Caminada, J. ([1895] 2017) *Detective Caminada's Casebook*, Manor Vale Associate, Reading.

Crinson, M. (2022) *Shock City: Image and Architecture in Industrial Manchester*, Yale University Press, New Haven and London.

Cooper, G. (2007) *The Illustrated History of Manchester's Suburbs*, Breedon Books, Derby.

Dawson, A. (2017) *Early Railways of Manchester*, Amberley, Stroud.

Defoe, D. ([1724–1726] 1971) *A Tour Through the Whole Island of Great Britain*, Penguin Books, London.

Dobraszczyk, P. and Butler, S. (eds) (2020) *Manchester: Something Rich and Strange*, Manchester University Press, Manchester.

Dyos, H. J. and Reeder, D. A. (1973) 'Slums and Suburbs', in Dyos, H. J. and Wolff, M. (eds), *The Victorian City*, Routledge and Keegan Paul, London, pp. 359–386.

Dyos, H. J. and Wolff, M. (eds) (1973) *The Victorian City*, Routledge and Keegan Paul, London.

Engels, F. ([1845] 2009) *The Condition of the Working Class in England*, Penguin Books, London.

Engels, F. ([1872] 2021) *The Housing Question*, International Publishers, New York.

Faucher, L. J. (1844) *Manchester 1844: Its Present Condition and Future Prospects. Translated from the French with Copious Notes Appended by a Member of the Manchester Athenaeum*, British Library, Milton Keynes.

Fishman, R. (1989) *Bourgeois Utopias: The Rise and Fall of Suburbia*, Basic Books, USA.

Fraser, D. (ed.) (1982) *Municipal Reform and the Industrial City*, Leicester University Press, Leicester.

Fraser, D. and Sutcliffe, A. (eds) (1983) *The Pursuit of Urban History*, Edward Arnold, London.

Frow, E. and Flow, R. (1990) *The General Strike in Salford in 1911*, Working Class Movement Library, Salford.

Girouard, M. (1984) *Victorian Pubs*, Yale University Press, New Haven and London.

Girouard, M. (1990) *The English Town*, Yale University Press, New Haven and London.

Glinert, E. (2008) *Manchester Compendium*, Penguin Books, London.

Gregory, J. (ed.) (2021) *Manchester Cathedral: A History of the Collegiate Church and Cathedral, 1421 to the Present*, Manchester University Press, Manchester.

Gregory, R. and Millar, I. (2015) *Greengate: The Archaeology of Salford's Historic Core, Greater Manchester's Past Revealed 13*, Oxford Archaeology, Glasgow.

Gunn, S. (2000) *The Public Culture of the Victorian Middle Class*, Manchester University Press, Manchester.

Gunn, S. and Bell, R. (2002) *Middle Classes: Their Rise and Sprawl*, Phoenix, London.

Hayes, L. (2014) *Iron and Steel in Openshaw: Excavating John Ashbury's Carriage and Iron Works, Greater Manchester's Past Revealed 11*, SLR Consulting, Aylesbury.

Hartwell, C. (2001) *Manchester*, Penguin Books, London.

Hartwell, C. (2006) 'Manchester and the Golden Age of Pericles. Richard Lane, Architect', *Transactions of the Lancashire and Cheshire Antiquarian Society*, 102, 18–35.

Hartwell, C., Hyde, M. and Pevsner, N. (2004) *Lancashire: Manchester and the South-East*, Yale University Press, Newhaven and London.

Harvey, D. (1973) *Social Justice and the City*, Edward Arnold, London.

Harvey, D. (1989) *The Urban Experience*, Johns Hopkins University Press, Baltimore and London.

Harwood, E. (2010) *England's Schools; History, Architecture and Adaption*, English Heritage, Swindon.

Hewitt, M. (1996) *The Emergence of Stability in the Industrial City: Manchester, 1832-67*, Scolar Press, Aldershot.

Hewitt, M. (2000) 'Confronting the Modern City: The Manchester Free Public Library, 1850–80', *Urban History*, 27.1, 62–88.

Higgins, C. (2017) 'Phil Collins: Why I Took a Soviet Statue of Engels across Europe to Manchester', *The Guardian*, 30/06/2017, https://www.theguardian.com/artanddesign/2017/jun/30/phil-collins-why-i-took-a-soviet-statue-of-engels-across-europe-to-manchester

Hodder, I. (1986) *Reading the Past: Current Approaches to Interpretation in Archaeology*, Cambridge University Press, Cambridge.

Hunt, T. (2004) *Building Jerusalem: The Rise and fall of the Victorian City*, Pheonix, London.

Hunt, T. (2009) *The Frock-Coated Communist*, Penguin Books, London.

Hylton, S. (2003) *A History of Manchester*, Phillimore, Chichester.

Joyce, P. (2003) *The Rule of Freedom: Liberalism and the Modern City*, Verso, London.

Joyce, P. (2021) *Going to My Father's House*, Verso, London.

Kadish, S. (2015) *Jewish Heritage in Britain and Ireland: An Architectural Guide*, Historic England, Swindon.

Kellett, J. R. (1969) *Railways and Victorian Cities*, Routledge and Keegan Paul, London.

Kelly, E. and Kelly, T. (1957) *A Schoolmaster's Notebook: Being an Account of a Nineteenth Century Experiment in Social Welfare, by David Winstanley of Manchester, Schoolmaster*, Chetham Society, Manchester.

Kidd, A. (2002) *Manchester*, Edinburgh University Press, Edinburgh.

Kidd, A. (1985) '"Outcast Manchester": Voluntary Charity, Poor Relief and the Casual Poor 1860–1905', in Kidd, A. and Roberts, K. (eds), *City, Class and Culture*, Manchester University Press, Manchester, pp. 48–73.

Kidd, A. and Roberts, K. (eds) (1985) *City, Class and Culture*, Manchester University Press, Manchester.

Kidd, A. and Wyke, T. (eds) (2016) *Manchester: Making the Modern City*, Liverpool University Press, Liverpool.

Kirby, D. (2016) *Angel Meadow: Victorian Britain's Most Savage Slum*, Pen and Sword History, Barnsley.

Koditschek, T. (2006) 'Book Review, The Rule of Freedom: Liberalism and the Modern City by Patrick Joyce', *The Journal of Modern History*, 78.1, 182–184.

Krantz, M. (2014) *The 1842 General Strike: Richard Pilling and the Lancashire Chartists*, Bookmarks, London.

Loftus, D. (ed.) (2017) *Confidence and Crisis, 1840–1880*, The Open University, Milton Keynes.

Loftus, D. (2015) 'Politics and the People', in Loftus, D. and Tremlett, P-F. (eds), *Contexts*, The Open University, Milton Keynes, pp. 109–159.

Mackie, R. (ed.) (2017) *Decline and Renewal, 1880–1914*, The Open University, Milton Keynes.

McNeil, R. and George, D. (eds) (1997) *The Heritage Atlas 3: Warehouse Album*, The University of Manchester Field Archaeology Centre, Chester.

McNeil, R. and George, D. (eds) (2002) *The Heritage Atlas 4: Manchester—Archetype City of the Industrial Revolution, a Proposed World Heritage Site*, The University of Manchester Field Archaeology Centre, Loughborough.

Malm, A. (2016) *Fossil Capital*, Verso, London.

Mansfield, N. (2013) *Buildings of the Labour Movement*, English Heritage, Swindon.

Marr, T.R. (1904) *Housing Conditions in Manchester and Salford*, Sherratt and Hughes, Manchester and London.

Marsden, J. (2014) *Forgotten Fields: Looking for Manchester's Old Burial Grounds*, Bright Pen, Sandy.

Martin Zero (n.d.), *Home*, YouTube, https://www.youtube.com/@MartinZero

Marx, K. (1974) *Early Writings*, Penguin Books, Harmondsworth.

Merrifield, A. (2002) *Metromarxism: A Marxist Tale of the City*, Routledge, London.

Miller, I. (2011) *Rediscovering Bradford: Archaeology in the Engine Room of Manchester, Greater Manchester's Past Revealed 4*, Oxford Archaeology, Oxford.

Miller, I, Ward, C. and Gregory R. (2010) *Piccadilly Place: Uncovering Manchester's Industrial Origins, Greater Manchester's Past Revealed 1*, Oxford Archaeology, Glasgow.

Miller, I and Wild, C. (2015) *'Hell upon Earth': The Archaeology of Angel Meadow*, Greater Manchester's Past Revealed 14, Oxford Archaeology, Oxford.

Miller, M. (2010) *English Garden Cities: An Introduction*, English Heritage, Swindon.

Moore, J. R. (2004) 'Urban Space and Civic Identity in Manchester 1780–1914: Piccadilly Square and the Art Gallery Question', *The Historical Society of Lancashire and Cheshire*, 153, 87–123.

Morris, R. J. and Rodger, R. (eds) (1993) *The Victorian City: A Reader in British Urban History 1820–1914*, Longman, London and New York.

Navickas, K. (2017) *Protest and the Politics of Space and Place, 1789–1848*, Manchester University Press, Manchester.

Neocleous, M. (2001) *A Critical Theory of Police Power: The Fabrication of Social Order*, Verso, London.

Nevell, M. (2008) *Manchester: The Hidden History*, The History Press, Stroud.

Nevell, M. (2011) 'Living in the Industrial City: Housing Quality, Land Ownership and the Archaeological Evidence from Industrial Manchester, 1740–1850', *International Journal for Historical Archaeology*, 15.4, 594–606.

Nevell, M. (2013) 'Bridgewater: The Archaeology of the First Arterial Industrial Canal', *Industrial Archaeology Review*, 35.1, 1–21.

Nevell, M. (2017) 'Excavating "Hell upon Earth" towards a Research Framework for the Archaeological Investigation of Workers' Housing: Case Studies from Manchester, UK', *Industrial Archaeology Review*, 39.2, 85–100.

Nevell, M. (2018) *Manchester at Work: Peoples and Industries through the Years*, Amberley, Stroud.

Nevell, M. (2020) *The Archaeology of Manchester in 20 Digs*, Amberley, Stroud.

Nicholls, R. (1996) *Trafford Park: The First Hundred Years*, Phillimore, London.

O'Brien, M. (1995) *'Perish the Privileged Orders': A Socialist History of the Chartist Movement*, Redwords, London.

Old Ordnance Survey Maps, (1988–2020) *Manchester Large Scale Sheets / Lancashire Sheets*, Alan Godfrey Maps, Bolden Colliery.

Olusoga, D. and Backe-Hansen, M. (2020) *A House Through Time*, Picador, London.

Palmer, M., Nevell, M. and Sissons, M. (2012) *Industrial Archaeology: A Handbook*, Council of British Archaeology, York.

Parkinson-Bailey, J. J. (2000) *Manchester: An Architectural History*, Manchester University Press, Manchester.

Peck, J. and Ward, K. (eds) (2002) *City of Revolution: Restructuring Manchester*, Manchester University Press, Manchester.

Pickstone, J. (1985) *Medicine and Industrial Society*, Manchester University Press, Manchester.

Porter, R. (1989) 'The Gift Relation: Philanthropy and Provincial Hospitals in Eighteenth-Century England', in Granshaw, L. and Porter, R. (eds), *The Hospital in History*, Routledge, London, pp. 149–178.

Rees, J. (ed.) (1994) 'The Revolutionary Ideas of Frederick Engels', *International Socialism*, 65, http://www.marxists.de/theory/engels/index.htm

Robbins, G. (2022) '150 Years Ago, Friedrich Engels Correctly Assessed What's Wrong with Housing under Capitalism', *Tribune*, 24/07/2022, https://tribunemag.co.uk/2022/07/the-housing-question-friedrich-engels-renting-tenants

Rose, I. (2024) *The Rentier City: Manchester and the Making of the Neoliberal Metropolis*, Repeater, London.

Rose, M. E. with Falconer, K. and Holder, J. (2011) *Ancoats: Cradle of Industrialisation*, English Heritage, London.

Ruff, A. R. (2016) *Manchester's Philips Park*, Amberley, Stroud.

Rutherford, S. (2008) *The Victorian Cemetery*, Shire, Oxford.

Sandling, J. and Leber, M. (2000) *Lowry's City: A Painter and His Locale*, Lowry Press, Salford.

Stewart, C. (1956) *The Stones of Manchester*, Edward Arnold, London.

Taylor, S., Cooper, M. and Barnwell, P. S. (2002) *Manchester: The Warehouse Legacy*, English Heritage, London.

Taylor, S. and Holder, J. (2008) *Manchester's Northern Quarter*, English Heritage, London.

Thompson, E. P. (1968) *The Making of the English Working Class*, Penguin, Harmondsworth.

Thompson, F. M. L. (ed.) (1982) *The Rise of Suburbia*, Leicester University Press, Leicester.

Veblen, T. (1899) *The Theory of the Leisure Class: An Economic Study in the Evolution of Institutions*, New York, Macmillan.

Webb, S. (2024) *Engels in Manchester*, The Langley Press, Great Britain.

Woodman, D. (2022) *Central Manchester Pubs*, Amberley, Stroud.

Wyke, T. (1996) *A Hall for All Season*, Charles Halle Foundation, Manchester.

Wyke, T. (2004) *Public Sculpture of Greater Manchester: 8 (Public Sculpture of Britain)*, Liverpool University Press, Liverpool.

Wyke, T., Robson, B. and Dodge, M. (2018) *Manchester: Mapping the City*, Birlinn, Edinburgh.

Yorke, T. (2005) *The Victorian House Explained*, Countryside Books, Newbury.

Index

Albert Square 13, 149–151, 153–154, 156, 158, 169, 211, 219, 279
Alderley Edge 148
Alexandra Park 183–184, 252, 278
Ancoats 12, 30, 39–44, 52–53, 57, 65–67, 85, 114, 131, 134, 170–171, 179–181, 185, 192, 202, 250–251, 268, 270, 283, 288
Angel Meadow 52, 61, 107, 202, 268, 270
Anglicanism 24, 44, 55–57, 72, 101, 126, 133–135, 138, 151, 175, 185, 196, 198–200, 203, 210
archaeology 2–5, 13, 36, 52–53, 102, 289
  'living archaeology' 3, 13, 102, 289
architecture
  Art Deco 166, 216, 263
  Baroque 9, 22, 26, 211, 218, 223, 228–235, 242, 247, 249, 257–258, 266–267, 273–275, 280
  Gothic 13, 22, 57–58, 90, 110, 114, 133, 137–139, 142, 144, 147–148, 150–158, 165, 167, 169, 175, 180–182, 199–201, 203, 211, 214, 229, 235, 237, 244, 247
  Greek Revival 57, 74–75, 79, 88, 112, 142, 151
  Italianate 83, 98, 105, 112, 116, 127, 142–143, 148, 153–154, 162, 167, 169, 171, 182, 233, 235
  Neoclassical 18, 21, 56, 74, 77–78, 81, 85, 88–89, 110, 112, 117, 138, 142, 151, 216, 233, 247, 257
  Renaissance 13, 75, 98, 106, 112, 114, 116–117, 128, 131–132, 139, 151, 167, 185–186, 229, 243–244, 258

Ardwick 83–87, 107, 121, 131, 134, 140, 156, 176, 179–180, 182, 185, 188, 193, 227, 255, 258–259, 278
aristocracy 15–17, 19, 33, 83, 88–89, 92, 254
Arkwright, Richard 35, 37
Armenian Church 203–204
Ashton-under-Lyne 32, 64, 82
assembly room 206, 274
Athenaeum 75, 111–112

Bancroft, Joseph 29
bank 35, 58, 77–78, 100–101, 104–105, 111–112, 115–116, 144, 147, 168, 206, 210, 218, 223, 230–232, 276, 287
barrack 12, 35–36, 60, 62–64, 69, 164, 191, 251
Barry, Charles 57, 75, 88, 112, 138
Bateman, John Frederick 24, 119
bath. *See* public bath
Becker, Lydia 186
Belle Vue 125, 164, 202, 264–265
Bell, Rachel 166
Bentham, Jeremy 162–163
Berry, John 19–20, 26
Beyer, Charles 175, 188
Birley family 44
Birley, Hugh Hornby 44, 71, 158
Blackley 134, 164, 188, 208, 235, 251
Blake, William 45
Bland, Lady Ann 21
Blanketeers 61, 65
board school 13, 150, 185–186, 245, 247
Boggart Hole Clough 254–255, 278

bourgeoisie 6, 12–13, 16, 21, 36–37, 59–60, 68, 83, 86, 89, 92, 95, 98, 109, 112–113, 128, 139–140, 145–146, 150, 158, 166, 168, 179, 197, 211, 228, 256, 260, 280, 289
Bradley, William 53
brewery 188–190, 259
bridge 12, 32, 49, 53, 61, 63, 77, 92–93, 100–101, 106–108, 118–119, 161, 214, 269
Bridgewater Canal 12, 19, 32, 49, 125, 224
Briggs, Asa 6
Brindle Heath 56, 58, 207
Brindley, James 32
Brooks, Samuel 71, 78, 90, 139, 141, 145, 148
Brotherton, Joseph 128, 130, 209
Brown, Ford Madox 144, 152
burial ground. *See* cemetery
Byrom, Edward 21, 28, 32

Caminada, Jerome 193, 210, 255
canal 12, 14, 19, 32, 36, 39, 41, 43, 48–51, 94, 108, 125, 134, 150, 170–172, 176, 211, 213–218, 221–222, 224, 237–238, 241, 268, 274, 286–289
capital 5–7, 14, 16, 32–33, 35–36, 49, 56, 60, 69, 83, 100, 103, 141, 151, 177, 211, 217, 237, 290
capitalism 3, 6–7, 14, 36, 44, 61, 69, 79, 94–95, 117, 123, 154, 159, 217, 237, 268, 280, 287, 289–292
Cartwright, Edward 46
Casson, Russell 19–20, 26
Castlefield 31–32, 46, 49–51, 108, 139, 192, 223–224, 287–288
Catholicism 55–56, 101, 135–137, 151, 198, 200–203, 210
cemetery 13–14, 24, 56, 67, 81, 85, 124, 126, 138, 151, 202, 207–211
central business district 13, 100, 108–109, 112, 114, 133–134, 148–149, 216, 231, 280
Central Library 248, 286

chapel 16, 22–23, 25, 44, 52, 55–56, 58, 65–67, 72, 83, 85, 101, 107, 133, 135, 137–139, 142, 151, 161, 174, 178, 185–186, 192–193, 196–200, 203, 209–210, 244, 247, 258
charity 30, 179, 181, 269, 271
  charitable institution 13, 19, 29, 150, 179, 181, 219, 269, 271
Chartism 12, 36, 64, 66–68, 85, 94, 99, 123, 130, 267, 278–279, 291
Cheetham Hill 48, 56–58, 82, 121, 131, 137, 140, 151, 162, 181, 189–190, 204–207, 227, 267, 282
Chester 16, 43, 48, 74, 121, 125, 133, 183
Chorlton-cum-Hardy 16, 210, 235, 266, 282
Chorlton-on-Medlock 43–44, 52, 80–82, 85, 122, 138, 142, 146, 160–162, 166, 180–181, 190, 192, 200, 219, 244, 249, 272–273, 287
church 9, 16, 19, 21–22, 24, 26, 28, 33, 36, 52, 55–58, 65–67, 69, 71–72, 75–77, 80–83, 101, 109, 116, 121, 132–138, 151, 154, 172, 175, 177–178, 182, 185, 196–204, 216, 252, 258, 261, 269–270, 289
  Commissioners' churches 36, 55, 57–58, 67
cinema 14, 219, 256–259, 266
Civil War (English) 18
Clarion Club 268, 277
Clayton 172, 188, 198, 235
coal mine (colliery) 32, 174
Cobden, Richard 78, 98
coercion 12, 36, 59–61, 65, 69, 94
Collins, Phil 291
Collyhurst 132, 134
commerce 13, 21, 89, 98, 100, 109, 114–115, 166, 280
community
  Armenian 203
  Catholic 56, 135, 137
  Irish 38, 56, 202
  Italian 56, 202
  Jewish 56, 204, 206–207

Conservative club 150, 175, 187–188
consumption 130, 141, 166, 189, 211, 234, 255
contextual analysis 4–6, 14, 289
co-operative movement 215, 219, 268, 271, 273–276
Corn Laws 98
cosmopolitanism 13, 150–151, 193, 197, 204, 280
cotton 12–13, 21, 27, 32, 35–36, 41, 45–46, 49, 60, 71, 82, 90, 94, 103, 110, 112, 114, 151, 157, 171, 173, 176, 239, 280, 286–287
Cottonopolis 35, 286
cricket 183, 253–254, 261–263
Crinson, Mark 8, 41–42, 113, 152–153
Cromwell, Oliver 18
Cross Street 4, 23, 44, 52–53, 65, 78, 138, 142, 169, 231–233, 260
Cross Street Chapel 23, 44, 52, 65, 138, 142
Crumpsall 161–162, 164, 207–208, 235, 246–247, 254
culture
  bourgeois 37, 59, 73, 91, 101, 139, 145, 168, 228
  civic 99, 148, 158, 218
  leisure 211, 256, 264–265
  material 4–5
  popular 14, 213, 217, 219, 255–256, 258, 260–261, 263, 265, 267, 271, 280, 290
Dalton, John 72, 85, 111
Deansgate 19, 66, 104, 106, 131, 156–157, 166–168, 186–187, 190, 222–223, 268–269, 272, 291
Defoe, Daniel 15, 19, 26
demolition 1, 5, 10, 28, 56, 67, 88, 120, 131, 151, 154, 163–164, 166, 182, 186, 194, 206, 209, 223, 249, 251, 256, 267, 277–278, 281, 286–287
department store 150, 166, 255
Didsbury 16, 88, 139, 141, 146–147, 214, 235, 246–247

discipline 4, 12, 35, 39, 41, 57, 60–61, 66, 123–124, 159, 161, 190–191, 247, 261, 270
domestic ideology 89, 141, 146
Dyos, H. J. 83

education 75, 128, 133, 139, 150, 185, 218, 242–243, 245–246, 287
Education Act 133, 185–186, 245
Egerton, Francis 19, 32
Egerton, Thomas 18
electricity 218, 237, 241–242
Eliot, T.S. 1–2, 285
empire 190, 215, 217, 247–248, 258, 280, 291
Engels, Friedrich 2, 6–7, 13, 15, 36, 52, 59, 68, 79, 107, 109, 111, 121, 140, 146, 172, 290–292
  Condition of the Working Class in England 2, 6, 292
engineering 13, 32, 35, 108–109, 119, 143, 150, 171–174, 214, 217, 280, 283, 286
exploitation 36, 47, 60, 94, 124, 292

Fairbairn, William 111, 128, 173
Fairhurst, Harry 216, 231–232, 234
Fallowfield 88–89, 143, 194, 207, 225, 235, 242, 254
Faucher, Leon 79
Fishman, Robert 91
football 253–254, 256, 261–264
Free Trade Hall 13, 97–98, 111, 116, 257

garden 10–11, 14, 28–29, 69–70, 84, 88, 90, 111, 125, 140, 145, 176, 195–196, 209, 219, 232, 240, 264–265, 278, 281, 286
gas 41, 100, 119–120, 122, 153, 166, 218, 237–238, 241, 291
Gaskell family 142, 194
Gaskell House 142, 145–146
Gaskell, William 52
General Strike 64, 94, 267, 279, 291

Gorton 47, 108, 119, 132, 150, 164, 171–175, 177–179, 188, 198–199, 201, 211, 235, 254, 261, 264, 266
governmentality 100, 117, 120–121
Great Depression 217–218, 286
Greater Manchester 14, 24, 106, 192, 218–219, 226, 228, 235, 242, 274–275, 278
Greek Orthodox Church 203
Green, William 27, 29, 32, 37, 39, 83
Greg, Samuel 37
greyhound racing 263, 265
Grimshaw, Robert 47
Gunn, Simon 98, 159, 166, 168

Halle, Charles 144, 209
hand-loom 46–47, 53, 289
Harpurhey 125–126, 132, 134, 179, 192, 210, 235, 250, 266
Harrison, Thomas 74–75, 77, 79, 110
Harvey, David 7, 217
health 125, 127–128, 153, 159, 164, 179, 240, 287
Heathcote, Charles 231–232, 234, 272
Heaton Hall 18, 254
Heaton Moor 241–242, 257
Heaton Park 78, 235, 254
heritage 3, 32, 44, 46, 112, 154, 204, 207, 275, 287–288
Hewitt, Martin 127
Heywood, Abel 23, 130, 152
Heywood, Benjamin 23, 51, 115–116, 128
Hodder, Ian 4
horse racing 263
hospital 10, 13, 19, 29–30, 33, 70, 111, 150, 156, 159, 164–165, 179–182, 233, 273, 286
hotel 90–91, 114, 190, 218, 228–230, 263
Hough End Hall 16–17
Houldsworth, William 150, 176–177, 187
housing
  by-law 1, 10, 13, 100, 121–124, 133, 142, 150–151, 178–179, 194–195, 215, 225, 242, 248, 250, 274–275, 280–282
  council/municipal 242, 250–251, 282–284
  middle-class 83, 134, 140–141, 145, 194–195, 197, 207, 225, 281
  working-class 51, 56, 58, 66, 121, 132, 140, 178, 194–195, 250
Hulme 2, 44, 57, 62–63, 121–122, 127–128, 131, 133–137, 146, 161, 179, 185, 192–194, 258, 283, 287

immigrant 202–203, 206
Independent Labour Party 184, 267, 277–278
industrialisation 6–7, 12, 36–38, 46, 51, 53, 60, 65, 68–69, 100, 103, 125, 159, 191, 211
industrialist 6, 29, 37, 44–45, 47, 74, 81, 86, 88, 98, 120, 147–148, 150, 157, 173, 175–176, 182, 210, 234, 247
Industrial Revolution 6–7, 14, 37, 66, 211, 217, 286
industry 15, 35, 39, 41, 46, 49, 98, 103, 108–109, 140, 150–151, 157, 166, 170–173, 176, 179, 206, 217, 263, 279–281, 286–287, 292
inn 26, 66, 260
insurance 168, 218, 230–232, 276, 280, 287

Joyce, Patrick 7

Kay, James 52
Kellet, John 108
Kempthorne, Sampson 161
Kennedy, John 41, 84
Kersal Moor 68, 127, 135, 139–140, 263
Kidd, Alan 286
King Street 19, 25–26, 69, 77–78, 112, 167, 169, 216, 232

labour 6, 14, 33, 35, 37–38, 46–47, 51, 56, 60–61, 69, 99–101, 124, 159–160, 176–177, 213, 219, 272, 277–278, 290, 292

Lane, Richard 58, 70, 72, 77, 81, 89–90, 107, 111, 113, 142, 155
leisure 14, 100, 211, 219, 226, 255–256, 259–260, 263–265, 280, 287
Levenshulme 1, 129, 134, 178, 188, 192, 194–199, 225, 235, 247–248, 254
liberalism 7, 13, 75, 97–98, 121, 146, 157, 237
library 12, 14, 19, 69, 71, 74, 79, 101, 111, 128–132, 156–157, 169–170, 182, 206–207, 218, 242–243, 246–249, 266, 286
Little Ireland 2, 52
Liverpool Road Station 37, 92–93, 103, 105
Longsight 90, 129, 132, 134, 178, 194, 255, 275–276, 283
Lowry, L.S. 172, 179, 198, 210, 244, 260, 285–286
Luddism 47, 289

Malm, Andreas 35
Manchester Cathedral 19, 21, 110
Manchester Corporation 14, 99–100, 117–121, 128, 138, 149–151, 153, 164, 183–185, 210, 214, 218, 224–225, 227, 237–243, 246, 249–252, 254, 274–275, 277, 280, 282–283
Manchester Free Library 130–131, 206–207
Manchester Grammar School 19, 165
Manchester Ship Canal 14, 19, 211, 213, 216–217, 221, 238, 268
Manchester Town Hall 13, 144, 149–155, 158, 162, 182, 189, 211, 254, 286
mansion 15–18, 81, 88–89, 92, 142–143, 146–148, 159, 182, 214, 254
maps (and mapping) 5–6, 19, 26–29, 32, 37, 39, 48, 51, 53, 56–57, 60–61, 63, 66, 83–84, 86, 90, 101, 103, 121, 124–127, 135, 174, 178, 189, 194, 197, 199, 215, 221, 223, 226, 259, 262–263, 280–281, 284

Market Street 71, 77, 110–111, 118, 166–167, 233, 277
Marsland family 44
Marsland, Samuel 44, 81
Marxism 2, 4, 6–7, 61, 267, 291
Marx, Karl 6, 22, 291–292
McConnel, James 41, 84
mechanics' institutions 116, 128–129, 158, 277
Merrifield, Andy 7
Methodism 24, 56, 72, 138–139, 185, 196, 198–199, 269–270, 273
middle class 10, 12–13, 16, 21–22, 24, 29, 33, 36–37, 52, 56, 65, 68–71, 74–75, 77, 83, 85–86, 88–89, 92, 94–95, 99–101, 107, 111, 114, 117, 124–125, 127–128, 130, 133–134, 137–142, 144–148, 150–151, 166, 168, 179, 183, 185–186, 189, 191, 194–195, 197, 200, 205, 207, 210–211, 217, 224–225, 242, 248, 258, 264, 281
Midland Hotel 218, 228–230
migrant 37–38, 51, 56, 135, 197
Miles Platting 51, 132, 171
militancy 47, 64–65, 267
mill (textile factory) 12, 23, 32, 35–37, 39–47, 51–52, 60, 64, 68, 82, 94, 98, 170–173, 176, 179–180, 182, 190, 198, 274, 289
Mosley family 16, 29, 85, 117
Mosley, Nicholas 16
Mosley, Oswald 21
Mosley Street 12, 37, 69–75, 77–78, 111–112, 114, 116, 128
Moss Side 122, 178, 183–184, 190, 194, 235, 262, 266
Murray, Adam 41
Murray, George 41
Murrays' Mills 39–41, 114
music hall 256, 258

Napier, General Charles 36, 64
Nasmyth, James 173
Navickas, Katrina 7, 65–66
Nevell, Michael 39

New Bailey Prison 12, 61–62, 162–163
New Cross 30, 65
Newton Heath 45, 108, 132, 171–172, 190, 261
Nonconformism 23–24, 55–57, 67, 101, 126, 137–139, 151, 185, 198, 200, 203, 210, 272, 278
Northern Quarter 28, 45–47, 53–54, 80, 279

Old Trafford 48, 125, 261–262
Openshaw 108, 132, 171–172, 174, 185, 187, 235, 268, 273, 277
Oxford Road 2, 10, 48, 82, 104, 134, 146, 155, 165, 200, 218, 220, 224, 227, 230–231, 233–234, 258–259

palazzo 13, 75, 98, 100, 112–113, 116, 128, 154, 169
park 2, 9, 13–14, 19, 32, 37, 45, 47, 63, 74, 78–79, 86–88, 90–92, 100, 119, 124–127, 132, 139, 141, 143–146, 150, 172, 181, 183–184, 197, 201, 209–211, 213, 215–218, 221–222, 232, 235, 242–243, 252–255, 263, 265, 274, 278–279, 286, 289
paternalism 13, 100, 148–151, 154, 157–158, 175–177, 179, 181–182, 197, 210–211
Peacock, Richard 175
Peck, Jamie 288
Peterloo Massacre 12, 44, 61, 63, 65–66, 71, 98, 123, 278
Pevsner, Nikolaus 18
Philips, Mark 88
Philips Park 88, 125–126, 183, 210
Piccadilly 10–11, 29, 69–71, 100, 104–105, 108, 110–111, 127, 150, 164, 167, 223, 230, 286–287
Piccadilly Esplanade 100, 110–111
Pigot, James 37–38, 48, 51, 55–57, 59–60, 83, 101
Platt Hall 17–18, 199
police (and policing) 61, 100, 121, 123–125, 127, 130, 150, 156, 164, 182, 184, 191–193, 210, 218, 230, 254–255, 267–268

police station 150, 191–193, 230
polite society 10, 12, 16, 21, 23, 33, 37, 68–70, 74, 79, 89
politics 3, 6, 11, 13–14, 16, 21–22, 30, 44, 47, 61, 65–69, 89, 99, 117, 127, 130, 141, 148, 150, 153, 157–158, 168–169, 175–177, 179, 184–189, 197, 211, 219, 237, 253–255, 267–268, 271, 278
   platform politics 65, 68, 127, 278
poor 29, 36, 52, 56, 61, 82, 85, 128, 159–160, 164, 179, 192, 206, 210, 250, 258, 268–269, 289
Poor Law 61, 159–162, 164, 189, 206, 269, 271
Porter, Roy 30
Portico Library 12, 71, 74, 79, 111
Port of Manchester 213, 215, 218, 221–222, 237, 286
Potter, Thomas 85, 88, 120
poverty 2, 30, 47, 52, 69, 79, 160, 181, 219, 251, 268, 271
power 7, 14, 21, 35–37, 39, 46–47, 59–61, 92, 98, 117, 150, 153, 161, 218, 224, 230, 235–236, 239, 241, 282
power-loom 35, 46
power station 239, 241
Prestwich 160, 162, 164, 207
Price, Henry 239, 247, 249–250
prison 12–13, 35–36, 60–62, 69, 150, 155, 159, 162–164, 192, 202, 206, 279
proletariat 6, 12, 158, 292
protest 30, 61, 71, 219, 230, 255, 278–279
pub 66, 85, 125, 150, 183, 188–190, 192–193, 219, 258–260, 266–267, 288. *See also* inn
public bath 14, 29, 52, 70, 100, 124–125, 127–128, 228, 242–243, 247, 249–250, 266
Pugin, A. W. N. 135, 154–155, 157, 201

Quakers 24, 56, 71–72, 138

Quay Street 19, 28, 165, 256–257, 259
Queens Park 125–126, 132, 183

radicalism 14, 30, 37, 47, 65–68, 98, 127, 130, 206, 277–278, 291
railway 12, 14, 37, 64, 92–94, 100–109, 112, 134, 140–141, 147–148, 170, 172–174, 197, 199, 218, 220–224, 228, 230, 261, 268, 281, 287–288
   railway station 12, 64, 100, 104–105, 114, 197, 221, 223, 228, 264
recreation 66, 124–125, 127–128, 132, 150, 157, 179, 183, 190, 219, 228, 246–247, 252, 254, 260, 263, 266
Reddish 150, 176–177, 188
Reeder, D. A. 83
reform 65, 99–100, 112, 117–118, 120–121, 123–124, 127, 148, 150, 158–159, 161–163, 168–169, 177, 179, 184–189, 208
Reform Act 99, 158, 168, 179, 185, 187, 189
reformer 116, 162
religion 6, 13–14, 16, 21–22, 36, 55–56, 69, 98, 101, 133, 135, 138, 154, 197–198, 200, 206, 208, 210, 268, 290
revolution 92, 95, 109, 166, 185, 291
riot 30, 42, 64–65, 94, 184
river 14, 19, 32, 39, 44, 49, 61, 63, 85–86, 92–93, 108, 126, 147, 202, 209, 211, 223, 240, 285
River Irk 39, 126, 202
River Irwell 19, 39, 49, 61, 63, 85–86, 92–93, 209, 219, 223, 240, 285
River Medlock 32, 39, 44, 219
road 9, 14, 36, 48–49, 86, 100, 118, 121, 134, 148, 178, 192, 206, 214, 220, 223–224, 226, 235, 280
Rose, Isaac 288
Royal Exchange 12, 21, 74, 76–77, 107, 110–111, 118, 167, 192, 218, 223, 230, 232–233, 286
Royal Infirmary 10, 12, 29–30, 69–70, 78, 110–111, 164–165, 232–234, 286–287

Royal Manchester Institute (Art Gallery) 75, 111
Rusholme 17–18, 81, 90–91, 135, 138, 165, 178, 194, 225, 235, 266
Ruskin, John 154
Rylands, John 156, 182, 210

Salford 8–9, 14, 20, 25–27, 32, 38, 45, 48–49, 55–64, 77–78, 85–88, 90, 99, 102–103, 106–108, 115–116, 118–121, 124–125, 127–128, 130, 132, 134–137, 140, 146, 155, 158, 160, 162, 164–165, 171–172, 179, 184, 186, 192–193, 200–201, 208–210, 213–214, 216, 221–223, 237–238, 240–241, 244, 250–252, 254, 258, 263–264, 267–269, 272, 280–281, 285, 288
   Broughton 58, 86–87, 121, 139–141, 146, 203, 207, 274–275
   Buile Hill 88, 254
   Charlestown 134, 172, 274
   Cliff, The 86, 139, 146
   Crescent, The 85–87, 90, 140, 267, 285
   Peel Park 125, 132, 183
   Pendlebury 164–165, 198, 268
   Pendleton 56–58, 88, 121, 140, 209, 274–275
Sargent, Francis J. 77
Schinkel, Karl Friedrich 41
school 13, 18–19, 24, 51, 57, 75, 133, 137–138, 150, 165, 175, 177, 182, 185–187, 198–199, 202, 207, 243–245, 247, 256, 269–271
shops (and shopping) 59, 81, 112, 150, 159, 166–167, 226, 251, 255, 260, 267, 273–275
Shudehill 2, 30, 49, 66, 77, 110, 118
slum 36, 51–53, 83, 94, 107, 118, 121, 123, 133, 178, 194, 206, 250, 269–270, 281, 283
Smithfield Market 100, 110, 117, 174
socialism 130–131, 206, 219, 237, 244, 267, 271, 277–279, 292

societies 13, 66, 121, 125, 150, 158, 168–170, 179, 189, 215, 260, 268, 271–277
space 2–7, 10–12, 14, 30, 37, 42, 49, 65–67, 69–70, 100, 109–111, 118, 121, 123–125, 127, 130, 133, 145, 150–151, 153, 158, 179, 185, 219, 247, 252–255, 264, 268, 278–279, 286, 290
spatial relationship 5, 7, 10, 14, 49, 53, 58–59, 67–69, 89, 92, 101, 123, 126, 132–133, 159, 218, 289
sports 14, 183, 256, 261–264, 266, 287. See also cricket; See also football
St Ann, Church of 9, 19, 21–22, 26, 28, 69, 76, 201
St Ann's Square 9, 19, 21–22, 115–116, 166–167
steam-power 32, 35–37, 41, 45–47, 60, 94
Stephenson, George 92
Stevenson Square 80, 278
Strangeways Prison 155, 163, 190, 206
street 2–4, 10, 15, 19, 24, 33, 37, 59, 70–71, 77, 79–80, 82, 90, 100, 111–113, 121, 124, 127, 140, 147, 166–167, 176, 178, 191, 195, 197, 216, 219, 227, 257, 289, 291
Stretford 121, 161, 182–183, 201, 211, 215, 265
suburb 10, 12–14, 36–37, 39, 44, 48, 69, 80–81, 83, 85–86, 88–90, 92, 94, 101, 107–109, 111, 123, 125, 129, 133–134, 137–141, 145–148, 150–151, 164, 166, 170–171, 175, 177, 181, 185, 192–195, 197–198, 205, 207, 211, 218–219, 224–226, 235, 242, 248, 251–252, 265–266, 274, 280–282
suburbanisation 13, 90, 141, 151, 193–194
surveillance 124, 159, 162
synagogue 55–56, 151, 197, 204–207

Taylor, A. J. P. 98
Taylor, James 45

temperance 183, 189, 193, 266, 269, 271–273
theatre 12, 14, 43, 69, 74–76, 111, 182, 219, 228, 255–259, 266
Theatre Royal 12, 74–76, 111, 256
Thirlmere Aqueduct 237–239
Thompson, E. P. 289
Thompson, F. M. L. 141
Tory 21, 44, 158, 160, 169, 177, 188
town hall 13, 78, 81, 107, 144, 149–155, 158, 162, 182, 189, 205, 211, 254, 286
township 13–14, 48, 82, 101, 108, 132–134, 148, 150–151, 160, 172, 178, 186, 193, 197–198, 204, 207, 211, 217–218, 224, 235, 242, 247–249, 252, 266, 277, 280, 287
Trades Union Congress 129, 158, 277
trade union 61, 66, 68, 129, 158, 160–162, 164, 189, 206, 217, 267, 271, 277–279
Trafford Park 9, 19, 211, 213, 215–218, 221–222, 232, 274, 286
tram 14, 218, 220–221, 224–227, 235, 237, 264, 279–280
transport 9, 11, 14, 21, 30, 32, 49, 92, 94, 103–104, 109, 216, 218, 221, 224, 227, 235, 237, 240, 268, 287, 290

union. See trade unioN
Unitarianism 23–24, 44, 72, 137–138, 142, 154, 174–175
University of Manchester 155, 165, 243
urbanism 1, 5, 9, 237, 282, 291

Valette, Adolphe 219–220, 224, 227, 230, 244
Veblen, Thorstein 255
viaduct 12, 100–101, 103–108, 220, 223–224
Victoria Park 37, 87, 90–91, 141, 143–144, 146
Victoria, Queen 111, 156, 214
villa 1, 13, 36, 58, 74, 82, 84–86, 88–90, 92, 101, 139–142, 144–148, 151, 166, 194, 197, 254

Walters, Edward 13, 88, 98, 113–114, 116, 139, 143, 155
Ward, Kevin 288
warehouse 13, 31–32, 35–36, 46, 49–51, 78, 92, 100–101, 109, 111–114, 116, 147, 151, 168, 207, 216, 221–222, 239, 267, 274, 287–288
Waring, Peter 26, 77
water 32, 35, 37, 39, 100, 119, 153, 183, 218–219, 237–241, 249, 253
Waterhouse, Alfred 13, 131, 151, 154–155, 163, 165, 177, 182, 211, 220, 230
Watts, James 114, 147
wealth 36, 50, 69, 79, 89, 94, 109, 114, 116, 150, 157, 178, 182, 234, 255, 268
weavers' workshop dwellings 36, 45, 47
Whalley Range 90, 138–139, 141, 148, 201–202
White, Charles 29
Whitworth, Joseph 143, 173–174, 234
Wilmslow Road 134, 139, 146, 228

Withington 135, 146–147, 161, 164, 190–191, 194, 207, 228, 235, 247, 250
workhouse 13, 35–36, 60–61, 69, 122, 150, 159–162, 164, 271
working class 12–15, 30, 36–37, 42, 45, 51–53, 56–59, 61, 63–66, 68–69, 82–83, 94–95, 100, 107, 109, 111, 121, 123–128, 130–135, 137, 140–141, 146, 148, 150, 157–160, 169, 172, 177–179, 181, 183, 185, 187–189, 191–192, 194–195, 197–198, 206, 211, 217, 219, 224–225, 230, 237, 248, 250–251, 261–262, 264, 267–268, 271, 273–275, 280, 282–283, 287, 291–292
World War II 1, 133, 217, 280, 284, 286
Worsley, Charles 18
Worthington, Thomas 86, 127, 153–154, 156, 162, 164, 175, 182, 237
Wyatt, James 18
Wythenshawe 10, 235, 282–284

zone 69, 108–109, 112, 123, 125, 132, 169, 226, 257, 280–281

About the Team

Alessandra Tosi was the managing editor for this book.

Adèle Kreager and Lila Fierek proof-read this manuscript. Adèle compiled the index.

Jeevanjot Kaur Nagpal designed the cover. The cover was produced in InDesign using the Fontin font.

Jeremy Bowman typeset the book in InDesign and produced the paperback and hardback editions and created the EPUB. The main text font is Tex Gyre Pagella and the heading font is Californian FB. Jeremy also produced the PDF edition.

The conversion to the HTML edition was performed with epublius, an open-source software which is freely available on our GitHub page at https://github.com/OpenBookPublishers

Laura Rodríguez was in charge of marketing.

This book was peer-reviewed by Dr. Mike Nevell, the Industrial Heritage Support Officer for England at the Ironbridge George Museum Trust and President of the Lancashire & Cheshire Antiquarian Society, and an anonymous referee. Experts in their field, these readers give their time freely to help ensure the academic rigour of our books. We are grateful for their generous and invaluable contributions.

This book need not end here...

Share

All our books — including the one you have just read — are free to access online so that students, researchers and members of the public who can't afford a printed edition will have access to the same ideas. This title will be accessed online by hundreds of readers each month across the globe: why not share the link so that someone you know is one of them?

This book and additional content is available at
https://doi.org/10.11647/OBP.0459

Donate

Open Book Publishers is an award-winning, scholar-led, not-for-profit press making knowledge freely available one book at a time. We don't charge authors to publish with us: instead, our work is supported by our library members and by donations from people who believe that research shouldn't be locked behind paywalls.

Join the effort to free knowledge by supporting us at
https://www.openbookpublishers.com/support-us

We invite you to connect with us on our socials!

BLUESKY
@openbookpublish
.bsky.social

MASTODON
@OpenBookPublish
@hcommons.social

LINKEDIN
open-book-publishers

Read more at the Open Book Publishers Blog
https://blogs.openbookpublishers.com

You may also be interested in:

Thomas Annan of Glasgow
Pioneer of the Documentary Photograph
Lionel Gossman
https://doi.org/10.11647/OBP.0057

William Moorcroft, Potter
Individuality by Design
Jonathan Mallinson
https://doi.org/10.11647/OBP.0349

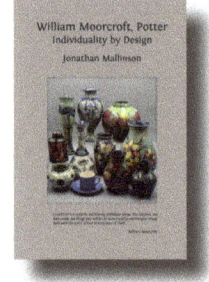

A Fleet Street in Every Town
The Provincial Press in England, 1855-1900
Andrew Hobbs
https://doi.org/10.11647/OBP.0152

Tangible and Intangible Heritage in the Age of Globalisation
Edited by Lilia Makhloufi
https://doi.org/10.11647/OBP.0388

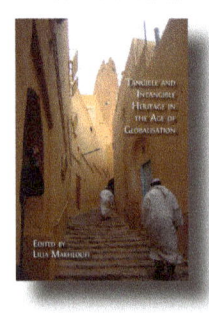

www.ingramcontent.com/pod-product-compliance
Lightning Source LLC
Chambersburg PA
CBHW040323300426
44112CB00021B/2860